EDITED BY DAVID LITTLEFIELD

SPACE CRAFT:
DEVELOPMENTS IN ARCHITECTURAL COMPUTING

RIBA ⊞ Publishing

© David Littlefield, 2008

Published by RIBA Publishing, 15 Bonhill Street, London EC2P 2EA

ISBN 978 1 85946 292 8
Stock Code 63560

The right of David Littlefield to be identified as the Author of this Work
has been asserted in accordance with the Copyright, Design and
Patents Act 1988, Sections 77 and 78

All rights reserved. No part of this publication may be reproduced,
stored in a retrieval system, or transmitted, in any form or by
any means, electronic, mechanical, photocopying, recording or
otherwise, without prior permission of the copyright owner.

British Library Cataloguing in Publication Data
A catalogue record for this book is available from the British Library.

Publisher: Steven Cross

Commissioning Editor: Matthew Thompson

Project Editor: Susan George

Copy Editor: Sara Parkin

Designed and typeset by Kneath Associates

Printed and bound by Cambridge University Press

We make every effort to ensure the accuracy and quality of
information when it is published. However, we can take no
responsibility for the subsequent use of this information, nor for any
errors or omissions that it may contain.

RIBA Publishing is part of RIBA Enterprises Ltd.

www.ribaenterprises.com

CONTENTS

FOREWORD

Throughout history, architecture has been a manifestation and reflection not only of society but also the materials and tools available to architects and engineers. For example, the Gothic period reflects building methods and engineering including pointed arches, ribbed vaults and flying buttresses, which in turn allowed an emphasis on light and verticality. The Church's influence and dominance in daily life was embodied in Gothic cathedrals.

Similarly, Art Deco was a celebration of the Machine Age through conspicuous use of manufactured materials (particularly glass and stainless steel), symmetry, repetition, all modified by Asian influences such as the use of silks and Middle Eastern designs. It was widely adopted in the United States during the Great Depression for its practicality and simplicity and to evoke memories of better times.

When computers became more common and more affordable a decade ago, architects had a new tool for drawing and revising drawings. At that point, computers were seen as a new platform for designing, but not an enabler of new design abilities. In other words, the computer was used as an electronic drawing board to document then-conventional building plans and elevations.

With ever more powerful computers, more sophisticated software is emerging as an enabler of revolutionary new capabilities for architects and engineers. Architectural forms and structures that could hardly be represented, much less fully expressed, with 2-D drawings are now possible with computational design. One such software product from Bentley that has just moved from the research and development stage to a commercially released product is GenerativeComponents, which is used or referred to in many of the case studies and essays in this volume.

We at Bentley are proud not only to advance this new approach with our products, but also to champion the opportunities illustrated in this book, which we are underwriting. This volume gives us insight into radically new possibilities and a glimpse of the future of architecture and engineering.

Brad Workman
Vice President
Bentley Systems, Inc.

The Spacecraft has landed – and this is not just a play on words – for with the digital revolution, the art of creating form and space has once again become a craft. The use of digital media allows the artificial separation of art and science to become reconciled and both architectural education and practice have been quick to seize on the potential of extending digital design into digital manufacture. As a result we are seeing the emergence of a new breed of digital craftsmen, who are using technology to explore new connections between form-making and imagination.

The contributors are people so actively involved in their craft that they would normally never have the time or the opportunity to describe their experience. It is thanks to the encouragement and persistence of the author that we now have a collection which charts the progress of a movement at a point when it is gaining so rapidly in momentum and diversity.

This is not a text book or an instruction manual, but there is much to be learnt from all the references and case studies which carefully describe the underlying principles, motivation and philosophy behind the projects. Architecture today is increasingly becoming a team game. Often the clients are also teams, and so the level of consultation and involvement is requiring a more inclusive design process, based on a platform where anyone can be invited to play. The most liberating aspect of the technology is the possibility of combining a broad range of specialisation and skill sets.

Architect, engineer, surveyor, developer, artist, animator and educator – all are represented in a comprehensive series of snapshots which are likely to have a lasting value. They invite contrast and comparison which illuminate the present while hinting at the future. The writers range from individuals to members of large companies. Some of their ideas reinforce to form a consensus, while others are more radical and will prompt the reader to further research.

The collection of chapters, each from a different contributor, need not necessarily be read in sequence. Dip into it and it works like a kaleidoscope, composed of fragments which form different patterns and shades of meaning each time it is shaken. Most of the chapters have no conclusion, perhaps because they are written by people who recognise that we are all involved in a journey without end. Those who enjoy travel are often frustrated and disappointed by arrival, so if this book has a message it is – enjoy the journey!

Hugh Whitehead
Foster + Partners

ACKNOWLEDGMENTS

This book has been made possible by busy people giving up their time for free. The depth of their generosity cannot be overstated. Now that the book is here for all to see, I hope all the contributors can forgive me for the three years of pestering, begging and bullying to which they have allowed themselves to be subjected. Apart from thanking Hugh Whitehead of Foster + Partners for writing the book's preface, and Bentley Systems for backing the book, it would be unfair to pick out particular names for special mention. Thanks go to all those mentioned on the contents pages.

It is worth making the point, however, that all the people who have contributed to this book believe that developments in computing allow them to do their jobs better – that is, to design better buildings. By becoming masters of the tools at their disposal, they have never considered computing to be a limiting factor in their work. Architectural computing is, rather, a liberating force. And that is the point of this book.

David Littlefield

ARCHITECTURE AND STRUCTURE

Through the application of pure geometry and analysis from the very start of a building project, digital modelling can bring the disciplines of architecture and structure closer together. Like a medieval Gothic cathedral, the one is seamlessly an expression of the other.

This consequently triggers a more intimate relationship between what has become two distinct professions – architects begin thinking a little like engineers, and vice versa. It fosters an architecture of purity, robustness and rigour that is more than skin deep. A building's curves, the position and incline of its columns, the junctions between its surfaces – all are simultaneously aesthetic, practical and structurally considered moves. This is not an architecture of floors, walls and ceilings, but one of planes and geometric relationships.

ARCHITECTURAL STRUCTURE –
COMPUTATIONAL STRATEGIES.
LARS HESSELGREN, RENOS CHARITOU AND STYLIANOS DRITSAS, KPF

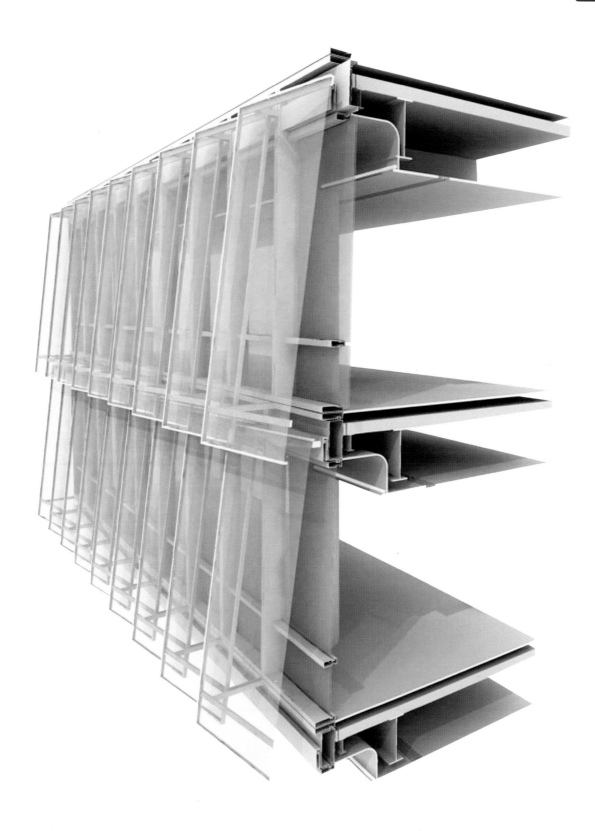

ARCHITECTURAL STRUCTURE – COMPUTATIONAL STRATEGIES.

LARS HESSELGREN, RENOS CHARITOU AND STYLIANOS DRITSAS, KPF

All architecture implies structure, but structure does not imply architecture. This is the first dilemma that faces the designer. In many minds, the simple act of creating a structure means creating architecture. In the case of buildings, however, there is a qualitative difference between something earning the label architecture and something that is simply 'building'. How the structural component of architecture is integrated into the overall concept is an important ingredient. It is one that the Modern Movement has increasingly put to the forefront. The argument that elegant structure is, by definition, architecture is somewhat suspect, however, as is the inverse – that compelling architecture necessarily has to resolve structure elegantly.

The advent of computing has renewed interest in 'free-form' design, and the ability to describe mathematically complex forms with complex curvature has resulted in a degree of experimentation that is only natural with the advent of this new technology. The current state of affairs is nevertheless a half-way house. Digital manufacturing has in no way kept pace with the formal possibilities given by the ease of access to mathematic libraries by modern CAD systems. As a result, many of the most interesting architectural techniques of today mediate between the ideal complex geometry and its manufactured manifestation in the real, full-sized world.

Following on from that is the expression of the manufacturing and assembly processes. The nuts and bolts of the assembly system do literally become architectural form, just as the extrusion process of material manufacture dictates the aesthetics of the total product. But an obsession with detail does not in itself make great architecture. The composition of the parts and the spatial manipulation lies at the heart of true architecture. So how do computational strategies help create a fusion between form, structure and an expression of material and process?

It is essential to approach the issues with techniques that actually enhance the product. One of the more spectacular failures is the notion of 'automated design' where some kind of process (random or inspired by, for instance, Darwinian selection) actually creates architectural forms. The architect is reduced to some kind of form selector rather than a designer driven by a self-given goal. Optimisation is a technique that promises more. In essence, the technique is one where a system delivers the 'most efficient solution'. The devil, as usual, lies in the detail. What is our evaluation criterion? If we have multiple criteria, how is one traded for the other? What are the inputs and variables that can be tweaked? The issue lies not so much in the computation, which nowadays is very efficient, even in massive multi-dimensional spaces, but in the definition of the problem.

The classic problem that illustrates optimisation is that of the travelling salesman – how to find the shortest path connection between a set of destinations across a two-dimensional plane. This problem turns out to be 'NP-hard' (where NP stands for Nondeterministic Polynomial time), which means that solution time explodes exponentially with the set of points. However, the great feat of optimisation theory is to verify that there are efficient ways of solving the problem. To understand how this works, visualise a closed body in three-dimensional space. All the possible solutions lie inside the volume; however (and this is the key), all solutions that could be minimal will lie not just on the surface, not just on the edges, but absolutely on the vertices. Optimisation travels along the edges (which connect the vertices) and compares the vertices' efficiency and then travels to the next more efficient vertex. This can lead to finding just a local optimum; surprisingly, in the case of the travelling salesman problem, this is exceedingly rare and the best solutions can be found reasonably quickly.

Most engineering problems are far more complex and need more variables to be evaluated against each other. These variables are connected by rules (just as Euclidian three-dimensional space is dictated by the rules of Pythagoras's theorem, and the transformation from three to two dimensions is governed by the rules of projective geometry). For mathematical convenience these variables are called 'dimensions' or 'degrees of freedom', and they are generally visualised in abstract form through equations and matrices. Multi-dimensional spaces tend to frighten the uninitiated. It is, however, important to understand the general concepts and mechanics because so much of modern mathematics and computing depends on it.

We all understand (we think) ordinary Euclidian three-dimensional space. Abstractly, the importance of the three dimensions is the set of rules that binds them together; for instance, the fact that (thanks to Pythagoras) we can calculate the shortest distance between two points. Embedded within three-dimensional space exist lower-dimensional objects: one-dimensional objects such as lines with lengths, two-dimensional surfaces with additional properties such as area and Gaussian curvature, and three-dimensional solids with properties such as volumes and hence mass.

Once we are properly in three-dimensional space, volumes (hence mass) and cross-section areas have utterly profound consequences. The strength of a material depends directly on its cross-sectional area, and its mass depends on its volume. If you double the (linear) size of an object its mass will increase as the cube of the transform, but its strength only as the square (given the same geometry, but there are subtleties as we shall see).

Large objects are effectively less strong and this phenomenon not only dictates how we approach structure as an architectural tool, but it determines the structure of the universe – from galaxies to quarks. In architecture the consequence is that large buildings are very different from small ones. The effort of supporting large spans or cantilevering tall objects rises as the cube of the size. We cannot expect similar solutions to work at different scales.

The solutions will all obey the simple structural concepts first appreciated during the nineteenth century. Beams don't get stronger by being thicker, they get stronger by being deeper. The distribution of material within the structural system is critical. We learnt all this in structure 101 and it is worth revisiting these fundamental rules for horizontal structural systems – the rules apply to every horizontal structure, be it a short beam or a large-span arch. The critical dimension is the structural depth, which translates into the 'second moment of area'.

The second moment of area states that the vertical distance within a horizontal structural system is proportional to the square of the vertical distance, that is the vertical separation between the top structural member (normally in compression) and the bottom structural member (normally in tension).This simple fact dictates the configuration of all horizontal structural systems. The most common example where this is made explicit is the I beam. On the face of it, the arch seems to behave differently. However, as a structural system it contains two components: the arch itself and the forces tying it together at ground level (explicitly as a tie or implicitly by a foundation). In an arched enclosure we use the space within the structural system, where the rise of the arch is the vertical distance of the second moment of area.

Materials behave differently under different loads. Tension as a system is very important because, unlike compression systems, there is no buckling and thus tension-based systems on a per-weight basis are more efficient. Tension-based systems have very different configurations, the principal issue being that tension has to be maintained under all load conditions. Tent-like structures therefore use curvature as a means to maintain form and are saddle-shaped so that the opposite curvatures can both be in tension and thus maintain their shape.

Curvature is one of the most critical issues of built form after the fundamental configuration. It is striking that as a species we choose to want the most difficult system of all on the horizontal: the flat plane. Flat floors have serious problems – span and deflections are the two limiting factors in any multi-storey design. Vertical walls, however, exploit gravity in a positive manner – we use gravity as a post-compression strategy. In walls, gravity does all the structural work for us.

But here comes the scale issue: on very tall buildings we use gravity on the system as a whole. The 'wall' is no longer a wall; it is literally a skin with very different design criteria. So we see evolving classes of solutions. Within each class we can use optimisation techniques to find local solution minima: least material for given height, least air resistance for given volume and, in the specific case of Bishopsgate Tower (now called 'The Pinnacle'), the minimum number of diagonal braces to support the system.

The greatest skill needs to be exercised in defining the class. The class is a set of solutions predicated on a system; the system definition is critical. System definition is what the architect does (or should do). In real life, system definition is a joint enterprise between architect and engineer, but we can sum it up in a simple statement: engineers solve problems, architects pose problems.

In the case of optimisation we are defining the boundary condition of the solution space. The boundary will directly dictate the result. Computing strategies can assist by helping to form a declarative system. Many architectural concepts depend on sets of dependent ideas and hence dependent geometries. In this area the idea of parametric design resides confidently. Parametric systems handle dependency mechanisms which govern large sets of architectural rules. The parametric model, because it handles dependencies, formalises design but also renders it more flexible. We no longer have to make decisions such as locking the dimension of the grid, or the size of the building, or the exact dimension of its footprint at a given stage of the process. The dependency model takes care of that.

In the following case study, which explains some of the geometric approaches of The Pinnacle, this becomes clear. The fundamental setting-out consists of tan arcs to a polygon. However, in this case subtlety exists in that the radii of the tan arcs are driven indirectly by specifying only the control polygon and the edge lengths. The output of this system is the radius of the arcs. In addition, the geometry is defined by inclined flat planes and a taper on each plane that defines the taper of the sheared cones. It is only now, having established some form of boundary, that the solution is amenable to computational strategies.

It is clear that, as we become more accustomed to the inherent power of computing, the mathematical models we develop will become ever more powerful and useful. The current trend is simple simulations for one-off proposals. Our current goal at KPF Research is to use simulations to evaluate thousands of alternatives and provide an increasingly comprehensive framework for increasingly generalised solutions.

ARCHITECTURAL STRUCTURE – COMPUTATIONAL STRATEGIES.
LARS HESSELGREN, RENOS CHARITOU AND ST.YLIANOS DRITSAS, KPF

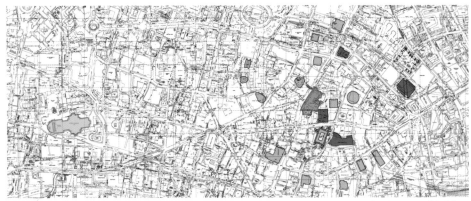

Fig 1 The site of The Pinnacle in the City of London showing proposed and existing tall buildings

Case study
The Pinnacle
(formerly the 'Bishopsgate Tower'), London

The Pinnacle is one of a number of tall buildings planned for the City of London (figure 1). The 100,000 square metre building has been configured with a visually fragmented profile to break down what could otherwise become a massive imposition on the London skyline; furthermore, a series of strategically important views, including views of St Paul's Cathedral, have had to be respected. The design, therefore, has grown from a consideration of a number of key factors, including planning constraints, aesthetic considerations and commercial demands (figure 2).

The tower was designed primarily with Bentley's Generative Components parametric modelling software (then in Alpha release stage, now a released product), while our 'Bishopsgate-System' was implemented in the C+ programming language as an in-process server to the parametric platform. The interactive system is composed of a series of object-oriented assemblies specialised on specific aspects of the design space. The drivers for the selection of this development configuration were dictated by the need for high-performance, interactivity and flexibility for accommodating the scale and complexity of the project.

The primary design focus for the tower was to produce geometry that could be relatively easy to manufacture and communicate. The fundamental decision was taken in summer 2004 to build the tower's geometry entirely from lines and arcs. Subsequent design development has substantiated this approach. It has, among other things, yielded straight columns, together with beams that are either straight or simply bent to a radius (figure 3).

Fig 2 View of the cluster of towers from the Tate Modern

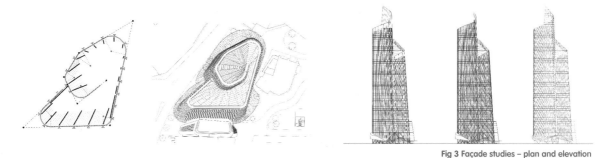

Fig 3 Façade studies – plan and elevation

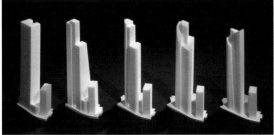

Fig 4 Building mass study models

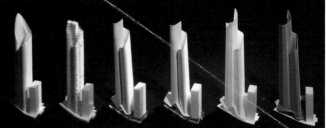

Fig 5 Façade design study models

The geometric approach is based on a number of simple constraints, while including flexibility in the design process. This need for flexibility means that the focus in the design process moves away from designing the object towards designing the system that designs the object. The tower is therefore built on a sequence of parametric dependency models, always responding to the demands of the process.

The original form-finding search (early 2004) was essentially manual, when a wide variety of options from very simple geometries (cylinders, prisms, etc.) were evaluated (figure 4). From this original work it became clear that a roughly triangular floor plate provided the only reasonable solution for this particular site, capable of accommodating the floor space required to make a viable project. The problem with a triangular floor plate is that its townscape impact when viewed edge-on is essentially benign; however, when viewed face-on the visual impact is large.

The design team approached this problem by creating an envelope which divided the volume into two visual components. This pair of components was then tamed in townscape terms by creating a helix which cuts into the wrapped surface (figure 5). The helical cut starts at the height set by the adjacent Tower 42 and 30 St Mary Axe (at approximately 180 metres). The cut then traverses the surface to the pinnacle of the building (at around 288 metres). One advantage of the form is that its asymmetry allows clear orientation in relation to the city. The overall form is thus designed to achieve maximum slenderness for the considerable bulk of the building.

The geometric problem was one of finding a coherent geometric schema allowing for a tapering building where each face slopes differently to be built from simple geometry capable of simple construction. One of the team proposed a design consisting of flat tapering planes joined by sheared cones. This schema was applied to the whole building and became the foundation of the overall geometric system. Such a system has many degrees of freedom and we had to make choices as to how the dependency mechanism should be structured.

The first move was to create a polygon defining the springing points of the tapered planes (the control net). Each corner has a chamfered tangential arc. The first question that arose was how to control the circular fillet. There was no intrinsic advantage in controlling the arc radius explicitly, particularly since the radii at each corner would vary as a function of the sheared cone. A linear set-out was chosen, where the arc radii were controlled indirectly by giving a length to each flat face which established the tangent position.

The issue then was one of direction and the origin of setting-out. The obvious origin point was at the edge of the envelope self-intersection/wrapping. That point itself is located arbitrarily in space in relation to the complex site boundary. The first model set out the building anti-clockwise. This method inevitably resulted in the wrap intersection point not aligning with a putative division system.

At this point of the design it was assumed that the façade module would taper in alignment with the building. Hence, each linear façade segment was made of a multiple of a standard bay (which was varied between 1500 and 1800 grids and a number of variations between). It was obvious that

ARCHITECTURAL
STRUCTURE –
COMPUTATIONAL
STRATEGIES.
LARS HESSELGREN,
RENOS CHARITOU
AND STYLIANOS
DRITSAS, KPF

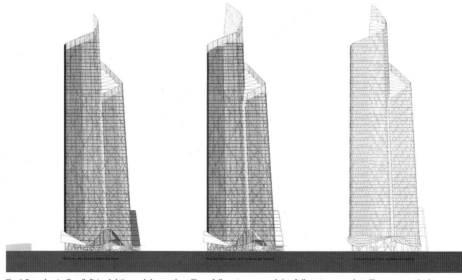

Fig 6 Façade studies (left to right): modules and mullions follow taper; modules follow taper and mullions are vertical; modules are based on 1.5m grid and mullions are vertical

7

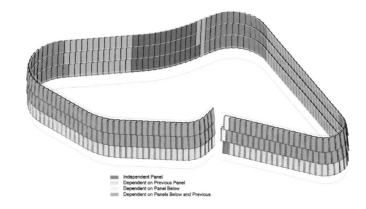

Independent Panel
Dependent on Previous Panel
Dependent on Panel Below
Dependent on Panels Below and Previous

8

Fig 7 Snake-skin topology, showing algorithmic dependencies

Fig 8 Snake-skin optimisation results

Fig 9 Snake-skin geometry showing geometric dependencies

9

this geometric schema would need somewhere to 'take up the slack'. In September 2004, the decision was taken to reverse the setting-out, starting from the wrap intersection point (which would therefore coincide with a notional mullion and, more importantly, column one of the structural system). This created a variable dimension at the wrap intersection, an architecturally satisfying solution. The centres of the sheared cones all lie on a single vector. This vector (and the intersection with each floor plane defining the actual arc) can be computed by constructing the vector on the plane and its intersection with the next plane. Hence, only a single vector on a plane drives the taper of the cone. In a linear setting-out system, the only additional variables that need to be supplied are the inclination and taper of each plane. These two parameters indirectly control the radii of the sheared cones. While the design assumption was that the mullion system would taper in sympathy with the tapered planes, it was important that the taper was the same on each plane.

The initial design concept of tapering modules was abandoned in late 2004 in favour of a linear setting-out on a regular 1.5 metre module (figure 6). This new 'snake skin' of overlapping panels was configured with the help of a specialised optimisation algorithm (figures 7, 8 and 9).

The structural column setting-out is generated from the design skin, but the columns have combinatorial issues of their own. The arcs at corners had chord lengths added, rounded to the nearest possible module. Combined with an offset from the design surface, these provided location points for the columns. In addition to regular spacing, the decision was taken to position the columns symmetrically with respect to the principal arc corners. Even within this constrained set there

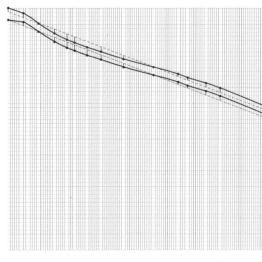

Fig 10 Law curve governing the spiral termination at the top of the building

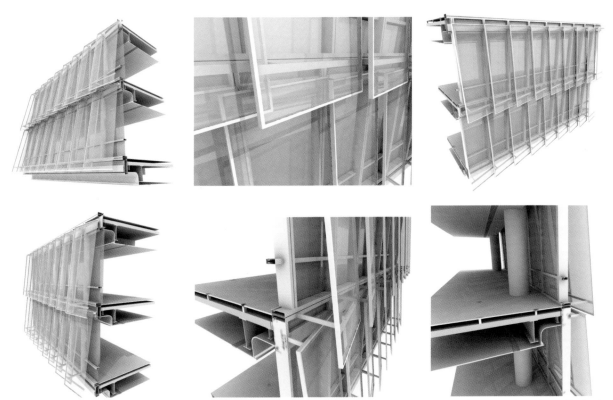

Fig 11 The double-skin façade - study of panel overlaps, cavity size and assembly details

were many possible combinations, most of which were evaluated. In addition, there were constraints imposed by foundation conditions and access roads. These resulted in a number of columns being born off by v frames. The final number of columns was 21, although solutions ranging from 19 to 23 columns were investigated. The huge benefit

of the original design geometry is that every column is straight. However, no column is vertical – their inclination is governed by the design surface.

The shape of the helical cut was the next principal design element. In order to control the shape of the cut, a 'normalised law curve frame' was built (figure 10). Rather than representing the true

10 ARCHITECTURAL
STRUCTURE –
COMPUTATIONAL
STRATEGIES.
LARS HESSELGREN,
RENOS CHARITOU
AND STYLIANOS
DRITSAS, KPF

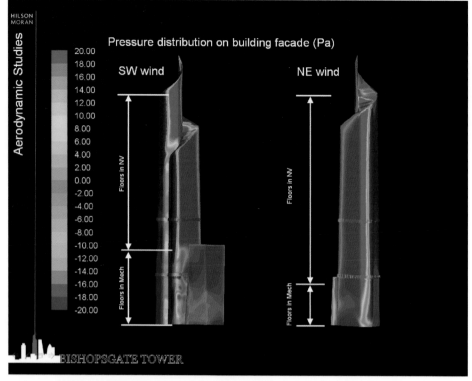

Fig 12 External wind pressure analysis assists the design of an externally ventilated cavity façade, one of the sustainable measures of the tower

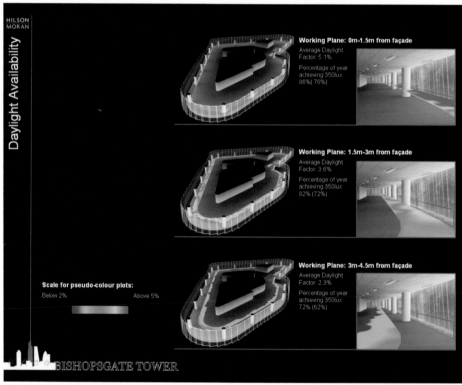

Fig 13 Daylight analysis of the tower

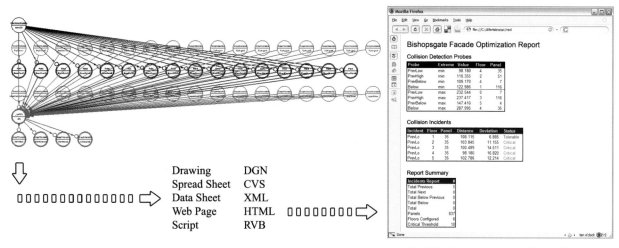

Probe	Extreme	Value	Floor	Panel
PrevLow	min	98.180	4	35
PrevHigh	min	110.355	2	51
PrevBelow	min	109.170	4	7
Below	min	122.986	1	116
PrevLow	max	232.544	0	7
PrevHigh	max	237.417	3	116
PrevBelow	max	147.410	5	4
Below	max	287.995	4	35

Drawing   DGN
Spread Sheet   CVS
Data Sheet   XML
Web Page   HTML
Script   RVB

Fig 14 Building information modelling workflow diagram

unwrapped surface on the diagram, all near-vertical mullion lines and inflection points to arcs are represented as vertical lines. Equally, the heights are represented as true z heights ignoring the effect of the tilted planes. The law curve is controlled by a set of points such that the planes are cut by a straight line and the sheared cones have a smooth transform. This schema gave rise to a large set of variations driven by client and regulatory body input, and was explored on top of varying base forms. Each form was evaluated from a large number of critical street-level views; it was essential that the helical form could be appreciated from all important views.

As this description of The Pinnacle's design demonstrates, the process of architectural design is one that sets the stage for the structural analysis. Analysis is simple if the design–analysis feedback loop is simple – given this shape and these constraints, which structural solution is 'best'?

But design isn't like that. Structural strategies impact on the design and how the designers think of the design. Some visible design aspects are vital; others can be finessed in various ways. The interesting fact is that with evolving design technologies, the loop can be far more close-coupled; structural analysis really can adapt form in a visible manner and in a fashion that enhances architectural concepts.

Lars Hesselgren is a senior associate partner and director of research at Kohn Pedersen Fox Architects. Renos Charitou is a project coordinator at KPF. Stylianos Dritsas is a member of the Computational Geometry Group, KPF.

THE EFFICIENTLY FORMED BUILDING.
JALAL EL-ALI, BURO HAPPOLD

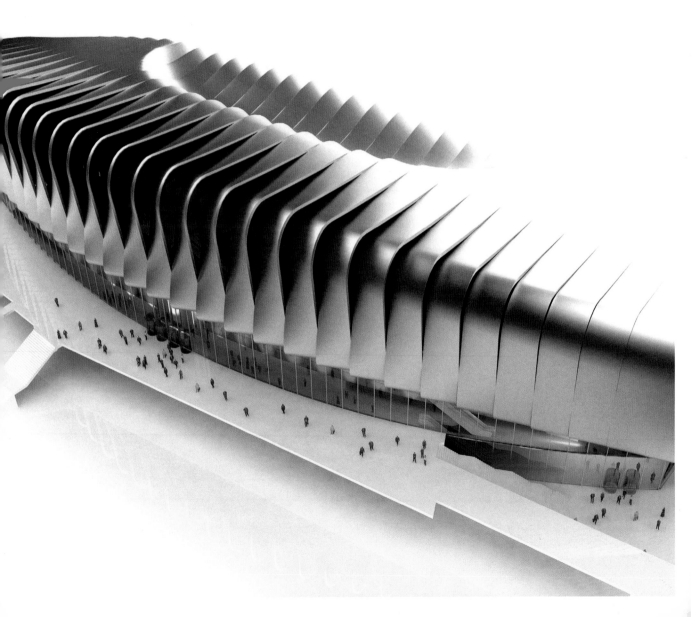

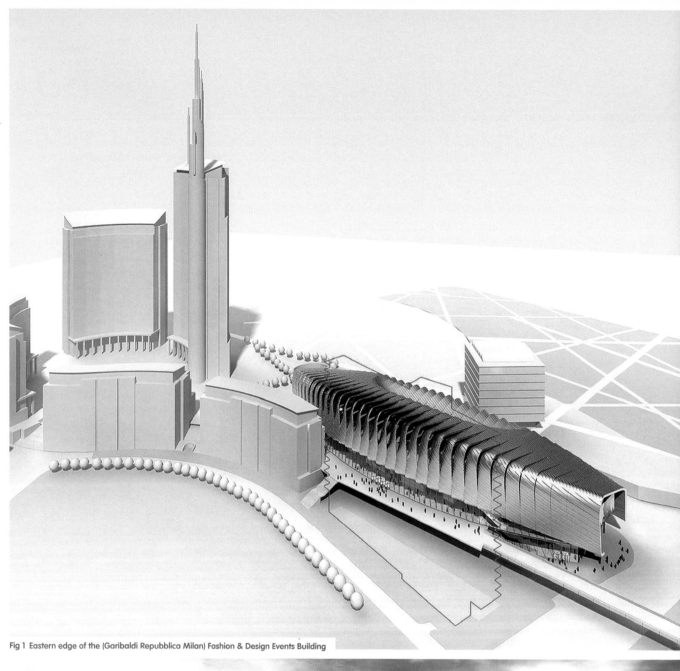

Fig 1 Eastern edge of the (Garibaldi Repubblica Milan) Fashion & Design Events Building

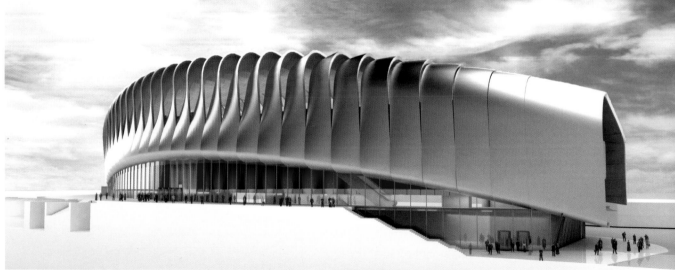

Fig 2 The south elevation of the Grimshaw design, a timber-framed, metal-clad structure

Designing free-form buildings and blobs is the new trend in architecture. This is due to newly evolved software tools and the ease in creating such objects. Complex-shaped buildings are obviously more expensive to engineer, build, operate and maintain, providing a motivation for researching procedures to simplify the process of designing them.

The techniques used by the Generative Geometry Group at Buro Happold allow us to realise and engineer free-form buildings through making both the process and the buildings more efficient.

Complex designs are those that cannot be described in basic geometric terms; they consist of interlocked simpler parts, the 'geometric components'. Complex models could be a result of experimental design processes or simply an architectural design concept. In either case, the design team has to be innovative and inventive in order to extract and design a building strategy to engineer the architectural object.

Complexity can be a structural solution in itself; a pure, efficient structure is usually a complex-shaped one. Catenaries are pure structural forms but they are expensive to build due to their complex geometries; beams are simple and cheap but are not an efficient form. Simulation, optimisation and modelling provide ways of identifying a solution that meets these multiple demands.

A distinction between free-form designs and form-found designs should also be made. 'Free-form' designs are shaped by the architect without referring to material and structural behaviours. 'Form-found' designs, however, are evolving structures, created through a dependency on physical forces, the constraints of materials and the effect of spatial boundary conditions.

Free forms, with the large and complicated structures necessary to keep them aloft, can be realised at a high price. As complicated building systems are employed, maintenance, access and installation become difficult and yet another expensive undertaking. Form-found structures are more efficient, as competing principles are

assimilated and optimised throughout the design process – by employing a parametric computational environment, there is an inherent flexibility allowing different design options to be explored. The use of parametric tools has become important, allowing us to explore multiple design alternatives in an interactive environment; this permits us to evaluate and compare different design solutions and to choose the most efficient one that pleases all parties and fits within the budget.

Efficiency through the modelling process

Grimshaw Architect's Fashion and Design Events Building will anchor the eastern edge of Cesar Pelli's masterplan of the 'Garibaldi Project' and address the 92,000 square metre public park to the north (figure 1). The two levels of exhibition space at the core of this project needed to be rectangular in both plan and section, thus giving little more formal opportunity than that of a large box at the core of the building. However, the architects created a complex roof form enveloping these boxes, inspired directly from fabric design in the fashion industry (figures 2 and 3).

The model of this complex form-found building was parametrically modelled and managed by Buro Happold using Generative Components, the plug-in for MicroStation. The process started with iterative design workshops involving the architects, multidisciplinary engineers and design managers concentrating on defining the initiating parameters of the design. It was agreed by all teams that only one model should be built and shared by all disciplines. This process led to a dramatically reduced workload, while leading to a design that is both structurally sound and architecturally unique.

The form of the roof is achieved through a number of parameters set by different site constraints. The overall shape of the building is extracted from its location, the maximum width of the site and height regulations. The roof geometry is defined as a combination of circular profiles in plan and elevation, creating asymmetrical arcs for the setting-out. The shape of the roof is then smoothed by filleting the edges of the box (figure 4).

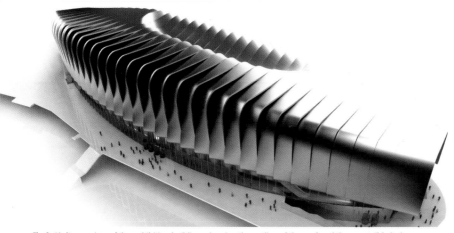

Fig 3 Bird's eye view of the exhibition building, showing the outline of the roof and the accessible balcony area

THE EFFICIENTLY
FORMED BUILDING.
JALAL EL-ALI,
BURO HAPPOLD

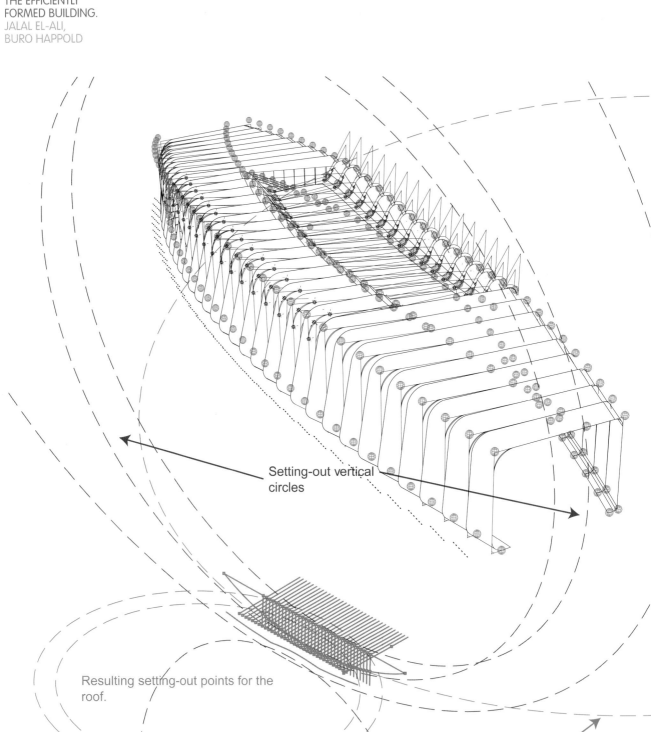

Setting-out vertical
circles

Resulting setting-out points for the
roof.

Setting-out planer
circles

Fig 4 The setting-out points for the complex geometry that underpins the building envelope

The roof is split into parallel strips, or ribbons, in a linear array in plan, each of which responds to its local condition (figure 5). At each end, where the form is lowest, the ribbons create a sun canopy over the external billboards; each ribbon then progressively twists to allow bands of daylight to penetrate the building. The direction and angle of these twists corresponds to the orientation of potential views. From the escalator foyers the important views are skyward, owing to the narrowness of the adjacent external space; from the ground-floor foyer the views are of the main square; and from the roof-top cafe they are of the park. On the north side of the building this device is used to conceal escape stairs and air-intake louvres from the park.

The ribbons are equal in width and are modelled as ruled surfaces between the curves that slice the roof. They also twist, an effect achieved by offsetting the fillets of the strip constructors; depending on the value and orientation of the twist, the strips will be distorted to reach out of the building or blend into it. We have constrained the control of the offsets to the fillet arcs on the centre strip of the roof; this value represents the maximum twist as the remaining strips will gradually twist to blend with the original surface of the roof. The value of the twist is achieved by the number of openings needed in the building; this factor is directly linked to the amount of required light and, potentially, environmental parameters.

We have also created a strategy to find the most effective and efficient structure to support the roof and achieve the pure form the architect intends. Using Generative Components we were able to construct a number of simple elements to communicate the roof geometry to the structural analysis software, Robot, allowing us to analyse and evaluate different building materials, and various structural spans, material thicknesses, support conditions and spacing. At this stage, timber beams were selected as the supporting structure for the roof. Modelling these beams was essential, as we needed to study connection details, interfaces and their appearance (they will be exposed internally). The external cladding of the roof will be constructed of folded metal double-seamed sheets, assembled to comply with the twists of the roof and allow effective drainage.

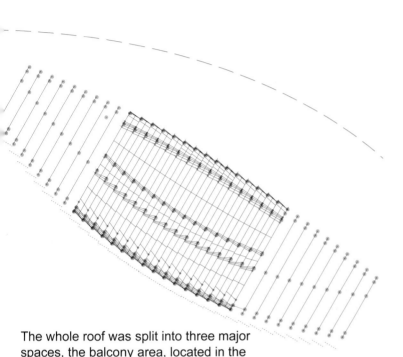

The whole roof was split into three major spaces, the balcony area, located in the middle of the roof and the two sides. They use different components as the level of complexity varies, but to simplify, the same parameters were needed for both of the components.

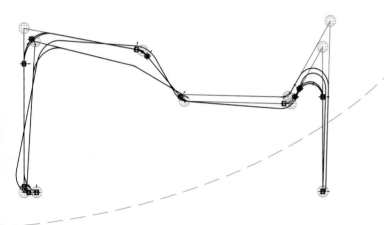

This section was built to easily control the whole roof, changing specific points in that section, will interactively affect the whole points on the roof. The gradual variation of the roof twist was acheived by linking it to custom law curves.

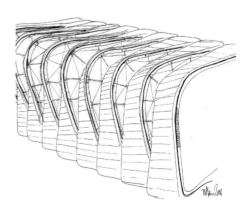

Fig 5 Architect's sketch illustrating the build-up and materiality of the building's gill-like structure

THE EFFICIENTLY FORMED BUILDING.
JALAL EL-ALI, BURO HAPPOLD

Fig 6 Model showing how the roof structure is draped over a series of buildings beneath National Academy of the Arts.

**Fig 7 Initial structural optimisation of the roof.
Far left:** creating a surface by lofting the edges. This is the minimum surface capable of covering the required area.
Second left: Simulating the roof as a plastic material, enabling engineers to see the areas of maximum deflection.
The simulation was permitted to accept a high level of deflection.
Second right:
The displaced shape was inverted, although multiplied to achieve the right amount of curvature.
Far right: Simulation of the deflected shape was used to analyse its behaviour and optimise its shape.

Optimisation process, Bergen National Academy of the Arts (KHiB)

Snohetta Architects' design for the Bergen National Academy of the Arts incorporates a roof structure that spans the entrance and main sculpture court of the art school (figure 6). Buro Happold was contracted to supply geometric information from computational means to aid the development of this roof. The efficiency of this single-span network is determined by the geometry. We have, we believe, executed multiple optimisation strategies to achieve a buildable and efficient structure.

The roof was designed as a steel-grid structure clad with glass. Two factors defined the cost of the roof: the weight of steel and the area of glass. The optimisation process in the weight of steel involved applying a new method in form-finding (figure 7). The developed method uses the same concept as hanging chain models, but extends it to digital simulation. The concept was to simulate the behaviour of the roof and 'relax' it until the optimum shape was achieved. The main objective for this optimisation was to minimise the deflections and stresses in the roof, allowing a parallel decrease in beam sizes.

The initial design considered homogeneous beam sizes across the whole roof; these sizes were altered in every iteration, where a direct relation between the stress and thickness was defined. The process led to beams which were tapered in section – thicker when next to their supports and thinner when suspended in space. All load conditions were considered within this optimisation process. The optimised roof proved to be 40 per cent lighter than the original form; simultaneously, the height of the roof grew by 3 metres, representing an increase of 2.3 degrees in the pitch angle.

As mentioned above, form-found geometry is more complex to build than a flat shape. It is obvious that complex form construction is a serious challenge to engineers and fabricators, although complex forms have their virtues. Meanwhile, research into designing and proposing fabrication techniques is now being done as early as possible in the design process. For the Bergen roof project, multiple contractors were consulted on how best to implement the design in a cost-effective way. Fabrication parameters were simplified into geometrical constraints, including glass sizes, properties and thickness, as well as warping factors (figure 8).

These factors were included in a parallel iteration routine, where different tessellation options were explored (figure 9). The results were exported to the structural form-finding routine, allowing the structurally optimised form to be evaluated against various fabrication criteria. This process is capable of producing an infinite number of variations of the design, incorporating key alternatives, and requires the use of an evaluation matrix. This matrix involves giving certain parameters a hierarchy of importance – budget is the first filtering parameter employed, reducing the number of options. Further parameters include tessellation options, materials, support conditions and load patterns. When this information is eventually presented as a spreadsheet we will be able to diagrammatically observe the differences between one solution and another, allowing a final choice to be made.

Jalal El-Ali is a Senior Designer in Buro Happold's Generative Group

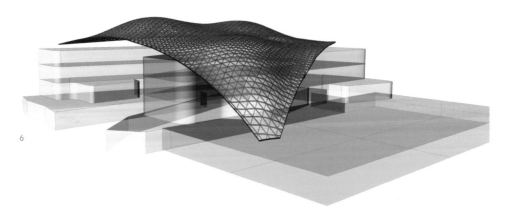

6

7

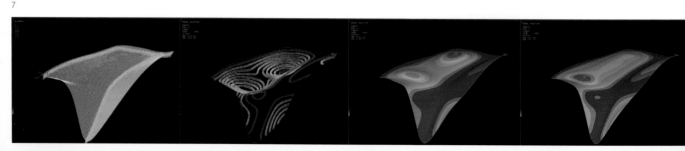

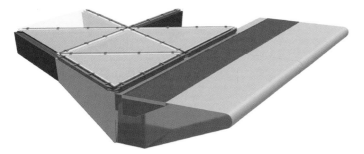

Fig 8 Drawing showing the edge beam of the roof, and the glass detailing

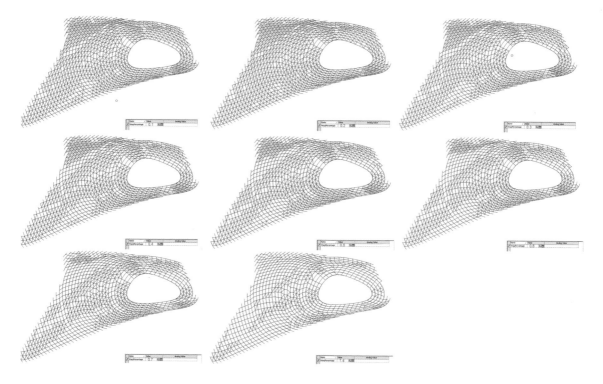

Fig 9 A series of images showing variations in the subdivision of the glass panels, depending on their twist value

Fig 10 Computer-generated rendering showing the final shape of the roof

GEOMETRY,
FORM AND COMPLEXITY.
HUGH WHITEHEAD
AND BRADY PETERS,
FOSTER + PARTNERS

GEOMETRY, FORM AND COMPLEXITY.

HUGH WHITEHEAD AND BRADY PETERS, FOSTER + PARTNERS

Part 1

Is geometry the essence of form –
or just a convenient means of description?

At the level of philosophy or of science this is a question that could be debated without ever reaching a conclusion, while to most architects the question would be almost rhetorical. However, in the digital age, where computers are increasingly used in design, fabrication and construction to explore the art of the possible, the answer is no longer clear cut. This is because the approaches to design are as much a matter of style as the resulting form. The choice of medium for design exploration and the materials and methods used for construction to a large extent determine the most effective means of description.

Historically, the use of geometry and mathematics to describe built form provided a common basis for communication between the processes of design, fabrication and assembly. This meant that the theories of proportion and harmony – and also the precision required to coordinate delivery by large numbers of people under a legal contract – could both be specified within the same system. The implication was that the application of rationale would not compromise creativity or the creation of a beautiful form. This is now being challenged by the use of digital technology to produce free-form buildings which, by transcending the limitations of Euclidean geometry, can deliver an aesthetic that appears more organic but which can also achieve higher levels of performance.

Ultimately the creation of form is about the resolution of forces – some physical and some metaphysical. While engineers may use form-finding techniques to deploy material in a way that minimises stress, architects explore trade-offs between considerations which are much harder to quantify or balance. In terms of aesthetics there can be no absolute measure. The appeal of a building may lie in the delight of experiencing a habitable sculpture in which the exterior celebrates the play of light across curved metal panels, while the interior uses digitally fabricated timber to provide superb acoustics, yet the complex structure that supports it is never seen. On the other hand the honest expression of structure and detailing can be seen as symbolising an intellectual rigour which permeates the whole design, so the complex qualities of form and space can be decoded in terms of an underlying simplicity which makes it possible.

Accepting the constraints of a limited palette of surfaces that can be described in terms of simple projections of lines and arcs has advantages that cannot be easily abandoned. A system of geometry constructed with a ruler and compass can also be marked out with nothing more than pins and string, so that the design intent can be reliably conveyed to fabricators and contractors by means of conventional drawings and a rule-based method statement. However, free-form designs developed with digital 3-D models can be implemented using only surveying equipment based on laser technology and fabrication processes dependent on computerised numerical control systems. The higher levels of skill required are also often accompanied by higher risks and greater cost.

Since the mid-1990s, Foster + Partners have explored the potential of free-form design with a series of six seminal buildings (see below) for which geometric principles were relaxed and gradually extended rather than suddenly abandoned, so that a systematic approach still ensured delivery on time and on budget. The necessary research was undertaken by the formation of the Specialist Modelling Group as an in-house consultancy, setting a trend that has been followed by many architectural and engineering practices. At the time, each project was a voyage into uncharted waters, but in retrospect they can be seen as part of a progression in which new design ideas were supported by new approaches to rationale which helped to make the projects buildable.

Design can also be described as an evolutionary process in which the result, the intended route and even the starting point cannot be predetermined. The way in which potential solutions are generated, evaluated and selected is extremely Darwinian, yet both logic and intuition play roles that are inextricably combined. In his book *Lateral Thinking*, Edward de Bono famously described logic as the management of 'no'. The process of design requires a counterpart or corollary – inspiration is the management of 'yes'.

However, before construction can commence, a design has to be described in terms of a set of procedures which are to be performed in a sequence that is entirely logical and based on some system of geometry, mathematics or numerical control. In nature there is no such clear distinction between process and procedure – at a conceptual level the development of form is all process, while at a material level it is all procedure, but they occur simultaneously as growth. The use of computers is helping designers to blur this distinction by using procedural techniques earlier in their design process. As a result, buildings are starting to appear more organic, not as an issue of style but because they are beginning to behave more like organisms, which are both responsive and even adaptive to their environment.

30 St Mary Axe, London

The Swiss Re Headquarters (figure 1), now known as 30 St Mary Axe but commonly referred to as 'the Gherkin', was the first of these six seminal buildings and its radical form was derived primarily from a response to context. At first sight the unusual shape might appear to be a wilful gesture attempting to

Fig 1 30 St Mary Axe, London, colloquially known as 'the Gherkin'

Fig 2 The Sage, Gateshead. A wave-form profile swept around a spiral cross section

be iconic, but it would never have succeeded on this basis. True iconic status cannot be designed, but is conferred by the people who use or appreciate the building. While the Gherkin has now become the film maker's first choice of a location shot for London that symbolises the adventurous use of technology, the general public is probably unaware that the design logic is so tight that, in retrospect, the resulting form was almost inevitable. The building was, in effect, pre-rationalised, making it possible to develop parametric control systems which, in turn, made the detailed design, fabrication and construction possible. Coordination and accountability were ensured by issuing all consultants and contractors with a formal geometry method statement, from which they were required to build their own 3-D models and extract coordinates as part of checking procedures.

Learning from the experience of Swiss Re the next two buildings in the series, the Sage centre and GLA City Hall, were essentially exercises in post-rationalisation. Both projects began as competition schemes where the design called for a free-form double-curved skin; the panelisation of the surface – required in order to deliver an affordable building – was developed only after the concept stage. The challenge was to find a geometric rationale that would not compromise the original design concept. Whereas any curved surface can be easily subdivided into a triangular mesh, a quadrilateral mesh may result in panels that are twisted and therefore difficult to fabricate as a cladding system. Designers, however, tend to prefer quadrilateral rather than triangular panels in terms of visual appearance and there are also compelling economic considerations that result from simpler

node connections, fewer framing members and less material wastage. While there is now a large body of research into techniques for transforming quadrilateral meshes into planar facets, they generally use iterative calculations which converge to a solution that is within tolerance limits, but there are relatively few approaches to deriving a precise solution by means of formal geometry. These two projects are based on a different principle, but they illustrate two of the primary strategies for creating curved surfaces for which there is a natural flat panel solution.

The Sage, Gateshead

The cladding surface for the Sage (figure 2) is based on a wave-form profile swept around a spiral cross section. However, an arc swept around an arc produces a 'torus patch' which can always be subdivided into planar facets. By rationalising the spiral curve into three tangential arcs and the wave-form into seven, the resulting surface is composed of 21 torus patches, which all fit together with perfect tangency across the boundaries. This surface could then be unfolded into a flat pattern development, making it easily scheduled and economically fabricated because there is repetition in the sweep direction. Furthermore, because the profile remains constant, the supporting ribs could all be formed to the same curvature. By setting up a parametric control system for the two defining curves the whole envelope could be continually varied in response to design changes in the shape of the auditoria. Significantly, rather than compromising the original concept, the approach of developing geometry that could perform as a rule-based mechanism provided the flexibility to progressively refine the design, even at a relatively late stage in the project.

Fig 3

Fig 4

Fig 5

Fig 6

GLA City Hall, London

The shape for City Hall (figure 3) began as a sphere, which had the advantage of providing minimal surface area for a given volume, but was then transformed into an egg shape with its central axis inclined towards the sun. This greatly reduced solar irradiation and hence the cooling load. Slicing this form with a set of horizontal planes produced floor plate shapes that were all close to elliptical. The proportions changed progressively up the building, with the long and the short axes becoming transposed through a circular floor plate at mid-height. This surprising result could have provided a way to rationalise the geometry, but the twist in the cladding surface could only be resolved by triangulation, which would have made it difficult to accommodate office partitions. However, by making all the floor plates conform to a circular plan the complex surface became a family of 'sheared cones'. While it is obvious that a cone with a vertical axis will have a simple flat panel solution, it was not widely known that when the cone axis is inclined the facets become trapezoidal, but they remain planar. Circular floor plates also allowed the internal space planning to be coordinated with a regular radial grid, while the partitions could be connected to inclined mullions with triangular closer pieces, each cranked to the required angle. As the design concept evolved, the guiding principles emerged through experimentation, rather than being imposed as a formulaic solution.

Albion Wharf, London

The series of six buildings was a cumulative process, in which each project increased the repertoire of successful techniques, but also created new points of departure for the next exploration. The design of Albion Wharf (figure 4) was based on spiral curves for both plan and section. Like Swiss Re, the curvature produced a recessive form, in which the apparent mass reduces as the building is approached. Like the Sage, the façade was panelised with a torus patch solution, but the effect of double curvature was further enhanced by adding an outer skin of tubular rods to provide solar protection. The roof, however, was designed as an undulating form with a soft silhouette, rising smoothly over the service cores to enclose the plant rooms. For this surface, twist was inevitable, and a new approach had to be found for controlling the curvature. The idea was to use the Kalzip system, which could accommodate twist by means of pre-curved and tapered sheets with a standing seam joint, but the process of prefabrication required a design surface that could be precisely defined in a digital model. The solution was to use radial beams with a standard curvature but pivoted from the top edge of the façade. Controlled undulation of the roof could then be achieved by varying the rock angle of a standard profile according to a simple sine-wave function. This technique employed a combination of parametric control systems together with a generative script, so that both the design and the construction rationale became embedded in the tools that produced the form.

Free University Library, Berlin

'Embedded rationale' was also used in the development of the Free University Library in Berlin (figure 5). This project provided a new infill to an existing courtyard, where the concept was for a bubble-shaped building. Column-free steel trusses produced a framework of hoops that support a double-skin enclosure, while the internal concrete floors are completely independent. A flat-panel solution was required for both the inner and the outer skin, so a rule-based variational profile was developed to control the truss geometry at every cross section. The curvature is defined by three tangential arcs for which the segment angle is constrained to remain constant so that, as with City Hall, each portion of the surface conforms to sheared cone geometry. The transformation was controlled by using a bi-directional solver, which accepts both geometric and algebraic constraints and returns a 'degree of freedom' count. The concept of degrees of freedom is fundamental to any constraint management system, and allows designers to explore different types of behaviour resulting from different logical dependencies.

When the height of the cross sections was constrained by a profile curve in the long direction, it was found that the solver returned zero degrees of freedom, so that for any given height there was a unique solution to the section shape. However, this meant that the plan shape could not be directly controlled, but only varied by changing the long section curvature. The loose-fit relationship between the skin and the interior structure meant that this turned out to be an acceptable limitation. Although the use of embedded rationale is a very powerful technique, it is best applied when a design concept has already reached a stable configuration and just needs to be fine-tuned. There is always an element of compromise in adopting any rule-based approach. While a potential solution can be explored in more depth, its breadth will inevitably be limited by the acceptance of constraints, which it is also important to challenge.

In the evolution of design ideas the use of pre-rationalised, post-rationalised or embedded rationale remains a matter of choice. However, in the development of a system of descriptive geometry that will support the delivery of a project, the aim is to achieve integration between performance requirements, which are based on the selection of appropriate materials but also informed by fabrication and construction techniques.

Chesa Futura, St Moritz

Chesa Futura (figure 6) provided extreme challenges due to a combination of adverse climatic conditions and a desire to use traditional materials in new ways, creating a futuristic form that would optimise the potential of a restricted and steeply sloping site. The building is a timber shell shaped like a kidney

Figs 7 and 8 The Great Canopy, West Kowloon Cultural District, Hong Kong. Conceived as a smooth and seamless surface floating over the site

bean but raised above the ground on raking steel supports. Although clad with timber shingles, cut by hand and fixed on site, the frame and wall panels were prefabricated in Germany using advanced CNC machinery. This was driven directly by curves extracted from a solid model, which involved multiple offsets, cuts and difference operations, so that precise geometry could be derived for every component. Even with the experience of the previous five projects, it became apparent that in order to design Chesa Futura, it would also be necessary to design a modelling process that was based on a full understanding of the underlying technologies.

The free-form shape was controlled only by a schematic plan and section, which were rationalised as tangential arcs and then linked to act together as parametric templates. This provided a simple control mechanism which allowed the complex interactions between internal spatial and external contextual relationships to be explored and resolved in a fine-tuning process that took many months. To create the full design surface of the form, transition points between the arcs were locked to sloping planes to define paths along which a variational profile could be driven by a generative script. Any change in the two defining templates caused the whole form to regenerate, but always as a fair surface with continuous curvature and a precise definition. By using parametric templates composed of rational curves, the resulting form was interpreted by the solid modeller as a mathematical surface for which precise offsets are easily produced. This approach guaranteed the precision and robustness which was required to reliably drive the machinery in the fabrication workshop.

The following case studies illustrate how these design methodologies have been developed. The ability to define geometry as a rule-based mechanism has become extended through generative techniques based on an algorithmic approach. These studies demonstrate how computational skills empower designers to become both tool-builders and digital craftsmen by allowing them to communicate directly with performance analysis and fabrication techniques.

Part 2

Case study 1: The Great Canopy, West Kowloon Cultural District, Hong Kong

The Great Canopy is a key component of Foster + Partners proposal for the West Kowloon Cultural District. This masterplan provides an unprecedented collection of arts, performance and leisure venues for Hong Kong. The canopy (figures 7 and 8) unifies the whole development and is seen as the symbol for the whole development and as a new icon for Hong Kong. Conceptually, the canopy is a smooth and seamless surface that floats over the site.

The ability to quickly, easily and precisely control the form of the canopy surface was critical. A single design surface was the starting point; this surface was then used as a carrier for different component strategies. A series of parametric control systems (figures 9 and 10) and generative scripts were used to create multiple structure and cladding options; many of these control mechanisms were driven by performance criteria. This project developed techniques that had been introduced in previous projects. Computer programming was increasingly used throughout the project as a tool to develop architectural ideas. Critically, the architectural designer rather than the computer specialist created the algorithms and wrote the generative scripts, allowing the design rationale to be quickly and creatively embedded within the mechanisms of geometry creation.

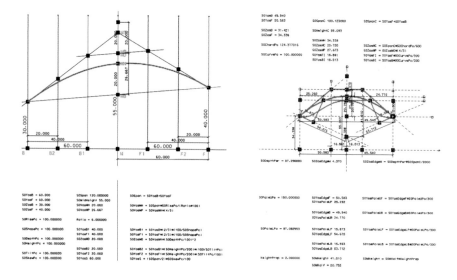

Figs 9 and 10 A series of parametric control systems guide the design process of this complex structure

GEOMETRY, FORM AND COMPLEXITY.
HUGH WHITEHEAD
AND BRADY PETERS,
FOSTER + PARTNERS

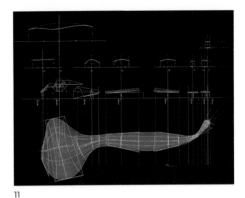

11

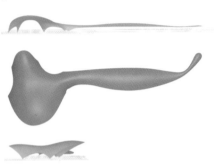

12

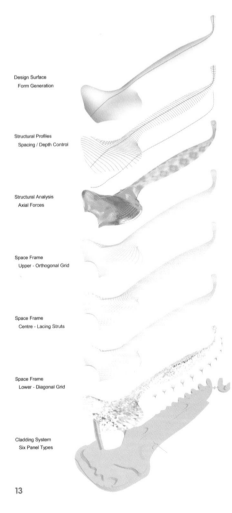

Design Surface
Form Generation

Structural Profiles
Spacing / Depth Control

Structural Analysis
Axial Forces

Space Frame
Upper - Orthogonal Grid

Space Frame
Centre - Lacing Struts

Space Frame
Lower - Diagonal Grid

Cladding System
Six Panel Types

13

Fig 11 A system of modular parametric controllers is used to control the complex geometry of the canopy's design surface

Fig 12 The design surface is generated in separate surface patches corresponding to the parametric control modules

Fig 13 Image illustrating the elements of the canopy, from design surface to cladding system

Design surface and form generation

The canopy's height, width and curvature vary over its length, presenting a smooth, undulating form when viewed both from above and beneath. A system of modular parametric controllers (figure 11) was used to control the complex geometry of the design surface. This modular system could easily be extended if a larger surface was required or if more detail was needed in a specific area. A plan, elevation and section controller constituted one module.

The design surface (figure 12) was generated in separate surface patches corresponding to the parametric control modules. These surface patches each contained the minimum number of control points needed to create the desired curvature characteristics – thus creating smooth, gently flowing surfaces. The parametric system automatically maintained tangency between surface patches; it allowed precise control over one of the most visually critical characteristics of the design surface geometry – its edge condition. Structural rules were built into this system by adjustable parameters controlling the section geometry. This parametric control mechanism produced an overall surface geometry that could be easily manipulated and precisely controlled. Once developed, this rule-based mechanism provided a flexible and lightweight solution that allowed for the rapid adjustment of the roof surface; this was important as adjustments to the canopy geometry were necessary on a near-daily basis until late in the design process.

Although the parametric control mechanism very carefully defined the design surface in terms of visual intent, the top design surface was rebuilt and a new offset bottom surface was created to embed structural performance criteria into the geometry of the canopy. A parametric section controller was developed to control the relationship between the top surface and a new offset surface, which defines the structural depth of the canopy. This amount of offset has been tuned to provide optimal stiffness in the areas where it is needed and minimal intrusion in less demanding zones. The variation in structural depth is controlled through the use of 'law curves', which provide a simple graphical interface to control complex relationships. The profiles were placed along a sinuous centre-line and their spacing related to the structural spacing and cladding module. The parameterisation of the surfaces generated from these profiles inherited this information (figure 13).

Generating structure – the designer as tool-builder

While many structural strategies were investigated, it was determined that a space truss solution was particularly suited to the varying geometry of the canopy. As a modular component-based system, it could be infinitely varied with minimal

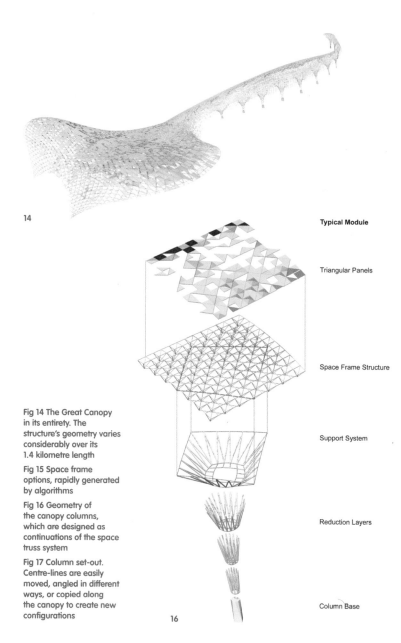

14

Typical Module

Triangular Panels

Space Frame Structure

Support System

Reduction Layers

Column Base

16

Fig 14 The Great Canopy in its entirety. The structure's geometry varies considerably over its 1.4 kilometre length

Fig 15 Space frame options, rapidly generated by algorithms

Fig 16 Geometry of the canopy columns, which are designed as continuations of the space truss system

Fig 17 Column set-out. Centre-lines are easily moved, angled in different ways, or copied along the canopy to create new configurations

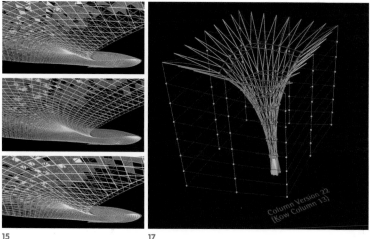

15   **17**

cost, and provided a unifying structural solution that accommodated the varying depths and spans in the head and tail areas. The top surface of the space truss allowed for direct cladding support and minimised the need for secondary steelwork.

The Great Canopy, stretching nearly 1.4 kilometres in length, incorporates a vast quantity of structural and cladding components; a single space truss option contains nearly 200,000 members (figure 14). As the geometry varies from one end to the other, all these components are potentially different. To draw every single one of these components using standard 3-D CAD tools would have taken an impossibly long time, even with a large team. However, the generating rules of these components can be easily defined and the algorithms can be translated into computer programs, which can then be used to generate many structure and cladding options (figure 15).

Through the use of parametric control mechanisms it is possible to generate and control hundreds of profiles or components; however, by using computer programs to generate geometry, the creation of hundreds of thousands of components is possible. While the definition of each algorithm is carefully considered, the geometric results are not always predictable. The effect of the rapid generation of these new geometric constellations of elements was profound, and new possibilities and forms began to emerge. Importantly, the generating scripts were written by an architectural designer. This approach allowed the definition of new digital tools, freeing the designer from the limited palette of commands available in the standard CAD package. These programmed generative tools were developed as the design progressed and altered on a daily basis. The computer scripts were developed in a fast and fluid way – a method termed 'sketching with code'.

Other team members and consultants were quick to realise the potential of this approach and became part of the process of creating these new tools, embedding their own ideas into the generating code. While detailed structural investigations took place, the geometry of the design surface was still changing. Scripting disengages one design problem from another, allowing the design to be developed in many areas simultaneously. Parametric models can be swapped, input geometry can be modified, variables updated and scripted modules can be inserted or removed without having a large impact on other parts of the process.

The canopy columns (figure 16) were designed to be continuations of the space truss system, both transferring the load of the canopy to the ground and appearing to grow out of it like trees, becoming the canopy overhead. The columns were generated by a computer script that used the column centreline and the canopy design surfaces as input.

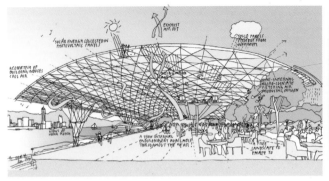

18   21

The column centre-lines could be placed anywhere under the canopy, in any direction (figure 17). These centre-lines were easily moved, angled in different ways, or copied along the canopy to create new column configurations.

Integrating environmental performance

The cladding of the canopy, which acts as a climate modifier for the semi-outdoor spaces underneath, is composed of an array of different panels distributed over the supporting structure (figure 18). The nature of the cladding is seen as an ephemeral cover that 'breathes' and has a distinctive surface pattern that serves to break down the scale of the expansive roofscape. Individual panels can be compared to the leaves of a tree, which combine to give a distinctive dappled effect (figure 19).

While structural rules were built into the generating rules of this canopy, the principles that governed the environmental strategy were more complex and a different strategy had to be employed. Environmental consultants developed a two-dimensional map locating the different panel types. Six different materials (figure 20) were selected for their ability to respond to the varying functional requirements of the canopy cladding: open trellis, glass, aluminium panels, ETFE cushions, louvres, and specials (i.e. solar thermal collection panels and photovoltaic cells). As it was not necessary to update the environmental analysis with each new canopy option, a loose-fit strategy was developed, by which this panel layout could be mapped onto the three-dimensional form. The geometry of the cladding components could then be generated from this information.

Digital fabrication

The computational techniques used to design this roof resulted in a very detailed structure with many components. But just as new techniques were needed to create the digital model, new ones were necessary for the fabrication of the physical model (figure 21). Using the information produced by the generative scripts, the canopy structure was printed in three dimensions using the selective laser sintering process. Because of the size limitations of this process, the canopy was produced in seven parts; glazing components were laser-cut from digital files. These elements were then assembled by our in-house model shop.

Brady Peters is an associate and member of the Specialist Modelling Group at Foster + Partners

Case study 2:
The Smithsonian Courtyard Enclosure, Washington DC

The Patent Office Building in Washington DC, built between 1836 and 1867, is considered one of the finest examples of Greek Revival architecture in the United States of America. Constructed to house the many scale models that patent law required inventors to submit, the building is now home to the Smithsonian American Art Museum and the National Portrait Gallery.

In 2003 the Smithsonian held a competition for the enclosure of its 2,600 square metre central courtyard. Our winning scheme (figure 22) encloses this grand space with a flowing glass canopy, an integrated design solution, the undulating surface of which efficiently deals with structural requirements,

Fig 18 Diagram showing the environmental performance of the canopy

Fig 19 The cladding of the canopy. Individual panels can be compared to the leaves of a tree

Fig 20 Foster + Partners developed six types of cladding panels for the canopy

Fig 21 Rapid prototyped model of the Kowloon canopy, produced in seven parts and assembled into a single structure

- Open trellis
- Glass
- Aluminium Tiles
- Elevated Aluminium Tiles Facing South
- Elevated Aluminium Tiles Facing South East
- Elevated Aluminium Tiles Facing South West
- ETFE
- ETFE Graphics
- Specials
- Fixed Louvres

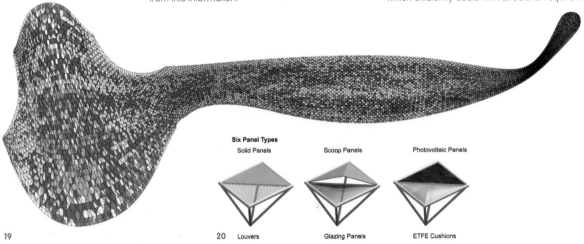

19

Six Panel Types

Solid Panels	Scoop Panels	Photovoltaic Panels
Louvres	Glazing Panels	ETFE Cushions

20

Fig 22 Norman Foster sketch proposal for a roof over the Smithsonian's central courtyard

Fig 23 Image of the Smithsonian roof, showing control polygons from which the structure is adjusted

Fig 24 Underside of the roof canopy, illustrating how the structural members curve across the courtyard (overleaf)

Fig 25 The Smithsonian canopy on site in October 2006. The creation of a 'geometry method statement' is designed to ensure that fabricators understand the geometric principles of the project and are less likely to misunderstand the geometry

Fig 26 The Robert and Arlene Kogod Courtyard will be enclosed by an undulating surface which deals simultaneously with structural requirements, acoustics, shading and lighting

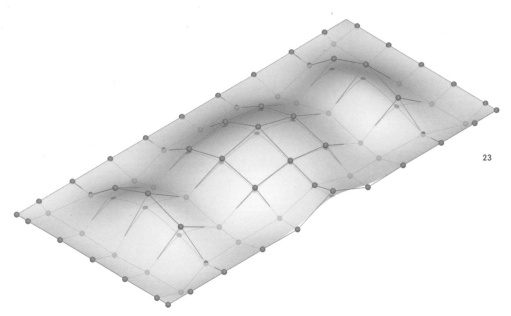

23

22

25

26

provides protection from the elements, acts a giant acoustic absorber and provides shading and natural lighting. This project develops many of the techniques and workflows of our Great Canopy project for Hong Kong. Simple surfaces and geometries were used as inputs for a generative script, an easy to control method of managing complex geometric relationships. Computer programming was used as the primary tool for design development from the project's initial stages, encapsulating knowledge into a single generative script.

A system of control geometries – a design surface, a set-out grid surface and line markers indicating column locations – were used as inputs into a computer program (figure 23). The design surface was created from the simplest possible control polygon – the 'minimal control polygon'. With fewer control points, it was easier to make fine adjustments to the canopy's geometry, making it difficult to end up with a surface of sharp, discontinuous or uneven curvature. The design surface controlled the form of the canopy and was the surface onto which the glazing and structural components were populated, while the grid surface controlled the spacing of the node positions in plan. The canopy's surface geometry changed throughout the project; the domes were adjusted to meet sightline restrictions, while the depths of the valleys were tuned for structural performance. The height of the design surface at the column locations was also adjusted to achieve reliable drainage, and the geometry at the perimeter changed as the edge detail developed.

The definition of the canopy surface considers structural, site, environmental and acoustic parameters while respecting the existing building by over-sailing at both the parapet and portico conditions. The form undulates through its long section, dividing the structure into three domed bays. The central bay is the highest and has the greatest span. When viewed across the long section, the four saddle points derive from the eight perimeter column locations. All water run-off occurs through the new columns; no water is discharged onto the existing structure. All structural forces are resolved through the columns. While the geometry at each structural node differs, the rules that drive that geometry are the same. At each node the structure is perpendicular to the canopy surface, and so the beams seem to gradually and elegantly twist as they diagonally traverse from one side of the canopy to the other (figure 24). The structure thickens gradually, both in depth and width, as it nears the columns.

The design evolution involved the use of many different media and techniques and an intense dialogue between the design team and many consultants. Computer programming was one of these techniques. This explorative approach required knowledge of both programming and architectural design combined with interpretative skills on many levels, and it proved to be a fast and flexible approach. Although the development of this computer program required specialist knowledge, its operation didn't. The design team could generate new options using the generating code and the simple and easy-to-manipulate control geometry.

The final version of the generating code was over 5,000 lines in length and had 57 parameters. Using only the set-out geometry as input, the script generated approximately 120,000 elements in about 15 seconds. Over 400 models were generated over six months.

Over the course of the project, many design studies were conducted via traditional CAD tools; however, once the design logic was determined, these algorithms were added to a single computer program. The entire roof structure and cladding components were generated by this one computer program written in MicroStation Visual Basic. Computer programming allowed for the independent development of canopy geometry and individual component strategies. The set-out geometry of the control surfaces could be altered without affecting the logic of the beam section or cladding system, and, likewise, within the generating code, different modules of source code could be inserted, removed or edited to create new canopy options. Using this approach, the long-chain dependencies of a fully associative CAD system did not exist, design modification was simpler and regeneration much faster. In this case, a dynamically parametric model was not necessary.

Rather than share the digital model directly, fabricators are required to develop their own digital model of the project. The design intent is conveyed to the fabricators through a 'geometry method statement'. This rule-based method statement explains how a 3-D model of the building can be developed on any CAD system, or even using a ruler, compass and perhaps a calculator. This approach ensures that the fabricators understand the geometric principles of the project and are less likely to misunderstand the geometry (figure 25). Furthermore, this approach ensured that what the designers proposed could actually be built. Now known as the Robert and Arlene Kogod Courtyard, the design will be enclosed by an undulating surface when complete (figure 26).

Hugh Whitehead is a partner and director of the Specialist Modelling Group at Foster + Partners. Brady Peters is an associate partner at Foster + Partners and a member of the practice's Specialist Modelling Group.

DISCOURSE NETWORKS AND THE DIGITAL:

STRUCTURAL COLLABORATION AT THE PHAENO SCIENCE CENTRE. HANIF KARA, ADAMS KARA TAYLOR, AND TIM ANSTEY, UNIVERSITY OF BATH

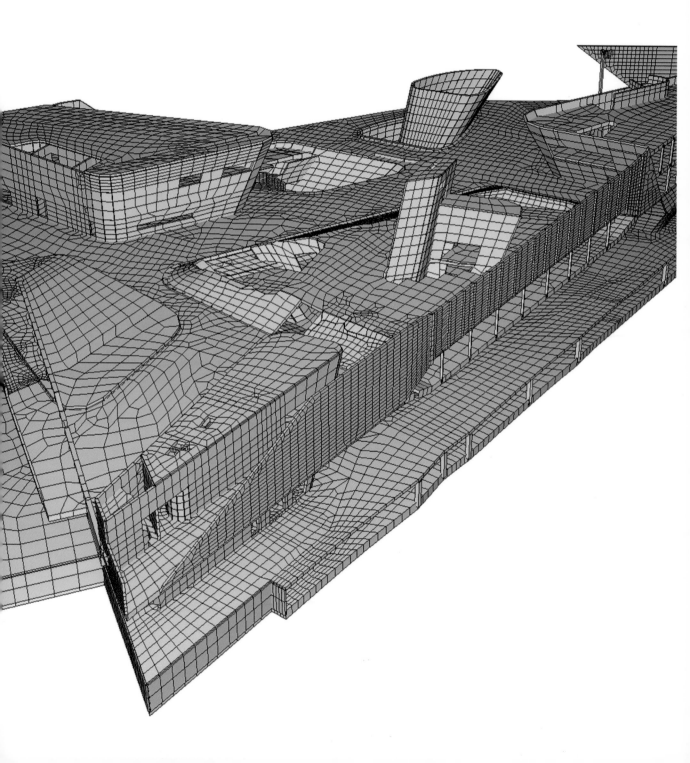

DISCOURSE
NETWORKS AND
THE DIGITAL:
STRUCTURAL
COLLABORATION
AT THE PHAENO
SCIENCE CENTRE.
HANIF KARA,
ADAMS KARA TAYLOR,
AND TIM ANSTEY,
UNIVERSITY OF BATH

The Phaeno Science Centre in Wolfsburg, Germany, like many 'centre-stage' buildings, is inevitably assimilated into architectural discourse in terms of the authorial contribution of a famous architect. Yet the ways in which such complex buildings are understood, and the extent to which that authorial ownership is annexed by the single 'name' architect, varies widely. Phaeno is important in several ways. Although the structural thinking of the project is one layer within a complex whole, it is clearly a highly significant one and at the heart of Zaha Hadid's experimental history. The building cannot really be explained, and certainly could not have been conceived, without acknowledging the way in which structure and structural engineering have been used as a means to develop architectural ideas. Discussions about this building have tended to stress the collaborative nature of the project. It is arguable that the habits of architecture–engineering collaboration that exist in London, which is where the thinking that created Phaeno was done, are unique. The discussion that began during the 1950s, following the establishment of Arup and Partners (1946) and F.J. Samuely and Partners (1956), created a discourse network that fundamentally affected how architecture was considered in post-war Britain. It was in this context of the technical – an invisible topography of contractual, physical and production conditions surrounding architecture as object – that informed architectural action in new ways. Adams Kara Taylor's collaboration with Zaha Hadid's office on the Phaeno building offers an integration with few parallels.

This culture of engineering–architectural collaboration has been served by the active role of the more experimental engineering offices in architectural education. Certainly, the dialogue that produced Phaeno (like that between Atelier 10 and Lab Architects that produced Federation Square in Melbourne, Australia) emerged from such a context. Thus, Phaeno's inception relied on a shared experience at the Architectural Association School of Architecture: Patrick Schumaker from Zaha Hadid's office and Hanif Kara as studio tutors, and project architect Christos Pasas as a former Design Research Lab (DRL) student. At one level this type of academic role invites the pursual of ideas for their own sake, and appears particularly important in creating a platform on which architectural and engineering culture can meet. At another level, academic collaboration alters the boundaries for problem solving between architects and engineers, setting up a very fluid condition for the interchange of information. At Phaeno this fluidity allowed the thinking systems that condition the building to be reclassified. The ten reinforced concrete cones that are central to the building's integrity are not quite one thing or another (they are part arch, part beam, part wall and part column) but, in order to analyse them both structurally and architecturally, one has to get away from the traditional ideas of thinking and naming. The result is more about topology than typology.

Yet that academic context – one not necessarily limited by the current envelope of technical possibility – has to meet another kind of discipline in order to change actual building construction and procurement, and to produce buildings like Phaeno. The maxim 'we shouldn't teach technology, we should change it' emerges from both the openness of academic discussions and the hard experience of practice. We believe that one of the most impressive aspects of the Adams Kara Taylor practice is its willingness to take on the grinding technical research that's necessary to support architectural ideas without grounding, wounding or

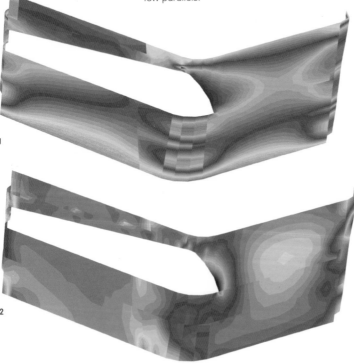

1

2

Fig 1 Phaeno Science Centre. Stresses in cone 2 due to dead load

Fig 2 Stresses in cone 2 due to thermal expansion

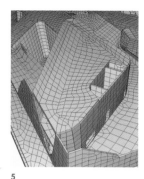

5

killing them. This research must be carried out at the level of material analysis (Which material will do the job? What do you have to do to an existing material to make it do the job?) and at the level of production and economy. This is research that will vary from project to project.

At Phaeno this research took on several levels. At the level of design, the organic process of form-making that defines the hybrid elements of the building (concrete and steel) produced questions about buildability that required a separate formal and creative analysis exercise. While the building was conceived to be stable as a complete assembly, its parts – particularly the ten reinforced concrete cones that organise the building – are unstable as separated elements, so a procedure of analysis had to be undertaken to vouchsafe the 'history' of the construction and ensure the building was stabilised at each point in its physical development. The need to define avenues of investigation and pursue them is also evident at the material level; there is a whole narrative around finding and rigorously testing a self-compacting concrete that could be cast into the complex forms developed for the lower parts of the building. The whole process involved a delicate balancing act in which ideas were allowed to remain sovereign while research into problem solving was pursued as far as possible.

Underwriting these various forms of research is digital analysis and form-making – the production of digital tools that can analyse problems in new ways as a means for interfacing with a discussion of architectural possibility. The way in which digital information is now exchanged between consultants challenges the traditional nature of drawing and representation of architecture. If the drawing has, through history, acted as a prosthetic device partly to guarantee the authority and genius of the architect – if architectural drawings have always had difficulty in escaping that rhetorical dimension – the nature of digital information exchange can be seen as a significantly freeing gesture.

In terms of disciplinary collaboration, the impact of digital technologies is fundamental, partly because they challenge existing ways of representing and explaining projects, and partly because they create another kind of 'space' in which the thinking about projects might be done. At Phaeno this exchange relied on finite element analysis software developed through Adams Kara Taylor by German software company SOFiSTiK specifically for the project. Again, the research story is important. At the outset of the project no software existed that could precisely analyse the combination of form and material that was emerging from the design. SOFiSTiK's product almost could, so Adams Kara Taylor tailored the parameters for the task-directed development of an existing product by the software company. Once the product had evolved, it then became central for both the structural and architectural design. SOFiSTiK could model continuing iterations of the form of the concrete cones and provide analytical

Fig 3 Global analysis model – isometric view

Fig 4 Global finite element analysis model – isometric view

Fig 5 Global finite element analysis model – isometric view of cone 2

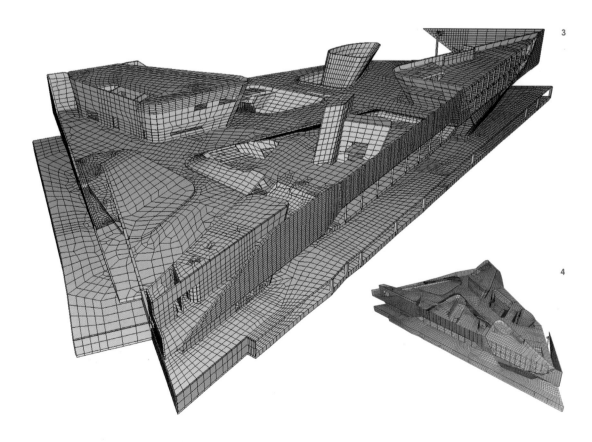

3

4

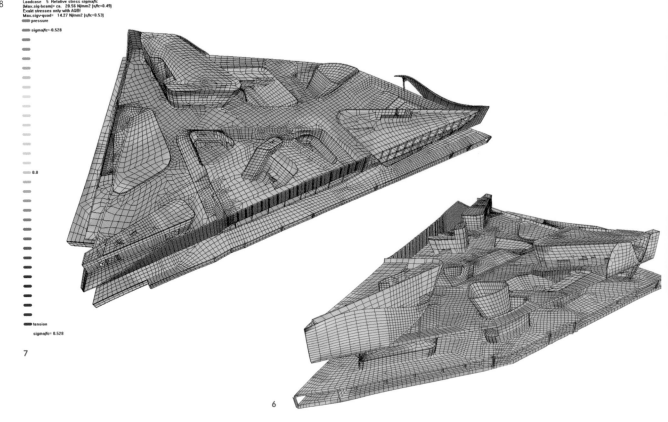

Loadcase 5 Relative stress sigma/fc
[Max. sig-beam]= ca. 20.56 N/mm2 [s/fc=0.49]
Exakt stresses only with AQB!
Max. sig v-quad= 14.27 N/mm2 [s/fc=0.53]
pressure

sigma/fc=-0.528

0.0

tension
sigma/fc= 0.528

7

6

Fig 6 Global finite element analysis model – stress distribution due to thermal expansion

Fig 7 Global finite element analysis model – stress distribution due to vertical and horizontal loads

information about stresses as well as a model of the formal result for the design team; material was slowly edited out of the design through this process of subsequent testing, a process that appears to have empowered both the architects and the engineers involved.

The 'thinking space' that emerges through using digital tools is fascinating. It is an 'in-between' place between disciplines that can be shared by architects, computer scientists, specialised analysts, material technologists and engineers in order to translate and enhance the first ideas about a project. The space varies from project to project and collaboration to collaboration. The aim is not necessarily always to optimise a design but to find a process that departs significantly from the ones both architects and engineers are trained in. The environment, then, demands 'new tribes' to be formed and new allegiances to be made, and is ultimately about research on projects as much as anything else. No one pays for it, so it has to be part of the work. Notably, there is a kind of inverse relationship between sophistication and accessibility, which becomes crucial. Frankly, the more complex the tool, the less fruitful the collaboration – only a very limited number of people can use specialist complex software, so it needs special projects and specialist operators. Writing project-specific software is an emerging and exciting trend but it is problematic in terms of

intellectual property rights. Where possible, Adams Kara Taylor aims to enhance and use tools that are easily available but also encourages the use of custom tools and hopes to eventually develop a 'tool box'. Another issue is the gap between design, manufacture and site. Few constructors are able to deal with the latest software and tools so, after a lot of effort, it is seen as a position where we have to boil everything down to something basic.

Our experience from Wolfsburg is essential in explaining our pursuit of design software that combines architectural modelling, structural analysis and evolutionary characteristics. And if the collaborative 'space' provided by digital technologies permits the integration of geometrical and structural analysis in new ways, it is clear that this is only one aspect of its significance. At the same time it changes traditional roles in relation to project representation, and allows other areas of analytical expertise to enter into, and impact on, the arena of the design. These possibilities exist at the level of design analysis (predicting how materials will behave in complex situations) and at the level of production. Digitally driven processes, such as printing concrete, could revolutionise both formal possibilities and building production methods.

Adams Kara Taylor has created an interest in interdisciplinary skills (rather than multidisciplinary) to enhance the core discipline of structures and in

2000 gave it the name of 'p.art' (Parametric Applied Research Team), an in-house research arm that seeks to develop structurally intelligent, formal modelling software. It is about geometry as just one strand, yet there are others that are critical such as off-stream work like artist collaborations or material research, analysis, graphic design, visualisation and computer science. This research team is also judged on the way its work is presented, which is a situation familiar for architects but not for engineers, who tend to distrust rhetoric as a non-scientific area outside the scope of their work; so the team affects all that is produced in the office to different degrees. The scale issue is such that there is a limited pallet of materials for building structures, and this pallet is unlikely to change dramatically – timber, steel, stone, concrete, glass are likely to remain at the centre of architectural production. However, we can now take a 'forensic' look at the nature of these materials and, although Adams Kara Taylor is unlikely to develop new materials, digital analysis provides the possibility for using existing ones in radically new ways. The concrete and the roof structure of Phaeno make use of this analytical potential to change material use. Here a bespoke use of two common materials is facilitated by the latest CAD/CAM methodologies. This kind of looking demands the interdisciplinary expertise over and above technical competences and flexible working structures that p.art provides for.

Do such initiatives set up tensions? Does the creation of new forms for consultancy around structures also speak of new possibilities for project ownership? Adams Kara Taylor – at the same time as promoting the creation of an interstitial space for thinking around architecture – clearly envisages that space is occupied by a multicultural population. It is clear, in our view, that architecture and engineering should be kept separate, as the basic thinking is different. One has the ability to diverge while the other wants to converge. What is most fruitful is to create a culture where both are educated in the other's discipline – so they know what to ask and when. Digital technology and analysis is here to stay. But is there anything it can't do? The homogeneous nature of some digitally driven projects, poured out of Maya and Rhino, for example, creates a shared illusion of reality that then risks separating it from creativity. We don't believe one should be using the latest technology for its own sake; to do so would be to produce monsters. As well as interrogating a project brief, clients and other consultants, it is sometimes important to ask 'why?'. Human transaction is the most crucial part of any creative process. After all the hard work on Phaeno, the basic component of the concrete is the reinforcement bar – where it is placed and how it is fixed – and no amount of digital analysis will remove the basic requirement of defining, placing and monitoring the processes by which large structures are erected.

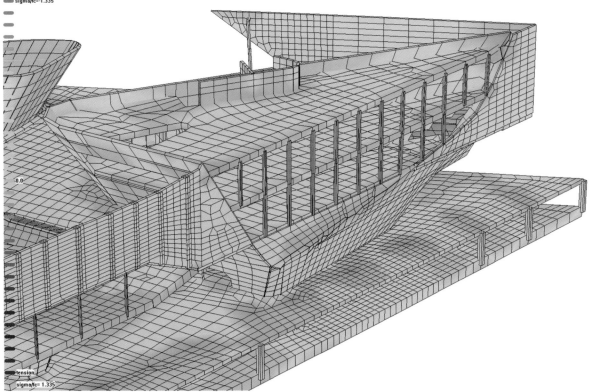

Loadcase 1 Relative stress sigma/fc
|Max.sig-beam|= ca. 62.86 N/mm2 [s/fc=0.80]
Exakt stresses only with AQB!
Max.sigv-quad= 36.04 N/mm2 [s/fc=1.33]
pressure

sigma/fc=-1.335

0.0

tension.
sigma/fc= 1.335

Fig 8 Global analysis model – stress distribution due to self-weight, cone 1

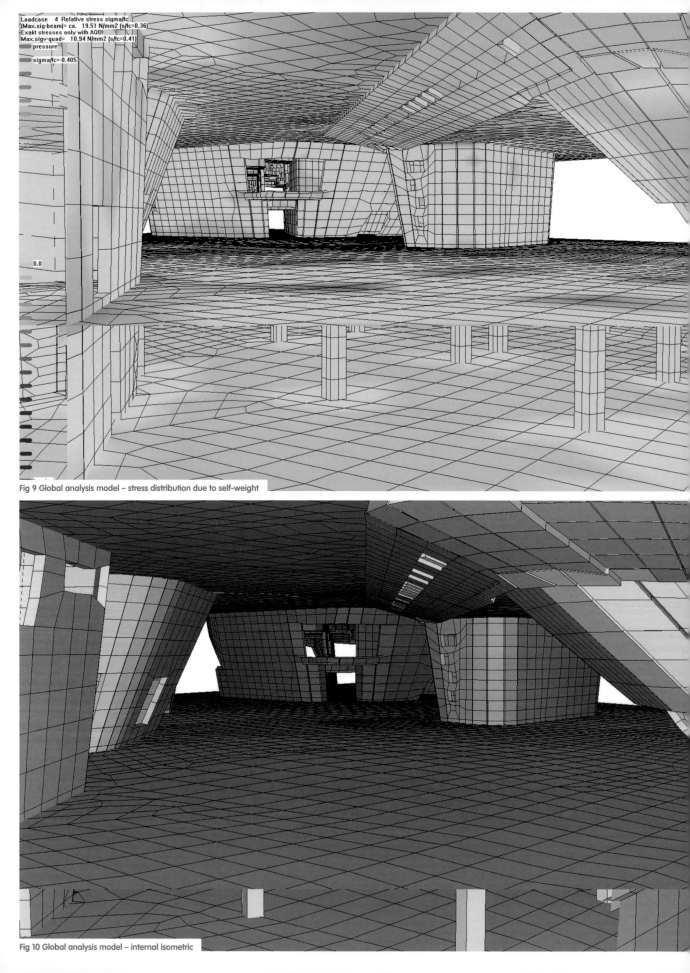

Loadcase 4 Relative stress sigma/fc
[Max.sig-beam]= ca. 19.51 N/mm2 [s/fc=0.36)
-Exakt stresses only with AQB!
Max.sigv-quad= 10.94 N/mm2 [s/fc=0.41)
pressure

sigma/fc=-0.405

0.0

Fig 9 Global analysis model – stress distribution due to self-weight

Fig 10 Global analysis model – internal isometric

We must always acknowledge the role of the 'social' and the importance of the human. Leon Battista Alberti praised Filippo Brunelleschi for the social achievement of vaulting the Dome of Florence, suspending ponderous masses 'on air' and creating a structure large enough to cover the people of Tuscany in its shadow. The social organisation required to achieve such feats will always be just that – social.

Analysis

Understanding the geometry and structural behaviour of the building is a complex task and almost impossible to perform without advanced 3-D CAD and FEA modelling software packages. In a first step the geometry of the building was defined in a 3-D CAD model, which was later used to derive several FEA models for analysis.

In order to analyse all structural members in an appropriate way it was decided to build several analysis models. A global model was built to analyse the behaviour of the ten cones in interaction with the floor slab. One of the reasons for using a global model was the challenge to design a monolithic concrete structure with continuous pours of up to 134 cubic metres without any movement joint. Several local models were used to design waffle slabs, steel roof structures, the façade structure and a bridge connecting the building to the Autostadt.

The global model comprises basement, ground floor and main floor – including the ten cones and mezzanine levels – and contains over 17,000 finite elements. The mesh was manually created using AutoCAD surface meshes and converting them into finite elements, since no mesh generator at the time was able to generate a valid mesh for such a complex 3-D structure. Loadings consisting of self weight, superimposed dead load, live load, shrinkage and thermal loads were applied to the structure. Special adjustment has been made to model the material behaviour on self-compacting concrete accurately, since it differs in some material properties from standard concrete mixtures.

The steel roof structure that covers the main floor slab was modelled using a frame analysis package. The steel roof consists of a special Vierendeel truss. Support is taken from just the four cones and perimeter structure, thus providing an obstruction-free exhibition space. The roof is fixed laterally in position at the most internal corners of the cones allowing the roof to expand horizontally with a minimum of constraint.

Hanif Kara is a founder partner of Adams Kara Taylor. Tim Anstey is an architect and lecturer at the Department of Architecture and Civil Engineering, University of Bath.

2.0

EVOLUTION AND EMERGENCE

At its most explorative, architectural computing hinges on a new relationship between the user and the machine. Here, the computer is treated not as a dumb slave at the beck and call of its operator-master; rather, it is treated as a thing of some intelligence. The architect or engineer is not a placer of lines and arcs but a writer of programs, a setter of rules and an asker of questions to which there are no obvious answers.

Perhaps these programs are constructed in such a way that they rewrite themselves according to what they have learned. It is a practice that seeks inspiration from biological systems, genetics, brain models and chemical processes. When applied to the architectural realm the results can be intriguing, surprising and challenging and often revealing and useful. Solutions do not necessarily reveal themselves suddenly; rather, they emerge over time as a result of a sequence of selective steps. Solutions evolve.

GENETICALLY
MODIFIED SPACES.
CHRISTIAN DERIX,
AEDAS AND UNIVERSITY
OF EAST LONDON

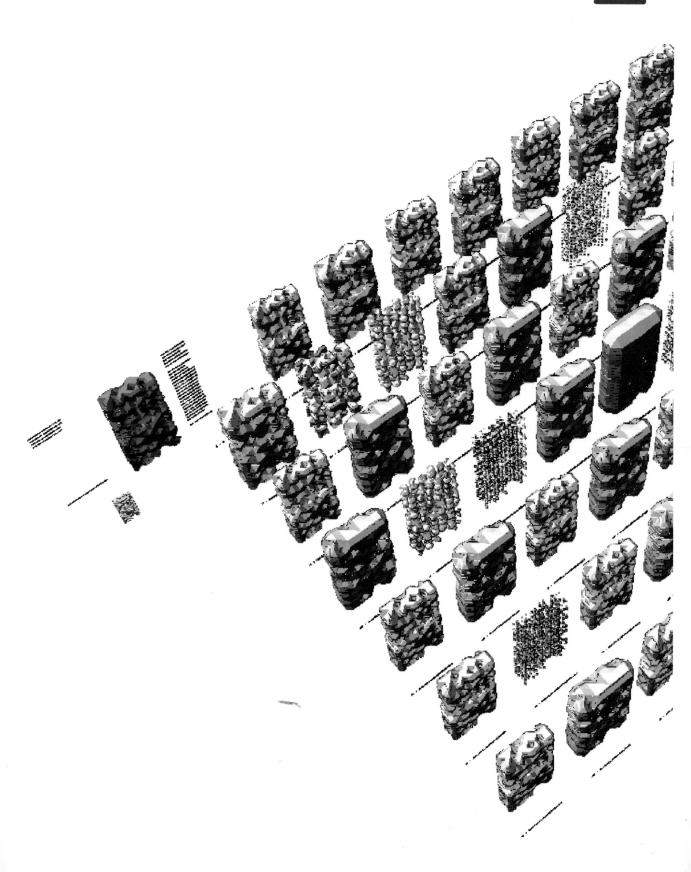

GENETICALLY
MODIFIED SPACES.
CHRISTIAN DERIX,
AEDAS AND
UNIVERSITY
OF EAST LONDON

With the introduction of cybernetics – the science of control (of machines) – principally by Gordon Pask to the architectural world in the 1960s (Pask, 1969; 1975), arrived the paradigm of systems design. The notion of a system with local rules and topologies generating undirected global configurations led to discussions about the existence of a design authority and a re-examination of the vernacular. Genuine hope that architecture could be coded as social and spatial relationships pervaded the scene, with architects like Cedric Price[1] and Archigram leading the way. Simultaneously, theories about architectural and urban spaces were thought out by architects and non-architects alike, such as Christopher Alexander (1967), Christian Norberg-Schulz (1965) and Rudolf Arnheim (1977).

The origin of systems thinking and the rise of the computer, however, paved the way for two camps that were and still are present in the sciences: a directed teleological approach and an undirected self-organising approach. The goal-driven paradigm for science, industry and architecture has always been a particularly strong feature of both camps. Scientific research, for example, expresses itself via artificial intelligence (versus artificial life), industry via expert systems and architecture via management systems and data-driven design.

Nicholas Negroponte (1970) experimented with computer system-supported design methodologies during the 1960s at MIT's Architecture Machine Group, but he couldn't avoid setting semantic and assumptive targets to the programs that the group was inventing. The machine was to emulate the human user – an approach that was being fostered simultaneously at MIT's artificial intelligence department, where neural networks and other methodologies such as 'construct elicitation' or 'case-based reasoning' were supposed to imitate human reasoning at its highest level.

This directed approach to computer-aided design continued into the 1990s with William Mitchell publishing *The Logic of Architecture* (1990), mainly based on George Stiny's 'shape grammars', which also try to emulate an architectural expression rather than spatial logic. The qualities of such expressions are back-propagated through the system to the mechanism and therefore don't provide any alternative to the algorithm; the expressions are already imbedded in the description. In fact, with the permeating paradigm of parametric design, which generally tends towards specific targets, we are still in the thick of goal-driven architectural computing.

Collective construction

An alternative approach kept alive over the 1970s and 1980s by some academics like Bill Hillier (Hillier and Hanson, 1984), John Frazer and Paul Coates involved the notion of undirected processes. These have spatial configurations in mind rather than explicit styles and expressions of architecture. Hillier's 'space syntax' tried to establish a connection between a simple evaluation mechanism of

geometric quantities and social occupations of space. Frazer and Coates, on the other hand, rather than evaluating and analysing, tried to generate spatial phenomena that manifested qualities not present in their description (on the basis of the interaction of simple processes with large quantities of simple elements).

When Cedric Price spoke about the 'death of the architect', it was assumed that visual and social qualities of space could not be 'authorised' explicitly within the representation of geometry, but that the systemic relationships of the elements and their mechanism embedded into some kind of context would give rise to expressions of space, unknown at the beginning. When properties arise without being described in the mechanism, or elements that produce them, one refers to 'emergence'. Emergent properties are unsupervised or undirected outcomes of self-organising processes.

Such qualities were discovered as machine analogies first and then mostly natural analogies by computer scientists like John von Neumann. Von Neumann wasn't satisfied with Norbert Wiener's cybernetic model of machine communication and wanted to simulate the logic of a machine that could reproduce its initial configuration. He used Stan Ulam's cellular automaton to reproduce virtual machines successfully (1995).

The cellular automaton is built on two fundamental structural aspects for emergent systems: a large amount of topologically ordered simple elements and simultaneous processing of information. The simple machines (or cells) communicate locally and simultaneously with their topological neighbours and calculate a new state for themselves on the basis of the gained information. From outside the system, it is possible to observe a global pattern, which is not present at the local cellular/elemental scale, but represents a consensus between all elements at a specific point in time. This globally observed pattern, or state, is the expression of the system. When transposed to an architectural or geometric system, the state can represent a spatial phenomenon.

In his interpretations of Gilles Deleuze, Manuel DeLanda highlights those essential aspects of self-organising systems by singling out population thinking, topological stability and intensity thinking (the last being a qualitative measurement of the system emerging from the propagation of elemental descriptions – an emergent outcome rather than an explicit quantity). DeLanda describes and proposes another natural analogy for the production of collective architectural spaces – a genetic algorithm (2002).

Genetic algorithms form part of evolutionary techniques that gained significance as search methods of design spaces after Richard Dawkins' introduction of the biomorph. Dawkins showed that Darwinian selection procedures from high-performing individuals within a population could form the basis of a fast convergence towards a 'best-fit' to a given environment (Dawkins, 1989). That environment can of course be an explicit problem such as an architectural brief.

1. *Cedric Price (2003) transferred the literary criticism of Roland Barthes (1977) – 'death of the author' – into 'death of the architect'.*

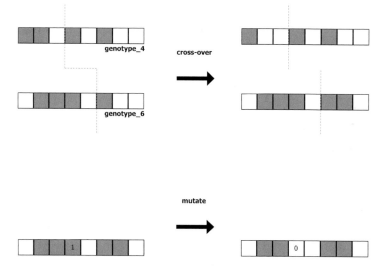

Fig 1 Genetics: the process of cross-over and mutation

Cellular automata and evolutionary techniques[2] are two of the most dominant natural analogies and self-organising methods available at present to a designer to generate alternative emergent design solutions. Further academic standard methods include agent-based systems or neural networks.[3]

As part of the research initiative at Aedas, we are testing and implementing self-organising computational methodologies on both live projects and experimental exercises. Some methods are developed as generic tools to support designers, such as agent-based adjacency diagram generators or visual integration mapping via 'isovists' developed by Benedikt (1979). The following text describes three projects that use evolutionary computing to generate design recommendations.

Evolution as design support

For many students, John Frazer's *An Evolutionary Architecture* (1995) opened the way towards a fascinating natural analogy for computing architectures. Genetic algorithms formed the basis for his experiments, along with those of Paul Coates, at the Centre for Evolutionary Computing in Architecture (CECA).

As mentioned above, evolutionary algorithms function on the Darwinian principle of selecting the best performing individuals from a population. The selected individuals of one generation form the basis for further development of the population. The development is based on crossing over two individuals of a generation in order to produce a new generation. During cross-over, chromosomes are cut into two pieces and exchanged between two individuals. Asexual cross-over is also possible where one individual cuts its chromosome and recombines it differently. Mutation within individuals (figure 1) is also used to help express non-inherited phenomena, even though the probability for mutation is generally kept low to guarantee hereditary continuity.

2. Evolutionary techniques include simulated annealing (mutation only), genetic algorithms (data-based evolution) and genetic programming (process-based evolution).

3. There are a large number of neural networks. They can generally be differentiated by being supervised or unsupervised.

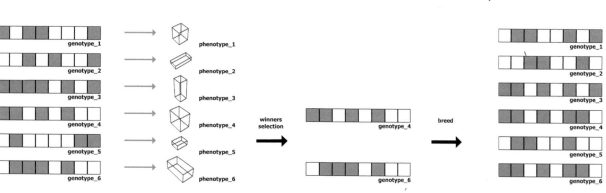

Fig 2 The embryology and development process

GENETICALLY
MODIFIED SPACES.
CHRISTIAN DERIX,
AEDAŠ AND
UNIVERSITY
OF EAST LONDON

Each generation of individuals is an expression of the previous selection (figure 2). They are called phenotypes (expressing the phenomena of the genes). At the beginning, a so-called embryology has to be created that encodes the topology and metric of the genes that make up the individuals. A gene represents a feature and is mostly encoded as a binary string. When linking several gene strings, one obtains the chromosome as a long binary string, which can be decoded into an individual. The first embryo constitutes the general genotype from which the first generation of phenotypes is produced. The 'best' individuals are selected to serve as genotypes for the next generation.

The selection process is governed by a selection criterion, called a 'fitness'. A fitness function analyses all individuals of a generation for their performance as measured against an encoded target. The 'fittest' individuals (in the basic version, only two) will be selected as genotypes for further development. There is a variety of standard selection functions, some of which will be mentioned later.

It is immediately apparent that setting a fitness is crucial for the development of the population. A complex expression can be measured either by an overarching fitness (although in this case one can't 'optimise' distinct genes, only the population as a whole). Alternatively, its constituent genes can be measured separately and amalgamated into an overall fitness, in which case the separate features are compared against other individual feature performances as well. Optimisation is no longer an option. One can only try to balance the features into a 'good' equilibrium and find a fitting compromise.

It has to be remarked that the fitness function is a global external evaluation setting. The population of individuals as such remains without intentions for

its development. The fitness function represents the environment that evaluates the system's adaptation.

The fitness function can be encoded into the program, a 'natural selection', as the population searches among itself to fit some virtual environment. Or the fitness function is represented by an external referee, like a user, who guides the population's development. In that case, one calls it an 'artificial selection'. Artificial selection is a much slower process as the program will have to stop to allow the user's inspection between generations. Natural selection can crunch on until all the fitness criteria have been met.

Experiment 1: Connected layout diagrams

An example of a natural selection is the program developed by one of the Aedas research group members, Pablo Miranda (2002), who experimented with Lionel March's Boolean description of space (1976) to generate well-connected layouts through a simple genetic algorithm.

The embryology consists of a 64-bit binary string where each bit represents a volume in a 4x4x4 matrix. 'On' bits represent volumes and 'off' bits represent voids. The population is searched by the fitness function for the individual where the volumes are most evenly connected with each other topologically (a measurement taken from network analysis) but at the same time are metrically as far away from each other as possible. To find the distances and connectivity between the volumes an agent attempts to reach all cells leaving a visible path. The fitness function is of the 'tournament' type where a number of individuals get selected and the best performing one gets paired up with a randomly chosen individual of the population. The worst performing individual of the population at the time is being discarded. That type of local evolution

Fig 3 Experiment 1: three stages of a converging population of Boolean spaces (all bar-coded) towards 'good' fitness. Boolean spaces are shown above; agent traces, part of a network analysis system, are shown below

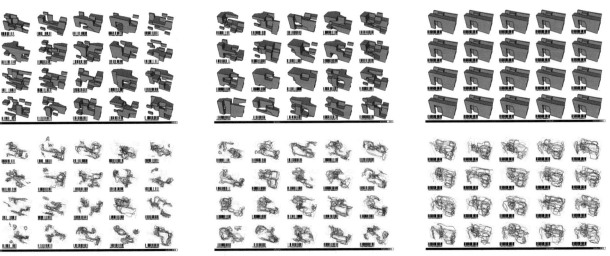

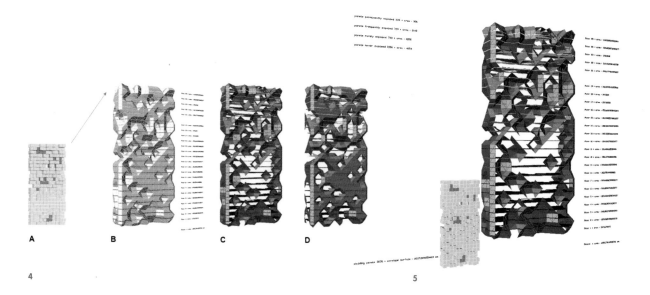

A   B   C   D

4   5

Fig 4 Experiment 2:
a sequence showing
how cellular automata
generate space,
providing topological,
solar analysis and
cladding solutions

Fig 5 Experiment 2:
a larger view of the
central tower in Fig
4, illustrating how
cellular automata
can help negotiate
building envelope
solutions

is 'steady-state' iteration rather than 'generational'
iteration.

The evolved diagrams share certain qualities
that are not encoded into the embryology. The
population eradicates layouts with isolated volumes
(that being coded into the selection) and the
layouts are folded bands of spaces rather than the
expected tree-like volumes.

The power of evolution is well exposed in this
experiment (figure 3). An exhaustive search through
all possible states of the 2^64 bits matrix would
take infinitely longer to find 'a' good solution than
the selection process employed by blind evolution,
which reaches a fairly stable state of 'good'
individuals rather quickly.

Experiment 2: Generative heuristics

In the 2004 Generative Towers experiment, we
wanted to concatenate some algorithms to
approximate a design heuristic for simple slab-
envelope spaces. The experiment didn't assume a
design brief as such.

Step 1: seeding topology. As a first step, the user
can weight a matrix of spaces interactively that
settle into a hypothetical arrangement of room
layouts in three or two dimensions stacked. The
mechanism to search for these configurations is
based on the above-described cellular automaton.
A cell contains probabilities for each possible
room type. Through a room-adjacency matrix
that evaluates each cell's context, the cells re-
weight their probabilities until all cells find their
arrangement agreeable. The default is set to three
general types: services, offices and atria. Generally
the cellular automaton distributes the functions
appropriately with services located centrally, and
offices and atria grouped next to each other. This
seeding process can be repeated by adjusting

the initial matrix until one is satisfied with the
adjacencies.

Step 2: building diagram. In a second step the
matrix of cells will be transposed into a metric
space where the cell types get an impact value,
which will translate into built or unbuilt space. The
metric derives from the user who can specify sizes
of plot, storeys and rooms.

Once the room nodes have been seeded as a
Boolean cloud of points in their appropriate metric
position, an algorithm called 'marching cubes'
calculates an isosurface that represents the
envelope of the diagrammatic spaces. Isosurfaces
map thresholds of densities within a specified
cubic matrix. The thresholds mapped here are
between 'on' or 'off' nodes within the metric space,
thus generating clusters of cohesive volumes.
Depending on the threshold variable and the size of
the cubic divisions of the volume, a finer or cruder
representation of the initial adjacency diagram can
be achieved. The size of the volumetric division also
hints at the envelope's structural division.

After the envelope has been generated, floor plates
are cut out from within the skin. The user can again
vary the parameters of the isosurface and floor
heights in order to arrive at a satisfactory result.
Additionally, solar exposure values can be mapped
onto the skin; a spreadsheet can contain all data
for generated spaces. If users are content with the
adjacencies, envelope, shape and solar exposure,
they can go on and develop further generations of
slab-envelope spaces from this prototype (figures
4 and 5).

Step 3: hybrid selection. The previously generated
prototype is encoded into a binary string with
the genes representing the room adjacency and
envelope parameters. The first generation is simply
produced through a mutation of the prototype's
genotype.

GENETICALLY
MODIFIED SPACES.
CHRISTIAN DERIX,
AEDAS AND
UNIVERSITY
OF EAST LONDON

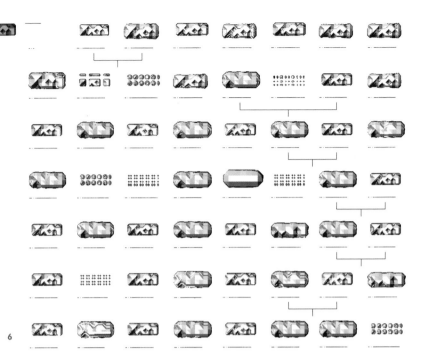

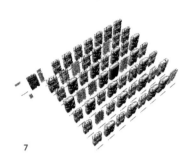

7

6

Fig 6 Experiment 2: the
'family tree' of tower
options, showing which
'parents' produced
which offspring

Fig 7 Experiment 2:
perspective view of the
generations of towers
produced

The innovation on this project was the combination of natural and artificial selection. The user selects one individual of a generation based on a subjective visual judgement, such as an aesthetically pleasing or a surprising individual which may express an unexpected feature that is valuable to the design. A second individual is selected by a fitness function that evaluates each individual's floor–wall ratio and picks the best ratio. Those two individuals are crossed-over to produce the next generation (figures 6 and 7). This hybrid selection process obviously doesn't necessarily produce the best individuals in the next generation, as the subjectively favoured fitness may, in fact, be relatively poor. The time for convergence towards an overall 'good' performing individual will therefore take much longer.

This hybrid selection process, of course, steers a path between natural and artificial selection. Natural selection needs explicit encoding and therefore quantitative data to work with. Artificial selection works on the 'black box' principle where only external qualities are selected. By hybridising the selection process non-descript qualities or phenomena can be kept and proliferated during the 'optimisation' process.

Apart from slow convergence due to weakening the well-performing chromosomes by crossing them over with mediocre hereditary material, the visualisation also slows down convergence as the program has to halt for user interaction. However, the visualisation of the generation gives an immediate feedback to the user and opens the possibility of taking advantage of novel combinations of genes which may produce unexpected individuals that fit a design brief particularly well.

Experiment 3: Compromising the masterplan

In 2006, a collaboration between Edward Finucane (a student of CECA), Aedas research and 4M Group was established (Finucane et al., 2006) where a masterplanning exercise was shadowed with a multi-objective genetic algorithm, called Pareto Optimisation. Vilfredo Pareto was a French–Italian economist who developed a method for optimisation between a multitude of parameters by gradual adjustments of single parameters resulting in the improvement of another until a state of optimality was reached where every further alternation between the parameters' values would lead to a degradation of any other parameter.

This type of optimisation seems to lend itself to urban settings where a large number of occasionally contradicting parameters have to be configured optimally, which mostly means that none of the parameters has fulfilled its optimum state but all parameters result in some kind of compromise. Therefore, the term optimisation could be misleading in the context of multi-criteria development.

Site rules: the site was an urban plot in Pristhina, Kosovo, and 11 objectives were identified that were

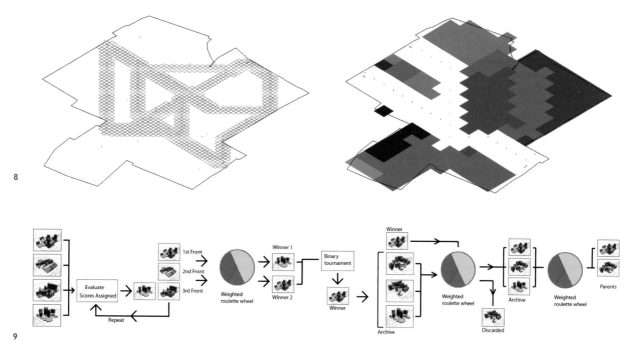

8

9

Fig 8 Experiment 3:
ant colony network (left)
and diffusion from paths
to massing (right)

Fig 9 Experiment 3:
the evolution and
selection process,
where well-performing
individuals create
successive generations

meant to be evaluated within the mixed-use master plan configuration. Among the objectives, or site rules, were areas for each use, storey limits, plan depth and build–void ratios. The fitness functions (described later) would evaluate every individual's compliance with those rules.

Embryology: every individual represents a massing option for the site. An individual is built up through various steps:

- an ant colony algorithm generates a circulation diagram in plan (figure 8). The ant-agents need to find 'good' routes from entry/exit points of the site to distributed public open spaces on site;

- the resulting non-circulation spaces are diffused by random land-use seed points in two and three dimensions to build a massing diagram.

Fitness functions: having set the first generation to random seeding points in the embryology for each genotype, a non-dominated sorting mechanism creates a hierarchy of well-performing individuals within the generation (figure 9). Each individual receives a score on overall error margins towards the site rules and how well each objective is reached compared to all other individuals' objectives (non-dominated being best as no other individual's object is dominating). The hierarchy into places is called the various Pareto fronts. When all individuals are mapped into a single scattergram front, the Pareto front shows which individual dominates for which objective. The individuals

situated at the centre of the front have the best average and are Pareto-optimal (after optimisation).

Selection: having ordered the population into a hierarchy (fronts), various selection processes filter out one very good individual which will be archived. The process works via the following steps:

- each individual is given a probability for selection according to their place or fitness front. Two are chosen by a weighted process that favours the best individuals with the highest probability (weighted roulette wheel selection);

- the two individuals are compared according to their individual performances by objective. The better individual is selected for the archive (binary tournament selection).

From the archive the best performing two individuals are selected again by weighted roulette wheel selection. Those two individuals are used to 'breed' the next population via cross-over (figures 10 and 11). The results of the experiments proved to be fairly successful in the sense that the evolution generated a population over many generations that approximated the objectives of the massing for the masterplan (figures 12 and 13). Error values for each individual in the final Pareto front are still present but had been drastically reduced from the beginning.

The embryology and number of site rules as objectives proved to be too large and complicated

52   GENETICALLY
MODIFIED SPACES.
CHRISTIAN DERIX,
AEDAS AND
UNIVERSITY
OF EAST LONDON

to handle appropriately within the short project time (just two months). One would also hope to work with affiliate objectives rather than highly divergent ones, as it would prove easier to improve the embryology and selection process. As with most generative processes, the seed geometry will play a large part in the visualisation and development of the population. A reduced slab geometry was used in this project to emphasise the diagrammatic massing.

Problems with the system designer

Although three models of evolutionary computing in an architectural context have been demonstrated here, there are many more possibilities for its application. Many other generative computing methods for architecture also exist.

Explorations of program methods which can help us generate non-quantitative phenomenological aspects of architecture seem to run into common problems at present. As the designer becomes system designer, he or she should try to remove personal assumptions from solutions by initiating only the mechanisms and setting a context; evaluation criteria can lead back into a similarly subjective fold.

In *Architecture's New Media,* Yehuda Kalay (2004) writes that an undeterministic process like a genetic algorithm still needs an unsupervised mechanism to pick out results that are truly emergent. He recommends unsupervised neural networks to be able to provide that ability by clustering solutions. With another former CECA student and now Aedas research member, Tim Ireland, in 2002 we tried

**Figs 10 and 11
Experiment 3:
Pareto-optimal massing
processes generated a
number of options**

**Fig 12 Experiment 3:
render of three Pareto
outcomes**

**Fig 13 Experiment 3:
three Pareto outcomes,
with notional building
uses indicated by colour**

10   11

12

13

to evolve self-organising feature maps with each other as context, so that each network would have to adapt to the other networks (Derix and Ireland, 2003). Fairly novel interpretations of spatial distributions of 'house' layouts emerged but the fitness criteria were too weak to establish whether the layouts were reasonable.

The idea, however, is reminiscent of co-evolution as proposed by Paul Coates or John Frazer. Coates and various students attempted models of co-evolution in the mid- to late 1990s. Some models were based on Lindenmayer systems and genetic programming (Coates et al., 1999). This combination is a very promising direction for evolutionary design as it points towards the avoidance of two main problems:

- for co-evolution the fitness evaluation is not an explicit description of an optimal condition but a description of a 'good' condition for either environment. Thus, theoretically, either system has the freedom to evolve any solution that doesn't undermine the other system's performance. An increased redundance is built, therefore, into either system's scope for development;

- genetic programming evolves function trees which decode into algorithms, whereas in genetic algorithms the flexibility of the developmental process is non-existent. Genetic programming can actually produce emergent heuristics to a problem. If a 'lazy' fitness function is set, such an evolutionary process could potentially redesign the brief to generate only good solutions. Therefore, co-evolution lends itself well to genetic programming.

If we don't find a way of designing systems that can produce truly emergent autonomous solutions that are divorced from architects' assumptions, one can look to Frazer's proposition in *An Evolutionary Architecture* (1995) that an environment could be expressed as an evolved algorithm – evolving the context to fit the designer's ego.

Christian Derix is head of the research and development unit at architecture practice Aedas and lecturer on the Computing and Design MSc course at East London University's School of Architecture.

References

Alexander, C. (1967) *Notes on the Synthesis of Form*, Cambridge, MA, Harvard University Press.

Arnheim, R. (1977) *Dynamics of Architectural Form*, Berkeley and Los Angeles, CA, University of California Press.

Barthes, R. (1977) 'Death of the author' in *Image, Music, Text*, New York, NY, Hill.

Burks, A.W., "Essays on Cellular Automata", University of Illinois Press, Chicago, 1971.

Benedikt, M. (1979) 'To take hold of space: isovists and isovist fields', *Environment and Planning*, B 6.

Coates, P., Broughton, T. and Jackson, H. (1999) 'Exploring three-dimensional design worlds using Lindenmayer systems and genetic programming' in Bentley, P. (ed.) *Evolutionary Design by Computers*, San Francisco, CA, Morgan Kaufmann.

Dawkins, R. (1989) 'The evolution of evolvability' in Langton, C. (ed.) *Artificial Life*, Boston, MA, Addison-Wesley.

DeLanda, M. (2002) 'Deleuze and the use of Genetic Algorithms' in Leach, N. (ed.) *Designing for a Digital World*, London, Wiley & Sons.

Derix, C. and Ireland, T. (2003) 'An analysis of the poly-dimensionality of living' in proceedings: eCAADe Conference, Graz.

Finucane, E., Derix, C. and Coates, P. (2006) 'Evolving urban structures using computer optimisation techniques' in proceedings: Generative Arts Conference, Milan.

Frazer, J. (1995) *An Evolutionary Architecture*, London, Architectural Association.

Hillier, B. and Hanson, J. (1984) *The Social Logic of Space*, Cambridge, Cambridge University Press.

Kalay, Y. (2004) *Architecture's New Media: Principles, Theories, and Methods of Computer-Aided Design*, Cambridge, MA, MIT Press.

Langton, C. (1995) *Artificial Life*, Cambridge, MA, MIT Press.

March, L. (1976) *The Architecture of Form*, Cambridge, Cambridge University Press.

Miranda, P. (2005) 'ArchiKluge', <www.armyofclerks.net/ArchiKluge/index.htm>.

Mitchell, W. (1990) *The Logic of Architecture: Design, Computation, and Cognition*, Cambridge, MA, MIT Press.

Negroponte, N. (1970) *The Architecture Machine*, Cambridge, MA, MIT Press.

Norberg-Schulz, C. (1965) *Intentions in Architecture*, Cambridge, MA, MIT Press.

Pask, G. (1969) 'The architectural relevance of cybernetics', *Architectural Design*, September.

Pask, G. (1975) 'Artificial intelligence – a preface and a theory' in Negroponte, N. (ed.) *Soft Architecture Machines*, Cambridge, MA, MIT Press.

Price, C. (2003) *Cedric Price: The Square Book*, Chichester, Wiley Academy.

DRAWING OUT
THE MODEL.
MICHAEL KOHN,
SLIDER STUDIO

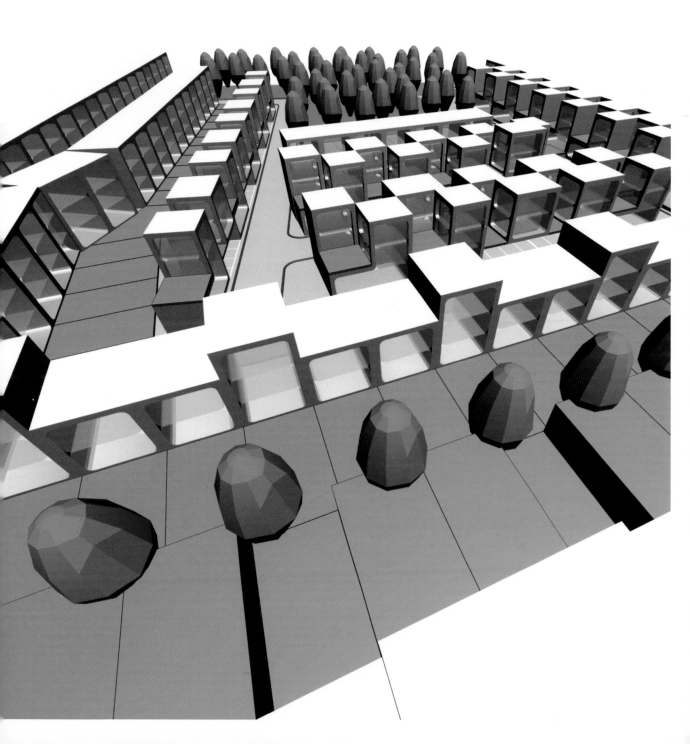

DRAWING OUT THE MODEL.
MICHAEL KOHN, SLIDER STUDIO

As part of my professional studies teaching at the University of East London, I ask students if they can count how many generic drawing types exist in architectural practice, or how many different types of drawing they have ever produced in their portfolios or in their work experience. This is not a question of drawing media, but one of drawing function. I'm talking about different types of plan, section and elevation, presentation drawings and more technical production information sets, and various scales of drawings depicting different levels of detail resolution. I'm talking about concept sketches, system diagrams, structural schematics and even procurement process maps. What is the specific role of a drawing type in the design process, and beyond? How does it work? What graphic code does it use to reduce what has to be drawn? How useful is the drawing? And, perhaps more challenging, when and why does a designer choose to create it in the first place?

A bright student might comment that there is now only the need for one type of architectural drawing; it is called 'a 3-D CAD model from which all good and accurate two-dimensional drawings can be extracted'. Smart answer, but it begs the question of how all that modelled information gets there in the first place. Is it sufficient to say that the design is simply and exclusively modelled? Is modelling alone a sufficient answer to producing better performing design information – leading to better designs? Before we can build information into a model, we have to use media in which we can abstract the design problem and explore it. That back-of-the-envelope sketching technique might still be useful. Moreover, a rapidly drafted, 2-D CAD abstract diagram might be full of undiscovered potential.

Emergence of generative drawings

Different types of drawing play different roles in the design process. Unlike an extracted section from a CAD model, traditionally abstracted architectural drawings can capture architectural intentions in ways which may not necessarily coordinate with each other. To some this may seem like waste, while others will recognise that different drawings form important 'process objects' within the larger complexity of design procurement. From initial concept to contractual instruction set, the specific role of the two-dimensional drawing is indeed hard to measure, but perhaps should not be underestimated in our fast-evolving world of three-dimensional design. Perhaps the most powerful characteristics of two-dimensional drawings are that they do not have the completeness of information of a 3-D model and that each drawing can suggest a variety of possible three-dimensional outcomes. Perhaps the most powerful characteristic of two-dimensional drawings is that they are fundamentally *generative* in nature.

A good example is provided by component distribution diagramming (CDD), a methodology of generating information-rich models built around a two-dimensional generative drawing type – the distribution diagram. The methodology is of a wide and general application in architecture, especially if you understand the architect's role as one of distributing both space and the building components that define that space. To date, Slider Studio has developed approaches for cladding and envelope design, and we are advancing with housing capacity models, site appraisals and masterplanning.

CDD methodology is supported by customised computational design software, authored in VBA for MicroStation, which we have developed in-house for different architectural typologies. The software facilitates a semi-automatic generative design search, enabling architects to draw simple diagrams – with just a few clicks of the mouse – in order to generate complex and complete designs

Fig 1 Typical library of components (tagged 3-D cells in MicroStation) representing the pool of individual components to be distributed by a diagram

Fig 2 Typical library distribution diagram sequence for a housing development comprising road layout, distribution markers and resultant information-rich model

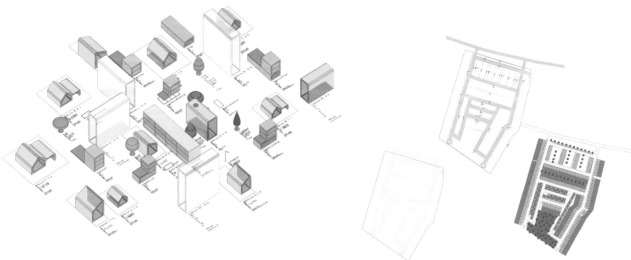

1

2

Strategy 4 / Scenario 12

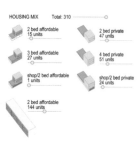

SUMMARY

Area:	3.15 ha
Dwellings:	310
Dwellings per Hectare:	98.4
Habitable Rooms:	1226
Habitable Rooms per Hectare:	389.2
Off Road Parking Spaces:	60
On Road Parking Spaces:	186
Total Parking Spaces:	265
Parking Ratio:	85%
Trees:	43
Trees per Hectare:	13.7

HOUSING MIX   Total: 310

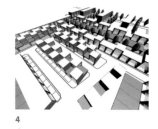

2 bed affordable
15 units

2 bed private
47 units

3 bed affordable
27 units

4 bed private
51 units

shop/2 bed affordable
1 units

shop/2 bed private
24 units

2 bed affordable
144 units

Housing Capacity Audit   sliderstudio

3

Fig 3 Typical automatic
report output from
each model, offering
key summary statistics
on the distribution

Figs 4, 5 and 6
Perspective images
of notional planning
and distribution
arrangements, drawn
from Slider Studio's
'component distribution
diagramming' software

4

in three dimensions. The process can take minutes not hours (and hours not weeks) compared to traditional CAD drafting or modelling methods. The hardest part, however, is the design thinking to make a good abstract diagram.

CDD is a useful design methodology, allowing an architect to describe the architectural problem at hand as a 'spatial distribution' of smaller components; each component contains architectural 'knowledge' of what it is, how it can be distributed (and ultimately how it must behave once distributed). There are many tricks one can play within the CDD process, but we will cover the four basic stages here. These stages are defined by the creation of (1) components and (2) diagrams, followed by the automatic generation of (3) information-rich 3-D models and (4) evaluation reports.

Capturing knowledge in a component: for the first stage, we will consider the components to be distributed. These may or may not represent actual constructional assemblies depending upon the approach adopted. They need to be identified and imagined by the designer as discrete objects which can be designed and modelled in either two or three dimensions, and added to a library of similar components. On creation, or after the event, information can be added to give them knowledge[1] of how they can be distributed (and in advanced applications, how they can behave once distributed). In this way the architect builds the building blocks to be distributed (figure 3).

The plan is the generator: [2] the second stage involves creating the diagram. Diagrams are made of different types of lines and shapes (we call these 'markers' after the felt-tip pen approach to design) and they have instructions embedded within them[3] explaining what types of components they can or should distribute, and how they should indeed distribute them. A small alteration in the instruction

of each marker can have a fundamental effect on the outcome of a model and, in this capacity, the diagrams become semi-generative. The distribution diagram does not need to be a plan, but the plan appears to us to be the primary abstraction of measurable habitable space, and records spatial function directly. If we want different architectural functions to have an influence on the distribution, the plan forms the basis for most of our distribution diagrams (figures 4, 5 and 6).

Model populations: the third stage is initiated by selecting the diagram to populate, pointing to the correct component library and pressing a button.[4] As the program is running, each marker in the diagram is examined and the distribution instructions are followed accordingly. These instructions will vary depending on the type of diagram marker and the type of components for a specific architectural problem.

Design metrification: the fourth stage in the process is one of evaluation. Once you have generated a component distribution model, fully populated with knowledge-based components, you can access its data to evaluate how good it is. Have you got the right housing mix or car parking ratio? Does your cladding solution meet the appropriate glazing ratios? Can you afford to build this solution? The component distribution model – generated programmatically by reading instructions within the original diagram – is similar to building information models in that it comprises a database which can be queried. Customised reports can thus be generated to provide the relevant metrics to assess the design quality and building performance for planning or building regulations. The metrification of design allows objective evaluation at a level not previously manageable with manual methods, but demands more and more as design performance and quality indicators. For better or worse, design measurement is here to stay.

1.
In MicroStation, CDD components are cells that have been tagged with information. The difference between information and knowledge may well be debated, and in the context of CDD it is arguable that the knowledge is really only found in successfully generated models.

2.
Le Corbusier's obvious but useful reminder of the generative qualities of the plan (Towards a New Architecture, 1923). If we are interested in distributing according to function, a 'feet on the ground' approach is still highly relevant in an ever complex three-dimensional world. Plan abstractions inevitably define function, so function-based generative diagrams are likely to be plan based.

3.
Diagram markers in MicroStation can be lines, shapes and polylines tagged with instructions as with the cells. Alternatively, a level-naming convention can be adopted to provide instructions for different markers. This later method was adopted for making diagrams in DoX.

4.
Our in-house tests on typical housing layout models of, for example, 1,500 components in MicroStation V8 on a moderate workstation take 45 seconds to distribute.

5

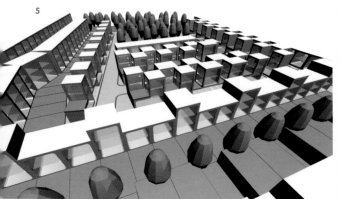

6

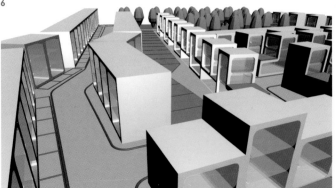

DRAWING OUT THE MODEL.
MICHAEL KOHN, SLIDER STUDIO

The design challenge by Make
Stuart Fraser, Make Architects

We have been working on a prestigious residential building in central London (figure 7). The fenestration concept of this building has been designed to reflect the differing functions of the rooms within each apartment. Accordingly, living rooms feature large, opening windows, maximising views out and drawing daylight in. By contrast, bedrooms are more intimate spaces requiring greater privacy and softer lighting; the fenestration for these rooms consists of a combination of slender vertical and horizontal apertures with opening lights.

Using this functional fenestration philosophy we developed the elevations to avoid repetitive façades yet provide an overall rhythm with a clear visual hierarchy of openings to suit different functions. To complete this idea, we believed the cladding panelisation itself should have a similar approach, where individual panels are sometimes aligned and sometimes offset from each other.

We had already developed our own generic drawing type for understanding different cladding solutions across entire façades, called 'functional elevations'. These drawings are stripped-back elevations, graphically recording the spaces (specifically the functions of those spaces, hence the drawing's name) behind the façade. The functional elevation provides a strategic reference to assist our composition of the façade, including positioning the fenestration followed by the panelisation. Our initial studies resulted in 11 different panel types on the building. The question was: can advanced computational methods help improve on this?

Slider Studio's response
Michael Kohn, Slider Studio

To tackle this problem, and problems like it, Slider developed the DoX software (short for 'Death of the glass box'). DoX uses the component distribution diagramming (CDD) methodology of using information-rich diagrams to distribute information-rich components. It naturally sits upon the architect's existing design methodology of 'functional elevations' and provides a powerful semi-automated generative design search software.

The DoX software has a 'cell builder' for making primary and secondary cladding components, which can differentiate between glazed and solid cladding types. Plan diagrams are created by tracing the envelope line and comprise markers that record the internal functions of the spaces behind the envelope. These diagrams are automatically converted into an elevation of scripted placeholders, indicating where different primary components (glazing) can go according to the function of the room behind. DoX places the primary components and then fills the remaining spaces with secondary components (cladding panels).

Alternatively, the architects can work directly in elevation mode, as Make's team chose to do (figure 8), by directly drawing placeholders and manipulating these to suit. By changing the cladding widths of individual components and setting different placement tolerances for each placeholder, a number of elevation variations can be generated until an appropriate solution with the required number of panel widths is found. Eventually, Make found a solution to their cladding problem using only four panel widths instead of 11. Make agrees this would have been unachievable without the help of DoX.

Role of the placeholder – the invisible visible variable

The fundamental computational concept required to understand CDD methodologies revolves around the coupling of component libraries with distribution diagram markers. The individual markers are essentially performing as 'placeholders' for different components. Drawing markers in CDD effectively places different types of placeholders with different rules attached to them. On this basis alone, the methodology is very open-ended.

A placeholder object can be understood as a kind of 'invisible visible variable'[5] as it very directly mirrors the function of the variable in the programming language that creates and subsequently controls it. Even more abstract, when viewing the completed architectural model, the placeholder isn't really there. The placeholder affords the architect a degree of decision deferral on the design, promoting the creation of strategic design relationships without having to worry about the specific design detail. When using a placeholder in a model, the architect effectively declares generic design intent without cutting out future options to change or refine specific component design.

Another interesting phenomenon of the placeholder is the idea that an architect can choose the degree of tolerance allowable in placing an object within the placeholder. That is to say, a placeholder can be much larger than the object or objects which are to be placed in it. Exactly where an object is placed within the placeholder can be subject to another set of rules – such as proportional rules in the case of a specific cladding algorithm – or it

---

5.
For those unfamiliar with variables in a programming sense, a variable represents an allocation of memory for a specified value; the placeholder represents an allocation of space for a particular component as is placed in the CAD package so can be considered more visible than a programmatic language variable from a text file. But placeholders are merely constructional graphical objects, not representations of real things like building components, so we don't necessarily want to see them represented – we just need them to preserve some space for a representational object. We would usually make them invisible in the CAD model by simply turning them off, hence the term 'invisible visible variable'.

Fig 7 Optimised scheme of a residential building in London, by Make

can be the subject of a random choice, executed manually with the role of a dice or generated using a computer's random number generator. This degree of placeholder tolerance is embedded in the software we built for Make to explore complex façade distribution patterns.

Model methodologies – diagrammatising architecture

The architect's relationship with the virtual 3-D model continues to mature as new technology is embraced. The photorealistic CGI has emerged as a now requisite drawing type to support the marketing of design proposals and ease their route through planning. But architects are also now testing the extended role of the model for design interrogation and evaluation, and embedding the use of 3-D models into their everyday design methodology. Methodologies for building models effectively would be helpful and component distribution diagrams may have a role to play here. It would be extreme to suggest that one could draw a useful component distribution diagram for every type of architecture, but there are clearly many examples of distribution systems within architectural design which could be identified and represented through CDD. Seen as process objects, such diagrams can be extremely valuable in an open-ended generative search for populations of what *could* be, as opposed to a singular, closed and manually modelled proposal of what a single designer suggests *should* be.

Drawing out the model

So, how many drawing types are there? Perhaps this is a bit like trying to find all the species of fish in the sea. As with architecture and the design methodology that generates it, drawing media are equally subject to evolution and mutation. There are probably hundreds of subtly different identifiable drawing types in architectural design processes, and many more yet to be invented. Some record and coordinate intent, while others – more generative in nature – may speculate on what might be. Some drawings will remain as simple scribbles on the back of an envelope or beer mat. Others will form the rich computational ingredients of a genuinely computer-aided twenty-first century design process.

Michael Kohn is an architect, computational designer and founder of the London-based design practice Slider Studio.

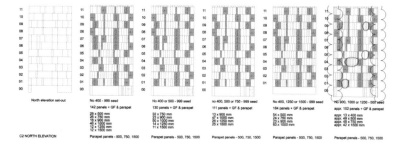

Fig 8 A depiction of Make's use of Slider Studio's software to solve a problem of façade composition

ARTIFICIAL INTELLIGENCE
AND THE
CONCEPTUALISATION
OF ARCHITECTURE.
ABEL MACIEL,
3DREID ARCHITECTS

62 ARTIFICIAL
INTELLIGENCE
AND THE
CONCEPTUALISATION
OF ARCHITECTURE.
ABEL MACIEL,
3DREID ARCHITECTS

In spite of the high degree of complexity in the built environment and the evolution of buildings from concept to construction, the drawing process can be 'parameterised' and artefacts can be 'mass-customised'. On the other hand, the design process is often a solo one and could be assisted by a parametric modelling tool, capable of creating intelligent agents which swarm over a digital concept model, interrogating it, refining it and collectively suggesting better ways to build it. This tool would take into account the aspirations of the designer by mimicking living systems – in particular, the purposive behaviour of interactions between multiple elements distributed in space and time. A useful characteristic of such systems is that complex behaviour can emerge as they adapt to changes in their local environments in the pursuit of minimally specified objectives. If one compares the restricted workflow of existing design tools with the richly interconnected chemical affinity of biological systems, a radically new approach to architectural design is suggested.

Parametric modelling tools support both dimension-driven and intuitive design. Working directly in 3-D, designers secure constant visual feedback and design control. Furthermore, coordination with other project participants is greatly facilitated. Advanced parametric and associative design systems help to explore design intent and dynamic configurations. This capability enables designers to concentrate on their design strategy, rather than on the mechanics of modelling. The model can be used to experiment with alternative design approaches, eliminating the need to rebuild the entire model at every iteration. However, the problem with parametric design is that, even though it is an articulated representation of the design, it does not respond to specific design issues – opening opportunities for further development.

Most parametric software used by architects is based on a two-dimensional drawing that feeds back alterations to a virtual 3-D model. The proportions of the drawing can be changed and this initial profile is, in essence, an alternative for sketching. This two-dimensional drawing or 'profile' of a potential model needs to be constrained in order to guide parameterisation. When this is achieved, the drawing is completely defined as an interrelated system that can be recalculated coherently, from which a 3-D model can be generated.

However, present design software does not constrain design by the functionality of its features and spaces in response to human use, the environment, or any other external parameter. It is not the design process that is parameterised – just the representation of the design, which has a practically infinite accuracy. The two-dimensional profile contains a set of interdependencies that are organised as either 'global' or 'local'. Local variables are generated from the individual parameters of each feature that has previously been constrained and are affected by global settings. All the variable names and equations are defined by the user from a nomenclature within the CAD system.

Ongoing research at Reid Architecture attempts to demonstrate the advantages of the design process having local variables that are automatically processed by the computer to acquire intelligent behaviour. This can be made to work by using a compound biomimetic system that interprets the external and internal constraints of a 3-D model in a continuous feedback loop. This method could be applied as a geometry solver that considers the effect of ambiguous design issues. It could also generate geometry without the requirement of setting up a constrained profile.

It is important to note that programming is a creative process; an understanding of a concept that informs a software development method like genetic algorithms and programming is crucial to the implementation of the solutions that these tools might propose, especially when dealing with abstract concepts. Genetics of population and genetics of molecules are two distinct approaches to software code development for artificial creativity. As in biological research, the use of both methods leads to the discovery and control of their mechanisms.

In genetic algorithms and programming there is a strong insistence on the concept of the 'survival of the fittest'. This was a mid-nineteenth century philosophy proposed by Herbert Spencer and known since then as 'Social Darwinism', though in fact Spencer began developing the idea before Darwin published the *Origin of Species*. This misguided Victorian naturalistic fallacy of what is and ought to be natural can blind us to many useful metaphors for the development of new methods of structuring genetic programming. Emergence has, in genetics, a character of a predictable and unpredictable morphogenesis. It operates within tolerances set by the inherent qualities of its parts.

One facet used as a metaphor for the proposed artificial creativity method described here is observed on the interaction of real life with real environments. A genotype is not static but a dialogue with the phenotype and the processes to which the life-form is exposed. In cases of direct adaptations, for instance the human skin, genes that favour responsiveness will prevail against the fittest phenotype. The DNA molecule itself is not a static blueprint for life, but it is constantly changing and adapting to external forces. The proof of that is what are called 'introns' or 'junk DNA'. There are, for example, portions of chromosomes which code for proteins; some portions are vestigial, others are intriguing incorporations of other live-forms (like viruses) within genomes.

'Transposons', or 'jumping genes' lead to a constantly reconfiguring gene sequence, discovered by Barbara McClintock in the 1940s. This had a profound effect on the Darwinian concept of life as a unit, and genes as a subservient of that unit. A new model was conceived where genes have their own internal processes, some quite anarchic. If 'transposons' insert themselves on a coding region of the chromosome, they might cause damaging mutation; however, they operate more like molecular drives on 'introns'. Their existence produces variations of a different nature – a self-design method.

This process was first observed in corn, a 'heterozygous' life-form like ourselves. On heterozygous genomes, as observed by Gregory Mendel in 1865, the genes expressing phenotype are composed of non-symmetrical 'alleles'. This notion takes us to the territory of polymorphic adaptability where genes reverberate across the genome. This behaviour is responsible for the effective deployment of adaptation rather than delegating it to chance events like mutation.

Using these metaphors, the proposed modelling system is composed of internal and external emergent constraints applied to a closed 3-D surface. It is then explored, colonised and modified by different orders of agents composing the emergent systems. In principle, this surface wouldn't need to represent the quantitative changes of the original briefing applied to the design but, acting more like a territory mapping, it tells you the location of solution zones embodied in the representation. This is conventionally done by entering numeric information for each factor of the surface constraints.

For example, in the case of a dwelling, any design has to perform on a number of different levels, including response to environmental factors, cultural space configuration, structural strategy, and so on. All these considerations coexist in the model's ability to display different levels of solution. The levels of reading can overlap and migrate. For instance, a room with a door has embodied within its representation an indication of the building system, social depth, environmental strategy and possible alternative uses and space recoding. This recognition depends on the ability of the architect to read the drawing both in local and global levels and share assumptions between the two scales.

The global form can represent the simplified version of the design. The problems represented by the features on the surface of the global form need to be solved for specific zones of the design using an inverted priority tree – the global topological distortion is related to the local topology. It can work both in top-down mode as well as bottom-up. Working in top-down mode would enable the architect to be intuitive, dealing with the global manifestation of the design in a sculptural manner.

This means that the computer would assist the interpretation of the surface into architectural sub-settings. Using the bottom-up approach, it could function as an analytical device to qualify and quantify geometry.

The necessary constraints of this 'intelligent surface' could be considerably different from an industry-standard package. Rather than giving a purely Euclidean and/or Riemannian representation of space, this type of geometrical solver would need to consider other representations like topology and space use, the connected dimensionality of such networks, the attendant building systems related to the dimensional layout, material properties of the architecture's physicality and a collection of simulation engines reassessing the functional performance of the surface. The definition of parameters to enable the system to propose intuitive strategies are based on two key points:

- the 'agents' produce geometric interpretations of the surface based on time-based modifications of the external envelope;

- a separate set of agents restructure the inner zones of the architecture as the surface is modified.

This dual system is composed of 'real' and 'abstract' agents; the real agents inhabit the 3-D surface and fill the interior of the enclosure created by this surface. The 'abstract' agents compute information and do not appear in the 3-D environment. The term 'agent' refers to any object with autonomous behaviours which interacts with its environment and other agents in the virtual world.

The draft simulation of this system was written in Breve, a freely available 'artificial life' programming environment with an OpenGL interface. Breve has a similar structure to C++, and is an object-oriented language with classes for development of complex interactions of swarms and auto-constructive genetic algorithms. Breve supports the Python scripting language and can be called into a C++ script.

Auto-constructive genetic algorithms in general have some interesting capabilities: they are an evolvable language, well suited to evolution simulation because of their extremely simple syntax, and they operate as a stack-based typing system. The simple syntax helps to ensure that any kind of genetic operator (including the commonly used cross-over and mutation) will produce a syntactically valid individual. The stack-based typing system – in which instructions look for operators on typed stacks – ensures that all 'push programs' are semantically valid.

Arguments are passed to instructions using a set of stacks, one for each variable type. When an instruction is executed, it reads and removes argument values from the tops of the relevant

ARTIFICIAL
INTELLIGENCE
AND THE
CONCEPTUALISATION
OF ARCHITECTURE.
ABEL MACIEL,
3DREID ARCHITECTS

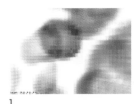

1

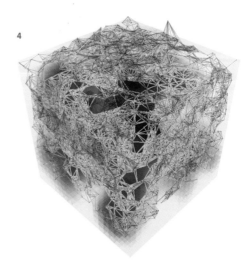

3

**Figs 1 and 2 Agents'
simulation of a Grey–
Scott reaction–diffusion
model**

**Fig 3 Agents colonising
the surface of a sphere
and tessellating a
mesh. They compute
light exposure, and
migrate and adapt to a
given shape guided by
neighbourhood rules.
Parameters of the agents'
behaviour vary from
velocity, cruise distance,
collision and acceleration
to energy requirement,
age and species**

**Fig 4 Internal and
external agents installed
in a cube. This combines
the diffusion–reaction
simulation with the mesh
tessellating agents.
On the interaction, the
external agents follow the
diffusion concentrations
of the internal agents**

stacks; it performs a computation, and then it 'pushes' any output values onto the relevant stacks. If a stack is empty, the instruction performs a 'NOOP' and does nothing. This scheme ensures that instructions are always provided with input data of the correct type.

This 'push program' is made up of lists of the elements like instructions, literal values and sub-lists. Execution of a push program begins by placing the entire expression onto the code stack and proceeds recursively as follows:

To execute program P:

    If P is a single instruction then execute it.

    Else if P is a literal then push it onto the
    appropriate stack.

    Else (P must be a list) sequentially execute each of
    the Push programs in P.

Here's a sample push program which does some mathematical and logical computations:

(2 3 INTEGER.* 4.1 5.2 FLOAT.+ TRUE FALSE BOOLEAN.OR)

After execution of the program, the stacks are left in the following states:

```
# the program we started with
CODE STACK: ( ( 2 3 INTEGER.* 4.1 5.2 FLOAT.+
TRUE FALSE BOOLEAN.OR ) )

# the result of the code TRUE FALSE BOOLEAN.OR
BOOLEAN STACK: ( TRUE )

# the result of the code 4.1 5.2 FLOAT.+
FLOAT STACK: ( 9.3 )

# the result of the code 2 3 INTEGER.*
INTEGER STACK: ( 6 )
```

Push programs can be somehow more complex, as in the case of this conceptualisation tool for architecture. Instructions are initially provided to allow the programs to modify their own code, perform logical and program flow-control operations and create and run new programs on the fly (automatically providing support for elements which resemble macros and 'automatically defined functions'). For example, a group of agents can be programmed to adopt the behaviour of a Gray–Scott reaction, which predicts chemical diffusion reactions. Generally, diffusion-reactions produce patterns reminiscent of those seen in nature, such as the marks on snake or zebra skins. The Gray–Scott equations model such reactions.

By using this technique, agents can communicate with a field of nearby neighbours with no a-priori synchronisation among them. They can target or avoid pre-programmed objectives, such as light or temperature. They collectively tessellate a surface based on a region's definition rules. These rules can be modified dynamically to affect the mesh tessellation. Finally, the different group of agents are 'frozen' and exported to a more advanced 3-D modelling package for re-meshing and optically complete rendering.

This interaction of agents on 3-D geometry suggests the possibility of organising amorphous computing systems in a developmental fashion by starting with particles in a random distribution to solve reaction–diffusion problems. The resulting regularly spaced 'zones' of particles could then serve as self-organising 'centroids' for subsequent stages of spatial and geometrical organisation. An emergent system alone is a partial answer, with the customisation of a contextual tool being a key issue. Programs can evolve, simulate and learn from other programs, consume resources and be tailored to

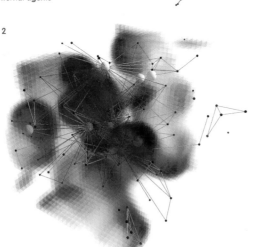

2

4

Fig 5

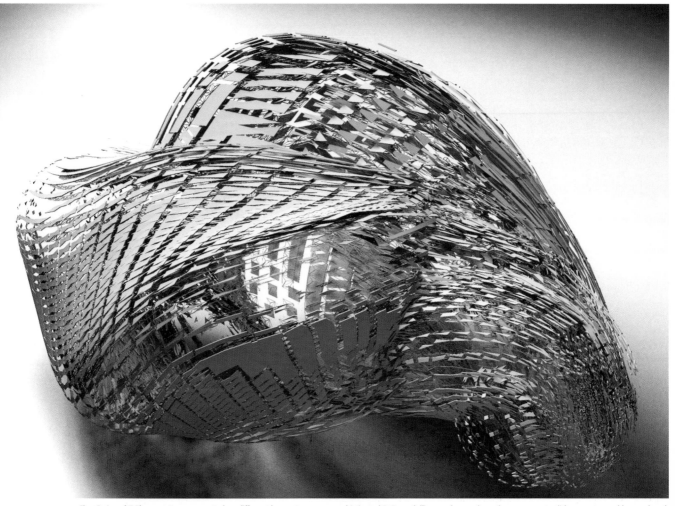

Figs 5, 6 and 7 The agents are exported as different layers to a more sophisticated 3-D modelling package where they can meet solid geometry and be rendered.

66 ARTIFICIAL
    INTELLIGENCE
    AND THE
    CONCEPTUALISATION
    OF ARCHITECTURE.
    ABEL MACIEL,
    3DREID ARCHITECTS

optimise the design. Further development of this tool should be able to generate millions of agents divided by more specific behaviours by using faster and more manageable algorithms, creating interactions of higher definition and accuracy.

The 27,000 particles randomly packed in a 3-D patch (30x30x30 voxels), starting with random concentrations, evolve to regular spots after few hundred time steps. The partial differential equations modelling this process use a forward Euler integration of the finite-difference equations that one obtains by spatial discretisation of the Laplacian. The applied equation is stated on the right, where:

U and V and P are chemical species;
u and v represent their concentrations;
r_u and r_v are their diffusion rates;
k represents the rate of conversion of V to P;
f represents the rate of the process that feeds U and drains U, V and P.

One may also simulate the underlying process, which is stoichiometrically conservative (accounting for the source of U and the drain of U, V and P.) The fact that all the interactions are local makes this a good candidate for a parallel implementation. Diffusion may be modelled by an explicitly conservative exchange process among neighbours where the reactions are locally modelled at each locus by a simulated processor.

Each particle's neighbours are those within a distance of 0.05 units from it. The constants for the Gray–Scott model here are k1=1.6, k2=0.4, c1=0.04, c2=0.1 and integration is performed using the forward-Euler method with Δt=1. The different gradient from black to colour + alpha of the particles indicates different values of μ1.

Abel Maciel is an architect and researcher based in London. He has a Masters of Architecture from Bartlett School, where he studied architectural computation, parametric modeling, biomimetics and sustainability. Maciel is currently pursuing a multidisciplinary Engineering Doctorate in Virtual Environments & Architecture at UCL and is a visiting tutor at the Architectural Association. Maciel has worked at Foster + Partners for many years and is now conducting research for 3DReid Architects.

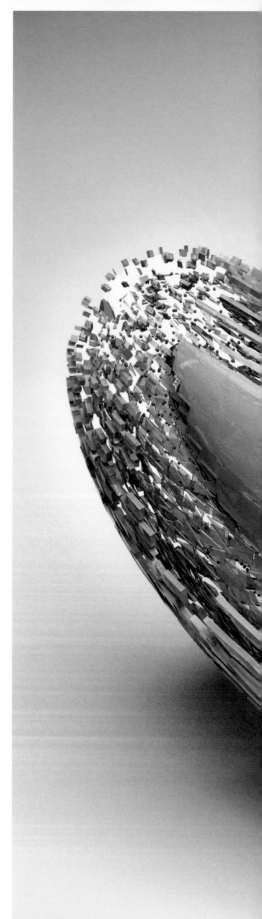

Fig 7

PRACTICAL
EMERGENCE.
CHRIS J.K. WILLIAMS AND
ODYSSEAS KONTOVOURKIS,
UNIVERSITY OF BATH

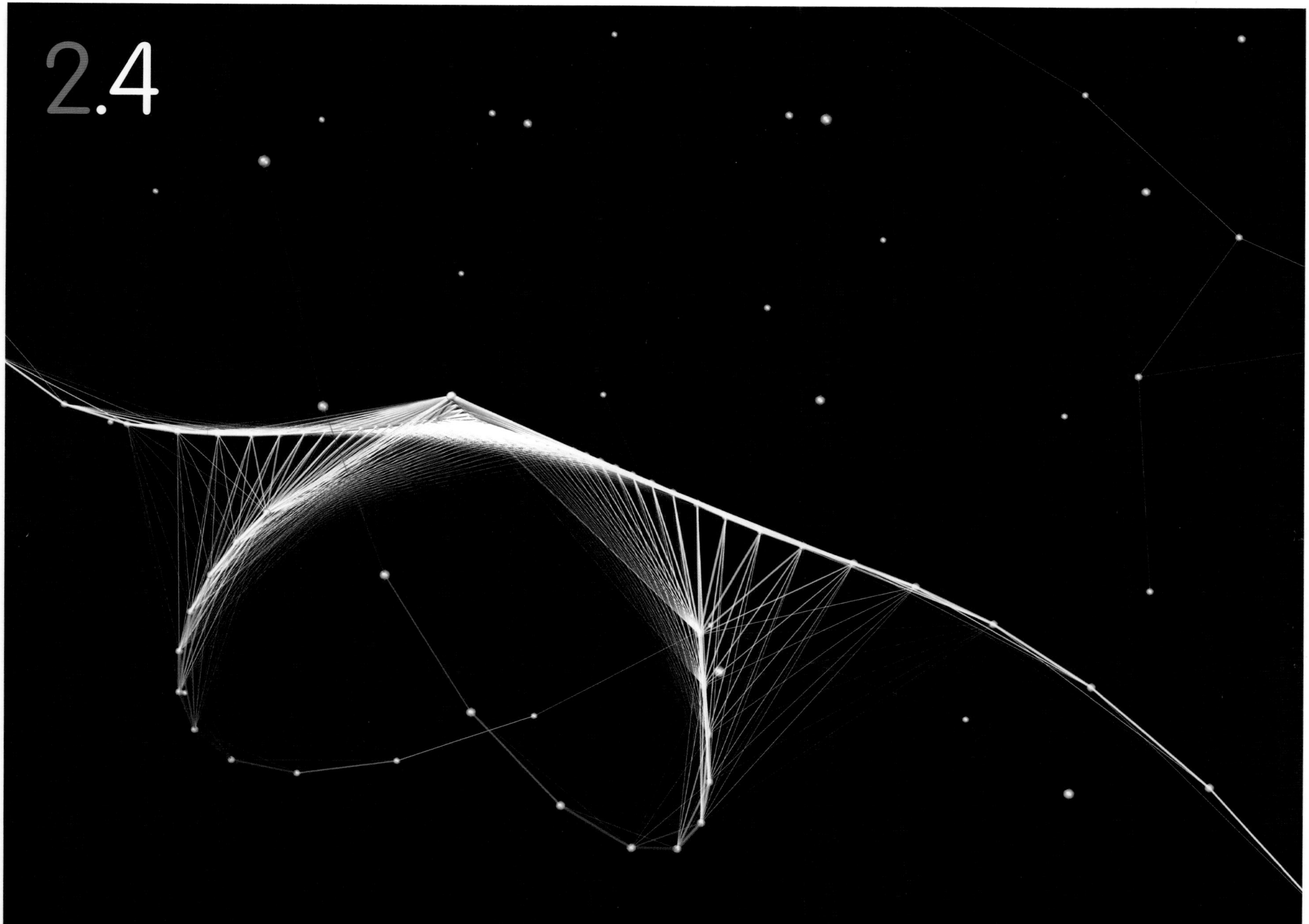

2.4

PRACTICAL EMERGENCE.

CHRIS J.K. WILLIAMS AND ODYSSEAS KONTOVOURKIS, UNIVERSITY OF BATH

The Latin *mergo, mergere, mersi, mersum* means to dip, plunge into a liquid, immerse. From *ex mergo* we have *emergo, emergere, emersi, emersum*: to rise up, to free oneself, to come to light, appear, emerge. *Nuttall's Standard Dictionary* (Wood, 1916) gives the two words 'emergence' and 'emergency' the same definition: the act of emerging; a sudden appearance; an unexpected event; exigence; pressing necessity.

In the first edition of the journal *Emergence*, Jeffrey Goldstein (1999) wrote:

Emergence, as in the title of this new journal, refers to the arising of novel and coherent structures, patterns, and properties during the process of self-organization in complex systems. Emergent phenomena are conceptualized as occurring on the macro level, in contrast to the micro-level components and processes out of which they arise.

In a wide variety of scientific and mathematical fields, grouped together loosely under the title 'complexity theory,' an intense search is now under way for characteristics and laws associated with emergent phenomena observed across different types of complex system.

Goldstein then describes the history of the concept of emergence, tracing it back more than a hundred years to the English philosopher G.H. Lewes. In this chapter we shall discuss emergence through practical examples, since it is only by looking at the results of emergence that one can assess its relevance, if any, to architecture.

Fig 1 Flow past a cylinder computed using smoothed particle hydrodynamics

Fig 2 Computational study of a spiral galaxy

Modelling reality

Perhaps the starting point should be the computer modelling of an emergent phenomenon in nature, that is the replication of a natural occurrence. Figure 1 shows a computer simulation of flow past a cylinder using the method of smoothed particle hydrodynamics (Monaghan, 2005). The von Kármán vortex street of alternate clockwise and anticlockwise vortices emerges out of the properties of the fluid and its motion. The fluid motion is at the same time random and highly structured.

This immediately shows the limitations of computers. A calculation (seen in figure 1) took two days on a MacBook with an Intel Core Duo and used 106 particles. However, Loschmidt's number (related to Avogadro's number) is 27×10^{24} molecules per cubic metre of air. Properties such as temperature, density, pressure and viscosity are explained by the kinetic theory of gases in which air molecules bounce off each other randomly due to thermal agitation. On average a molecule will travel the mean free path between collisions, about 70×10^{-9}m. On the large scale, the volume of the atmosphere is approximately 10×10^{18}m³. Thus if we start at the scale of one metre we have two impossibly large numbers – smaller scale (individual molecules) and larger scale (the atmosphere).

Computers are limited to storing and performing calculations on perhaps 10^8 numbers, so there is no conceivable way in which they will ever be able to analyse the motion of individual molecules. Instead, each particle used in smoothed particle hydrodynamics represents many air molecules

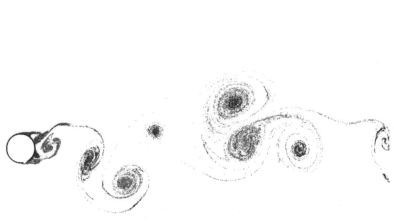

1

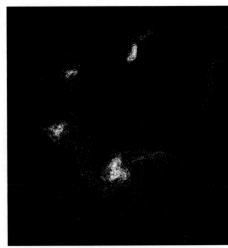

2

and is given more sophisticated behaviour than that of the molecules in the kinetic theory. Each particle is 'aware' of its neighbours and moves in a complicated way in an attempt to model the effects of pressure and viscosity.

Thus, in this case (figure 1), we have two scales of emergence, from the individual molecules of the kinetic theory to the particles of the smoothed particle hydrodynamics and then to the macroscopic scale of eddies, vortices, waves and smoke trails. The limitations of computer power will mean that the calculation of emergence will always be limited to highly simplified special cases.

A spiral galaxy simulated by treating each star as a particle (figure 2) moves under the influence of gravitational attraction from every other star. This simulation took one hour on a MacBook. As in the case of fluid dynamics, there is very little disagreement about the physical laws, although there is much discussion on the most efficient way of implementing the rules in a computer program.

A chain moves under gravity (figure 3). This program runs much faster – a few seconds. The reason is that each node, or link of the chain is only influenced by its two immediate neighbours. The program, written in C++ using OpenGL is listed in Appendix 1. The tensions in the links are calculated from their lengths and stiffness and then

```
for(i=0;i<=1;i++){
Velocity[i][Node]+=deltat*Force[i][Node]/(m*L[Node]);
x[i][Node][0]+=deltat*Velocity[i][Node];}}
```

in which the velocities and positions are updated

3

using the Verlet algorithm. The rest of the program is concerned with setting up the initial conditions and doing the drawing directly to the screen.

The form of the Mannheim gridshell (figure 4) was determined by Frei Otto's hanging model (figure 5) using the same technique that Gaudí had used for the Sagrada Família and the Church of Colònia Güell, that of the inversion of a hanging form to produce a structure in pure compression. In each case the shape of the model (or of an equivalent computer model) emerges out of the technique and the laws of static equilibrium. However, in this case there is no sense of the result being unexpected and so it would perhaps not be appropriate to use the word emergence. The computer modelling of a hanging chain net would simply be an extension of the hanging chain program.

Imaginary worlds

In Benjamin Bucknall's translation (1889) of Viollet-le-Duc's analysis of the Doge's Palace (1863–72) (figure 6), 'The Venetian architect has scrupulously fulfilled the conditions of this programme, and his work owes all its decorative effect to the genuine and forcible effect of the structure.' In other words the architectural form *emerges* out of the rules of structural behaviour. However, this suggests some form of overall intelligence and understanding of the rules of structure, whereas the concept of *emergence* would seem to carry with it the implication that things happen automatically. Thus, even though we would discount the neo-creationist idea of *intelligent design* in nature, clearly in architecture an intelligent application of the rules

4

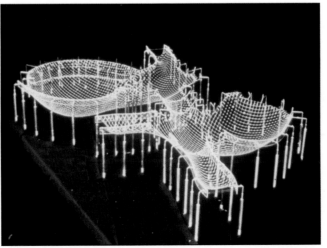

5

6

PRACTICAL EMERGENCE.

CHRIS J.K. WILLIAMS
AND ODYSSEAS
KONTOVOURKIS,
UNIVERSITY OF BATH

of structure, planning, and so on must accompany any attempt to use computer programs to cause a design to emerge out of some random process. Interest in emergence perhaps accompanies a lack of belief in the concept of rules of aesthetics in an attempt to bypass the application of such rules.

Emergent phenomena occur as a result of the repeated application of a set of rules. However, in the application of emergence to architecture, the rules are to a greater or less extent arbitrary – at least as arbitrary as the choice of rules of aesthetics. But because emergence is not predicable, the only way to test it is by trying it. Often the best results happen by accident, a serendipitous mistake.

A three-dimensional form (figure 7) is produced as a result of what we have called the 'Maud algorithm'. The particles started in a random arrangement and automatically moved themselves into a highly structured form. The jth particle repels the ith with

a force $f_{ij} = -f_{ji} = \dfrac{c(\mathbf{r}_i - \mathbf{r}_j)e^{-\frac{r_{ij}^2}{a^2}}}{r_{ij}^2}$ in which a and c are

constants and $\mathbf{r}_i$ is the position vector of the ith particle $r_{ij} = |\mathbf{r}_i - \mathbf{r}_j|$, the magnitude of $(\mathbf{r}_i - \mathbf{r}_j)$. The total force experienced by the ith particle is $\mathbf{p}_i = \sum \mathbf{f}_{ij}$ and the associated stiffness is the second order tensor

$$\mathbf{K}_i = c\,\frac{\partial}{\partial \mathbf{r}_i} \sum_j \frac{(\mathbf{r}_i - \mathbf{r}_j)e^{-\frac{r_{ij}^2}{a^2}}}{r_{ij}^2} = c\sum_j \frac{e^{-\frac{r_{ij}^2}{a^2}}}{r_{ij}^2}\left(\mathbf{I} - 2\left(\frac{1}{r_{ij}^2} + \frac{1}{a^2}\right)(\mathbf{r}_i - \mathbf{r}_j)(\mathbf{r}_i - \mathbf{r}_j)\right)$$

During each cycle all the particles are moved such that the ith particle is moved by a displacement proportional to $\mathbf{p}_i \cdot \mathbf{K}_i^{-1}$ in which $\mathbf{K}_i$ is the inverse of $\mathbf{K}_i^{-1}$. The principal values of $\mathbf{K}_i^{-1}$ may be negative, in which case a particle is moved in the *opposite* direction to that component out of balance force. Thus, even compression structures are stable and move themselves into backbone-like arrangements. This result was unexpected – the technique was developed to analyse ordinary, stable structures and its application to the generation of otherwise unstable forms was due to chance.

In what we have called the 'accumulation algorithm' (figure 8), white dots begin positioned randomly and move under a mutual repulsion and a repulsion from the fixed yellow dots and the red dot which is moved by the mouse. Each white dot is joined by a line to its nearest neighbour to form a maze. This time the program was written in Processing (undated) and an example of a Processing program is in Appendix 3. Processing is simpler to use than C++ and OpenGL, but does appear to be somewhat slower when there are many calculations to be done. Comparison between the two languages shows many similarities and so a beginner may chose to use Processing and then progress to C++ and OpenGL if need be.

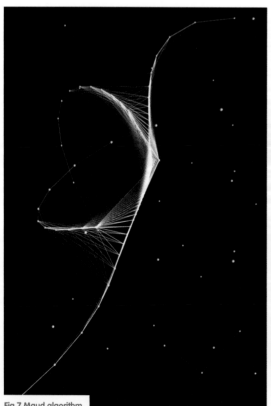

Fig 7 Maud algorithm

Fig 8 Accumulation algorithm

We have also written the same algorithm using Bentley Systems' parametric design program Generative Components, which is particularly suitable for integration into the architectural design process.

No discussion of imaginary worlds would be complete without mentioning fractals, in particular the Mandelbrot set (figure 9, shown in blue), plus a structure in grey that emerged from an error in the program. The Mandelbrot set is computed as follows. One starts with the complex number $z_0 = Z = X + iY = \text{constant}$ (where $i = \sqrt{-1}$) and repeatedly applies the rule $z_{n+1} = z_n^2 + Z$. Now only one of two things can happen, either you end up going towards infinity, or you jump around and stay close to the origin. The Mandelbrot set consists of those values of Z for which you stay close to the origin. The colours associated with the Mandelbrot set are formed by the number of cycles required to reach a certain distance from the origin. The grey (in figure 9) was obtained by mistakenly associating the colours with z_n rather than Z. The program is listed in Appendix 2; it writes a .tga graphics file directly.

Emergence is a dynamic phenomenon in which quantities change with time. A building is static and dynamic processes occur only through design, building and decay and through the movement of people and goods.

In the 1980s, Craig W. Reynolds created an artificial life program to simulate the flocking behaviour of birds (1986). Each bird ('boid') was treated as an individual (a 'cellular automaton'), applying simple behavioural rules of interaction, and the result was an aggregate motion of the flock.

A banding pattern arises as two groups of pedestrians cross. This phenomenon was studied by Helbing and Molnár (1995) and Helbing et al. (2005) and it is particularly pronounced here (figure 10) because our model assumes that people repel each other only when they actually touch. In practice, the bands would dissipate as people adjusted themselves after crossing the other group. This banding requires no intelligence, no overall view or any learning. The bands form due to random variations and, once formed, people are naturally funnelled into them.

Fig 9 Mandelbrot set

PRACTICAL EMERGENCE.

CHRIS J.K. WILLIAMS
AND ODYSSEAS
KONTOVOURKIS,
UNIVERSITY OF BATH

Fig 10 Banding of pedestrians

Helbing and his co-workers use a 'social force model' which can be traced back to Lewin (1951) and now these ideas have been taken further by institutions such as the Santa Fe Institute (2007). Any school of thought which treats people, or animals, as mindless automatons is to be rejected whether in politics, economics or religion. Following *L'affaire* Sokal (2007) one should also be wary of using well-defined concepts from the physical sciences loosely in the social sciences. However, provided the results of any analysis are treated with due scepticism, there is no harm in running numerical experiments just to see what happens and to use the results if they correspond to common sense – a very sophisticated thought process (try writing a computer program that exhibits common sense). The experiments we will describe here refer to a very simple building type, the airport. The building is simple in that the passengers have a very straightforward aim, to arrive or to depart, but the large number of people and their continual motion introduces complexity. We will focus on departure. Arrival is similar, but the passengers have fewer choices.

Our 'agents' will be subject to forces. The first is repulsion from other individuals and inanimate objects such as walls or tables. Immediately there is a problem; certain individuals will attract each other and then only repel each other when touching (they can't penetrate each other). If walking, one would avoid a table and walk round it, but if you have a coffee and sandwich you would be attracted to it. The force with which strangers will repel each other will depend on the people density – typically, they would sit next to each other only if most of the other seats were taken.

In mechanics the acceleration $\mathbf{a} = \frac{d\mathbf{v}}{dt}$ of an individual (a particle) is in the same direction as the force $\mathbf{f}$. $\mathbf{a} = \frac{\mathbf{f}}{m}$, where m is the mass. In the Maud algorithm (above) we effectively used $\mathbf{a} = \mathbf{f} \cdot \mathbf{Q}$ where $\mathbf{Q}$ is a second order tensor. This may seem like mathematical gobbledygook, but let us write

$\mathbf{Q} = \frac{1}{2m}\left(\mathbf{I} - \frac{\mathbf{v}\mathbf{v}}{\mathbf{v}\cdot\mathbf{v}}\right)$ (where $\mathbf{I}$ is the unit tensor) in which

case $\frac{d\mathbf{v}}{dt} = \mathbf{a} = \frac{\mathbf{f}}{2m}\cdot\left(\mathbf{I} - \frac{\mathbf{v}\mathbf{v}}{\mathbf{v}\cdot\mathbf{v}}\right) = \frac{1}{2m}\left(\mathbf{f} - \frac{(\mathbf{f}\cdot\mathbf{v})\mathbf{v}}{\mathbf{v}\cdot\mathbf{v}}\right)$ so that

$m\mathbf{v}\cdot\frac{d\mathbf{v}}{dt} = \frac{1}{2}\,m\,\frac{d(\mathbf{v}\cdot\mathbf{v})}{dt}$. Thus the magnitude of the velocity (and kinetic energy) remains constant, which would make sense for people walking. The number of possible rules is endless and whether or not a set of rules is suitable can be found only by trial.

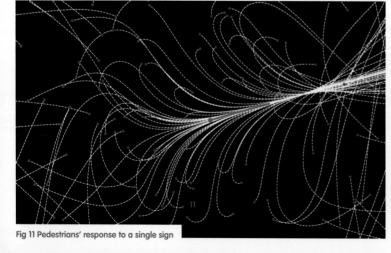

Fig 11 Pedestrians' response to a single sign

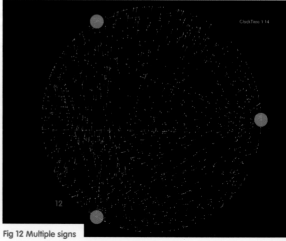

Fig 12 Multiple signs

Vision is a particular problem (Turner and Penn, 2002). An individual sees something and possibly decides to alter their motion as a result. In an airport, one can rarely see one's destination, such as a departure gate and one therefore relies on signs. But one's response to a sign is complex; if you want to visit the lavatory and you see a pointing sign directly in front of you 50 metres away, the correct response is to walk towards the sign and then turn as you approach it. If you turned straight away you would probably hit an obstacle, but you know that the 'line of action' of the sign will probably be along a path which will take you to the lavatory, or at least to another sign. Thus if your position is

$\mathbf{r}$ (so that your velocity $\mathbf{v} = \dfrac{d\mathbf{r}}{dt}$) and if the sign is at

$\mathbf{s}$ pointing in the direction of the unit vector $\mathbf{p}$, one

might use $\mathbf{f} = q \left(\dfrac{1}{c}\ (\mathbf{s\text{-}r})\cdot(\mathbf{I\text{-}pp}) + \mathbf{p} \right) e^{-\frac{1}{b^2}(\mathbf{s\text{-}r})\cdot(\mathbf{s\text{-}r})}$

in which b, c and q are constants. The vector $(\mathbf{s\text{-}r})\cdot(\mathbf{I\text{-}pp})$ is perpendicular to $\mathbf{p}$ and points towards its line of action.

Where paths taken by people responding to one sign (figure 11, in red), the blue dots represent their random starting locations and the equal spacing of the white dots along their paths show that they are walking at a constant speed. The Processing program which generated the image is listed in Appendix 3. To reduce its length on paper, this simple program does not include collision avoidance between people. However, a more complex image (figure 13) does include collision avoidance; the corresponding signs are also shown (figure 12).

One possibility is that one designs a plan layout and then uses this technique to position and analyse the signs. However, our preferred method is to use the signs to generate a circulation system and then plan the building around this pattern. Individual people are given 'agendas', some of which are just 'sitting, waiting' or 'browsing in bookshop' so that appropriate space evolves for these activities, as well as for circulation.

Chris J.K. Williams and Odysseas Kontovourkis teach at the Department of Architecture and Civil Engineering at the University of Bath.

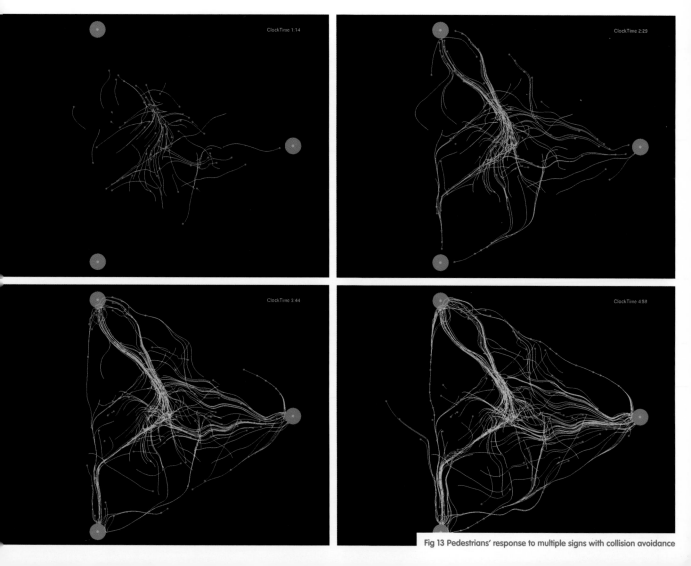

ClockTime 1:14

ClockTime 2:29

ClockTime 3:44

ClockTime 4:59

Fig 13 Pedestrians' response to multiple signs with collision avoidance

References

Bucknall, B. (1889) Discourses on Architecture, Boston, MA, Ticknor and Co., reprinted by George Allen & Unwin Ltd, London in 1959. The Doge's Palace is analysed in the XV Entrien, in volume 2.

Goldstein, J. (1999) 'Emergence as a construct: history and issues', Emergence, vol. 1, issue 1.

Helbing, D., Buzna, L., Johansson, A. and Werner, T. (2005) 'Self-organized pedestrian crowd dynamics: experiments, simulations, and design solutions', Transportation Science, 39, no. 1, pp. 1–24, DOI: 10.1287/trsc.1040.0108.

Helbing, D. and Molnár, P. (1995) 'Social force model for pedestrian dynamics', Phys. Rev. E 51, no. 5, pp. 4282–4286, DOI: 10.1103/PhysRevE.51.4282.

Lewin, K. (1951) Field Theory in Social Science, ed. by Dorwin Cartwright, New York, NY, Harper.

Monaghan, J.J. (2005) 'Smoothed particle hydrodynamics', Reports on Progress in Physics, 68, pp. 1703–1759.

Processing (undated) [online] <http://www.processing.org/>.

Reynolds, C.W. (1986) [online] <http://www.red3d.com/cwr/boids/>.

Santa Fe Institute (2007) [online] <http://www.santafe.edu/>.

Sokal, A. (2007) [online] <http://www.physics.nyu.edu/faculty/sokal/>.

Turner, A. and Penn, A. (2002) 'Encoding natural movement as an agent-based system: an investigation into human pedestrian behaviour in the built environment', Environment and Planning B: Planning and Design, 29, pp. 473–490, DOI: 10.1068/b12850.

Viollet-le-Duc, E-E. (1863–72), Entretiens sur l'architecture, Paris, Morel et Cie.

Wood, J. (ed.) (1916), Nuttall's Standard Dictionary, London and New York, Frederick Warne.

Appendix 1: C++ Chain

```cpp
#include <iostream>
#include <fstream>
#include <cmath>
#include <stdlib.h>
#include <time.h>
using namespace std;
#include <GLUT/glut.h>  // For Macintosh
//#include <GL/glut.h>    // For PC or Sun
#define   Macintosh 1  //1 for Macintosh any other number for PC or Sun
#define   LastNode   100
#define   LastCurve     500
void Calculation(void);
void ChrisGraphics(float BackGroundRed,float BackGroundBlue,float BackGroundGreen);
static void Draw(void);
static void Key(unsigned char key, int x, int y);
int argc;char **argv;GLUquadricObj *quadObj;
int HalfDimension[2],Node,i,Curve,points,lines;
float x[2][LastNode+1][LastCurve+1],Force[2][LastNode+1],Velocity[2]
[LastNode+1],deltax[2],
L[LastNode],LSq[LastNode],EA[LastNode],
PI,g,deltat,m,mg,ActualLSq,ToverL,mu,OneMinusmu,RedPeak,peak;

int main(void){
PI=4.0*atan(1.0);
cout<<"'esc' stops the program.\n'p' turns points off and on.\n'l' turns lines off and on.\n";
HalfDimension[0]=630;HalfDimension[1]=370;
m=1.0;g=0.001;mg=m*g;
for(Node=0;Node<=LastNode-1;Node++){
L[Node]=500.0*(Node+1)/(0.5*(LastNode-1)*LastNode);
LSq[Node]=L[Node]*L[Node];
EA[Node]=(Node+1)/(1.0*LastNode);}
deltat=2.0*sqrt((m*L[0])/(EA[0]/L[0]));
RedPeak=0.1;points=1;lines=1;
for(Curve=0;Curve<=LastCurve;Curve++){
x[0][LastNode][Curve]=600.0;
x[1][LastNode][Curve]=0.0;
for(Node=LastNode-1;Node>=0;Node--){
x[0][Node][Curve]=x[0][Node+1][Curve];
x[1][Node][Curve]=x[1][Node+1][Curve]+L[Node];}}
for(Node=0;Node<=LastNode;Node++){
for(i=0;i<=1;i++)Velocity[i][Node]=0.0;}
ChrisGraphics(0.0,0.0,0.0);
return 0;}

static void Draw(void){
glClear(GL_COLOR_BUFFER_BIT | GL_DEPTH_BUFFER_BIT);
Calculation();
glutSwapBuffers();}

void Calculation(void){
for(Node=0;Node<=LastNode;Node++){
```

```
Force[0][Node]=-mg*L[Node];Force[1][Node]=0.0;}
for(Node=0;Node<=LastNode-1;Node++){
for(i=0;i<=1;i++)deltax[i]=x[i][Node+1][0]-x[i][Node][0];
ActualLSq=deltax[0]*deltax[0]+deltax[1]*deltax[1];
ToverL=EA[Node]*(ActualLSq-LSq[Node])/(2.0*L[Node]*ActualLSq);
if(ToverL>0.0){for(i=0;i<=1;i++){
Force[i][Node ]+=ToverL*deltax[i];
Force[i][Node+1]-=ToverL*deltax[i];}}}
for(Node=0;Node<=LastNode-1;Node++){
for(Curve=LastCurve;Curve>=1;Curve--){
for(i=0;i<=1;i++)x[i][Node][Curve]=x[i][Node][Curve-1];}
for(i=0;i<=1;i++){
Velocity[i][Node]+=deltat*Force[i][Node]/(m*L[Node]);
x[i][Node][0]+=deltat*Velocity[i][Node];}}
glPointSize(5.0);glColor4f(1.0,0.0,0.0,1.0);glBegin(GL_POINTS);
glVertex2f(x[0][LastNode][0],x[1][LastNode][0]);glEnd();
if(points==1){
glPointSize(2.0);glColor4f(1.0,0.0,0.0,1.0);glBegin(GL_POINTS);
for(Node=0;Node<=LastNode-1;Node++)
glVertex2f(x[0][Node][0],x[1][Node][0]);
glEnd();}
if(lines==1){for(Curve=0;Curve<=LastCurve;Curve++){
glLineWidth(1.5);mu=(1.0*Curve)/(1.0*LastCurve);OneMinusmu=1.0-mu;
peak=exp(-20.0*(mu+RedPeak)*(mu+RedPeak));
glColor4f(0.5+0.5*peak,0.5-0.5*peak,1.0-0.5*mu-0.5*peak,(1.0-exp(-
100.0*mu*mu))*OneMinusmu*OneMinusmu);
glBegin(GL_LINES);for(Node=0;Node<=LastNode-1;Node++){
glVertex2f(x[0][Node ][Curve],x[1][Node ][Curve]);
glVertex2f(x[0][Node+1][Curve],x[1][Node+1][Curve]);}
glEnd();}}}


void ChrisGraphics(float BackGroundRed,float BackGroundGreen,float BackGroundBlue){
glutInitWindowSize(2*HalfDimension[0], 2*HalfDimension[1]);
if(Macintosh==1)   glutInit(&argc, argv);          // Remove this line for PC or Sun
glutInitDisplayMode(GLUT_RGB | GLUT_DOUBLE | GLUT_DEPTH);
glutCreateWindow("Chain");
glClearColor(BackGroundRed,BackGroundGreen,BackGroundBlue,0);
glViewport(0, 0, 2*HalfDimension[0], 2*HalfDimension[1]);
gluOrtho2D(-HalfDimension[0],HalfDimension[0],-HalfDimension[1],HalfDimension[1]);
glClear(GL_COLOR_BUFFER_BIT);
glutKeyboardFunc(Key);
glutIdleFunc(Draw);
glutDisplayFunc(Draw);
glEnable(GL_POINT_SMOOTH);
glEnable (GL_BLEND);glBlendFunc (GL_SRC_ALPHA,GL_ONE_MINUS_SRC_ALPHA);
glutMainLoop();}
static void Key(unsigned char key, int x, int y){
switch (key){
case 'p':if(points==0)points=1;else points=0;break;
case 'l':if(lines==0)lines=1;else lines=0;break;
case '\033':gluDeleteQuadric(quadObj);exit(0);}}
```

PRACTICAL
EMERGENCE.
CHRIS J.K. WILLIAMS
AND ODYSSEAS
KONTOVOURKIS,
UNIVERSITY OF BATH

Appendix 2: C++ Mandelbrot set

```
#include<iostream>
#include<fstream>
#include<cmath>
#include<cstdlib>
using namespace std;
#define W 1100
#define H 1000
int start[W][H],land[W][H],a,b,A,B,i,j,go,last;
double X,Y,x,y,x2,y2,lambda,mu;char s;
ofstream Q;
int main(void){
Q.open("MandelbrotSet.tga",
ofstream::binary);
s=0;Q.put(s);s=0;Q.put(s);
s=2;Q.put(s);
i=0;Q.put(i%256);Q.put(i/256);
i=0;Q.put(i%256);Q.put(i/256);
s=0;Q.put(s);
i=0;Q.put(i%256);Q.put(i/256);
i=0;Q.put(i%256);Q.put(i/256);
Q.put(W%256);Q.put(W/256);
Q.put(H%256);Q.put(H/256);
s=24;Q.put(s);s=0x20;Q.put(s);last=1000;
for(a=0;a<=W-1;a++){if(100*int(a/100)==a)cout<<a<<"\n";
for(b=0;b<=H-1;b++){start[a][b]=0;land[a][b]=0;
X=1.25*(2.0*a-1.5*W)/(1.0*H);x=X;
Y=1.25*(2.0*b-1.0*H)/(1.0*H);y=Y;
for(go=1;go<=last;go++){
x2=x*x;y2=y*y;y=2.0*x*y+Y;x=x2-y2+X;
if(x2+y2>4.0)break;start[a][b]++;
A=int(((x*H)/1.25+1.5*W)/2.0+0.5);
B=int(((y*H)/1.25+1.0*H)/2.0+0.5);
if(A>=0&&A<=W-1&&B>=0&&B<=H-1)land[A][B]++;}}}
for(b=H-1;b>=0;b-=1){
for(a=0;a<=W-1;a++){
if(start[a][b]==last)lambda=1.0;else
lambda=pow(1.0/cosh(0.02*start[a][b]),2);
   mu=pow(1.0/cosh(0.02*land[ a][b]),2);
i=int(255.0*lambda*mu);
j=int(255.0*mu);
Q.put(j);Q.put(i);Q.put(i);}}
Q.close();cout<<"File written\n";
return 0;}
```

Appendix 3: Processing signs

```
//HYPERLINK "http://www.processing.org/"http://www.processing.org/
import processing.opengl.*;
int LastPoint=200,LastPerson=100;
int Point,i,Person,LastStep,step;
float[][][] r;
float[][] v,a,f,rstart,vstart;
```

```
float[] s,p;
float theta,beta,b,c,q,deltat,m,factor,NodeSize,VectorLength;
FileWriter Julia=null;
void setup(){
  r=new float[LastPerson+1][2][LastPoint+1];
  rstart=new float[LastPerson+1][2];
  vstart=new float[LastPerson+1][2];
  s=new float[2];
  p=new float[2];
  v=new float[LastPerson+1][2];
  a=new float[LastPerson+1][2];
  f=new float[LastPerson+1][2];
  size(1270,740,OPENGL);
  ellipseMode(CENTER_RADIUS);
  smooth();
  b=250.0;
  c=100.0;
  q=0.1;
  m=1.0;
  LastStep=2000;
  deltat=10.0/float(LastStep);
  NodeSize=1.5;
  VectorLength=200.0;
  s[0]=0.0;
  s[1]=0.0;
  theta=PI/12.0;
  p[0]=cos(theta);
  p[1]=sin(theta);
  println("This program runs forever until 'esc' is pressed");
  println("Press right (control + button for Macintosh) button to write DXF file");
  println("DXF file is overwritten easch time");
  for(Person=0;Person<=LastPerson;Person++){
    rstart[Person][0]=(random(1.0)-0.5)*width;
    rstart[Person][1]=(random(1.0)-0.5)*height;
    beta=random(TWO_PI);
    vstart[Person][0]=cos(beta);
    vstart[Person][1]=sin(beta);
    startCondition();
    for(Point=0;Point<=LastPoint;Point++){
      r[Person][0][Point]=rstart[Person][0];
      r[Person][1][Point]=rstart[Person][1];
    }
  }
  frameRate(30);
}

void draw(){
  background(0,0,0);
  for(Person=0;Person<=LastPerson;Person++){
    for(step=1;step<=LastStep;step++){
      factor=q*exp(-
        ((s[0]-r[Person][0][0])*(s[0]-r[Person][0][0])
```

80 PRACTICAL
EMERGENCE.
CHRIS J.K. WILLIAMS
AND ODYSSEAS
KONTOVOURKIS,
UNIVERSITY OF BATH

```
    +(s[1]-r[Person][1][0])*(s[1]-r[Person][1][0]))/(b*b));
  for(i=0;i<=1;i++)
    f[Person][i]=factor*(((s[i]-r[Person][i][0])-
      ((s[0]-r[Person][0][0])*p[0]
      +(s[1]-r[Person][1][0])*p[1])*p[i])/c+p[i]);
  factor
    =(f[Person][0]*v[Person][0]+f[Person][1]*v[Person][1])
    /(v[Person][0]*v[Person][0]+v[Person][1]*v[Person][1]);
  for(i=0;i<=1;i++)
    a[Person][i]=(f[Person][i]-factor*v[Person][i])/(2.0*m);
  for(i=0;i<=1;i++){
    v[Person][i]+=a[Person][i]*deltat;
    r[Person][i][0]+=v[Person][i]*deltat;
  }
}
if(r[Person][0][0]>float(width)/2.0||r[Person][0][0]<-float(width)/2.0||
  r[Person][1][0]>float(height)/2.0||r[Person][1][0]<-float(height)/2.0)startCondition();
for(Point=LastPoint;Point>=1;Point--){
  for(i=0;i<=1;i++)r[Person][i][Point]=r[Person][i][Point-1];
}
fill(0,0,255);
ellipse(float(width)/2.0+rstart[Person][0],float(height)/2.0-rstart[Person]
[1],3.0*NodeSize,3.0*NodeSize);
fill(255,255,255);
for(Point=0;Point<=LastPoint;Point++)
  ellipse(float(width)/2.0+r[Person][0][Point],float(height)/2.0-r[Person][1]
[Point],NodeSize,NodeSize);
stroke(255,255,255);
strokeWeight(1);
for(Point=0;Point<=LastPoint-1;Point++){
  if((r[Person][0][Point+1]-r[Person][0][Point])*(r[Person][0][Point+1]-r[Person][0]
[Point])+
    (r[Person][1][Point+1]-r[Person][1][Point])*(r[Person][1][Point+1]-r[Person][1]
[Point])<400.0)
    line(float(width)/2.0+r[Person][0][Point],float(height)/2.0-r[Person][1][Point],float(widt
h)/2.0+r[Person][0][Point+1],float(height)/2.0-r[Person][1][Point+1]);
}
noStroke();
fill(255,0,0);
ellipse(float(width)/2.0+s[0],float(height)/2.0-s[1],5.0*NodeSize,5.0*NodeSize);
stroke(255,0,0);
strokeWeight(3);
line(float(width)/2.0+s[0],float(height)/2.0-s[1],float(width)/2.0+s[0]+VectorLength*p[0]
,float(height)/2.0-s[1]-VectorLength*p[1]);
noStroke();
if(mousePressed==true&&mouseButton==RIGHT)WriteDXF();
 }
}

void startCondition(){
  r[Person][0][0]=rstart[Person][0];
  r[Person][1][0]=rstart[Person][1];
```

```
  v[Person][0]=vstart[Person][0];
  v[Person][1]=vstart[Person][1];
}

void WriteDXF(){
 try{
   Julia=new FileWriter("/Users/Shared/ProcessingData/Signs.dxf");//Macintosh
   //Create folder /Users/Shared/ProcessingData/ before running
   //Julia=new FileWriter("C:\\Documents and Settings\\All Users\\Documents\\
ProcessingData\\Signs.dxf");//Windows
   //Create folder C:\Documents and Settings\All Users\Documents\ProcessingData\ before
running
   Julia.write("0\nSECTION\n2\nENTITIES\n");
   Julia.write("0\n3DFACE\n8\nBorder\n");
   Julia.write("10\n"+-float(width)/2.0+"\n20\n"+-float(height)/2.0+"\n");
   Julia.write("11\n"+ float(width)/2.0+"\n21\n"+-float(height)/2.0+"\n");
   Julia.write("12\n"+ float(width)/2.0+"\n22\n"+ float(height)/2.0+"\n");
   Julia.write("13\n"+-float(width)/2.0+"\n23\n"+ float(height)/2.0+"\n");
   for(Person=0;Person<=LastPerson;Person++){
     Julia.write("0\nCIRCLE\n8\nStartPoints\n10\n"+rstart[Person][0]+"\n20\
n"+rstart[Person][1]+"\n40\n"+3.0*NodeSize+"\n");
     for(Point=0;Point<=LastPoint;Point++)
       Julia.write("0\nCIRCLE\n8\nPoints\n10\n"+r[Person][0][Point]+"\n20\n"+r[Person][1]
[Point]+"\n40\n"+NodeSize+"\n");
     for(Point=0;Point<=LastPoint-1;Point++){
       if((r[Person][0][Point+1]-r[Person][0][Point])*(r[Person][0][Point+1]-r[Person][0]
[Point])+
        (r[Person][1][Point+1]-r[Person][1][Point])*(r[Person][1][Point+1]-r[Person][1]
[Point])<400.0)
        Julia.write("0\nLINE\n8\nLines\n10\n"+r[Person][0][Point]+"\n20\n"+r[Person][1]
[Point]+"\n11\n"+r[Person][0][Point+1]+"\n21\n"+r[Person][1][Point+1]+"\n");
     }
   }
   Julia.write("0\nCIRCLE\n8\nSignPoint\n10\n"+s[0]+"\n20\n"+s[1]+"\n40\
n"+5.0*NodeSize+"\n");
   Julia.write("0\nLINE\n8\nSignLine\n10\n"+s[0]+"\n20\n"+s[1]+"\n11\
n"+(s[0]+VectorLength*p[0])+"\n21\n"+(s[1]+VectorLength*p[1])+"\n");
   Julia.write("0\nENDSEC\n0\nEOF\n");
   Julia.close();
   println("DXF file written");
 }
 catch(Exception e){
   println("Error: Can't open file. You may need to create a folder in the appropriat
location:");
   println("Macintosh: /Users/Shared/ProcessingData/");
   println("Window: C:\\Documents and Settings\\All Users\\Documents\\
ProcessingData\\");
 }
}
```

ANIMATION, DESIGN INTERROGATION, DRAWING

Techniques of visualising and depicting buildings are moving closer to the mainstream design process. Indeed, it is a modern curiosity that design teams are having to show what their completed building will look like (its shadows, its reflectivity, its texture and impact on the environment) at every twist and turn of the design process. Verifiable views, the re-creation of context, the instant demonstration of how a designer's abstract idea will manifest itself … these are becoming design tools rather than post hoc illustrative ones. Moreover, any visualisation is often an amalgamation of a large number of techniques (not all of them digital) including laser mapping, stereo photography, rendering, montaging, scanning and even conventional drawing. The result will only ever be a representation *(à la Magritte's 'Ceci n'est pas une pipe')* so pretensions to realism are not always helpful. Sometimes the drawing shows more clearly the idea of a project than the final building itself. It is not a matter of 'does this image look realistic' but 'what is this image for?'

CONTEMPORARY
DIGITAL DESIGN
MATHEW EMMETT,
ARCHITECT AND
CONCEPTUAL ARTIST

I visualise architectural possibilities beyond the scope of this time: gelatinous membranes express a visceral luminescence of a self-aware architecture pluming with intelligence. It is essential to experiment with technology – bridging the gaps between science and creativity, making architecture a leading force in the application of innovative science and imagination. We can do this only by transgressing the boundaries, forging new links and focusing on the areas of uncertainty. There is a need for a pioneering architecture, shifting design away from today's unwieldy and cumbersome structures. The future of our cities is bound up in how successfully architects assimilate these frontier technologies while evolving a humane sensibility to their application.

These technologies do, however, need to be viewed with a critical eye, to form an understanding of their advantages and potential dangers; buildings have always acted as transmitters between human and material worlds. Yet materials are changing, science is evolving and architecture must transform with it, responding to changing values and meanings within contemporary culture. If architecture doesn't monitor and evaluate these progressions, architectural interpretation is left inconclusively vague and will fail to respond to our time.

Drawing is my primary agent for thinking about architecture. This is an essential discipline and underpins a personal language of seeing and investigation. An appreciation of space, light and

the fragility of form has grown through thousands of pencil studies. The tool of the computer has not diminished my drawing but has extended the experimental and exploratory nature of my work; it is most compelling to explore how digital tools can be deployed in various combinations in the making of architecture. The dexterity and fluidity of digital applications enables a creatively challenging design environment where the computer becomes a powerful ally in designing, testing and construction. However, basic principles such as design language and an intellectual framework pertain to all methods of design, whether using analogue or digital techniques. In the end it is up to the architects' skill to perform in a creative and natural way – empowered by an articulate and communicative platform.

Once beyond the white water of learning the software 'etiquette' and after the perspectival novelty has passed, questions and expectations escalate as the 3-D modelling software allows a more dynamic and direct link between the imagined and the envisioned. By digitising the physical the virtual model becomes the architect's three-dimensional world. The virtual model is more than just an image, it is information organised in a computational manner, algorithms that convey meaning and purpose. The building can be viewed from an infinite variety of points of view and depth of field, enhancing the viewer's perception of the design. The spatial orientation becomes fluid and limitless, providing the architect/client with a

Fig 1 Conceptual image of Mathew Emmett's competition entry for a permanent building for the Architecture Foundation, London

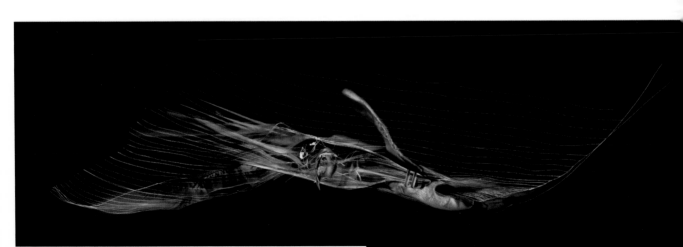

Fig 2 Part of a series of images being assembled by Emmett to illustrate the Book of Revelation

Fig 3 12 Portals

Fig 4 Throne of 24 Elders

Fig 5 The Throne Room

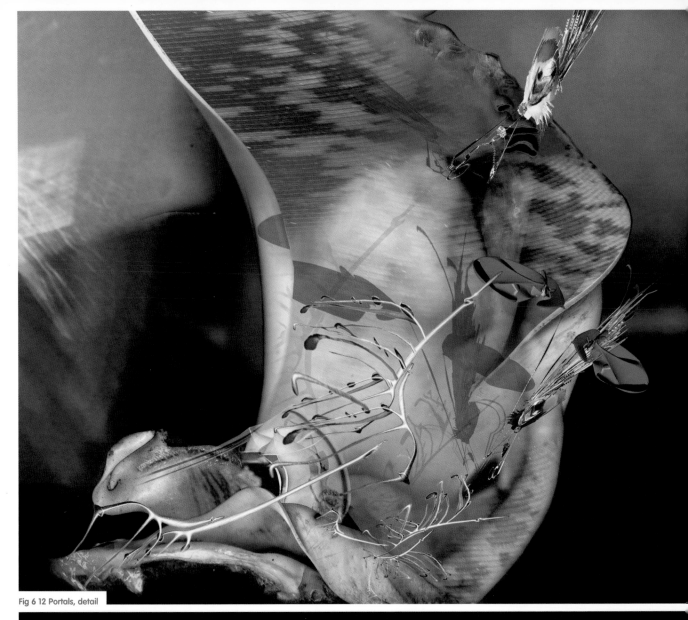

Fig 6 12 Portals, detail

Fig 7 Throne of 24 Elders, detail

viewing device to 'experience' the building prior to realisation. Animation/parametric software provides feedback mechanisms, providing the designer with a heightened sense of interactivity and revealing a closer interplay between thinking and constructing. In this respect the digital model enables the process of designing and articulation to become one, blurring the intellectual with the practical.

Done well, the freedom of digital expression gives a designer the power to express what they want, the geography of space no longer being a hindrance within the 'floating' reality of the virtual model. Improvisation and freedom lead to increasing levels of complexity and ingenuity of design. The morphological power of 3-D modelling – with its shape-shifting volumes – pre-echoes social and cultural conditions. Architectural design packages simulate multiple levels of experience from a myriad of viewpoints; they can be used in any variety of combinations to create any hierarchy of perception. Within this model framework, emphasis is put on the unity of design, as the composition and organisation of spaces within and around the building become more readily coherent and interconnected.

As the design is refined, details can be added and material properties developed. Atmospheric perspective can also be layered into the virtual model, bringing scenes to life through chiaroscuro and other visual effects. Tectonic properties and phenomenological intensity can be defined as a result of filter manipulation and colour saturation. Gradations of light and shadow establish material articulation and atmosphere. Depth of perception, scale and illumination combine to create an envisioned composition. The requirements are numerous, the tasks skilful, but with flair the virtual model submerges the mind within the architect's dream.

The methods and technical dimensions of my design practice uses a cross-processing discipline of digital and analogue technologies. Each project is a collaboration between the hand and the machine, a synthesis of multidisciplinary data supported by the computer-based environment where a variety of tools and applications are spliced to form a complex relational system of design processes. At the beginning, the work oscillates between these methodologies and avoids alienating any one tool or skill. As the design evolves, the different strains of technology mix and evolve into a hybrid language that is considerably more involved than a single operation; this language becomes a key element in the final success of the project.

Underpinning core design decisions is the site analysis, beginning with a site history and location plan. Then there is an in-depth mapping of the immediate context, undertaken at a variety of scales. This is a 'one-to-one' enquiry which provides the means by which one gains empathy for the site and a dialogue is developed. The site analysis incorporates three main actions: the survey, site documentation and atmospheric recordings. The site is modelled (in both CAD and reality) using materials that impart a poetic quality inspired by the haptic qualities of the original space. Two cameras are used to document the site, a digital SLR for general coverage and a large-format camera for key frame shots for superior-quality images. The site is then filmed to record the site's temporal qualities, while its sonic character is captured on a minidisc player. This data is collected and analysed to inform the development of the creative process, moving forward to constructing sketch models and explorative hand drawings.

The physical act of making a drawing or model by hand is my way of critically engaging with the design. The choice of paper, quality of line or weight of material provides a unique mix of technologies and, when spliced with the digital, generates an edgy and exciting fusion. This is where the work bridges gaps between theory, creativity and practicality. The actual and virtual models are worked and reworked simultaneously, providing an immediate and raw energy for sculpting space.

Mathew Emmett is an architect and conceptual artist.

Fig 8 Throne of 24 Elders, detail 2

Fig 9 Throne of 24 Elders, detail 3

Fig 10 Throne of 24 Elders, detail 4

Fig 11 Throne of 24 Elders, detail 5

8
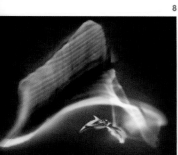

9
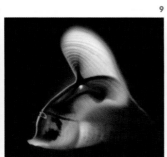

10
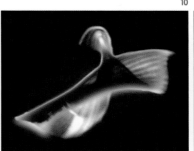

11

LONDON –
THE CREATION
OF A DIGITAL MODEL.
ROBERT GRAVES, GMJ

LONDON –
THE CREATION
OF A DIGITAL MODEL.
ROBERT GRAVES, GMJ

In 1986 Didier Madoc-Jones and I were working at Skidmore, Owings & Merrell (SOM) producing three-dimensional views of London's County Hall and a site behind it. We would take 35mm photographs, mark viewpoints, survey them, then use these coordinates, plus Ordnance Survey data, to superimpose wireframe models of architectural proposals into photography.

A few years later we created visualisation company GMJ and felt that the approach – with a few improvements – would add some technical verifiability to photomontages we were producing for planning applications. We swapped 35mm photography for professional 5x4 formats, replaced Ordnance Survey data with a full three-dimensional survey of each view and moved beyond wireframe CAD images. Now we were producing sophisticated renders that combined detailing, lighting and materials to create accurate representations of what a scheme would look like in context.

Over the last 15 years we have continually refined the workflow but, in essence, it is the same process we use today (as do many others in our industry). However, it is slow, painstaking work involving professionals from many disciplines – photographers, surveyors, architects, visualisers – and can often take days or weeks to produce a view. Then, being view dependent, if you want to see the building from a few metres to the right or left you have to start again. This is frustrating for our clients who often require 20 or 30 such views for a planning application.

It is a fundamentally inelegant process involving the reconciliation of two opposing technologies: the 'fuzzy' analogue world of lenses and optics and the Cartesian world of CAD modelling. We felt that there must be a simpler, more fluid way to let our clients and their professional teams evaluate digital models of buildings in the real world. The natural answer, albeit an intimidating one, was to use a digital model of the real world.

We looked about to see if anyone else was providing models commercially and were disappointed by what we found. The models that existed were either patched together from a variety of sources, thereby having no overall consistency of accuracy or detail; or they were built without respect to landscape (non-topographic); or, worst of all, they were based on Ordnance Survey data which, accuracy aside, created problems with licensing. None of the models looked like the city they were meant to represent – they had been abstracted so much for speed or to keep the size of the datasets down that they were at best uninspiring and at worse unrecognisable. As a result, we began to entertain the idea of taking on the task ourselves.

Like many others over the years we have modelled small areas of context for one-off projects, so we

were aware of the scale of the undertaking. We also knew that our client's expectations were high; 3-D contextual models had never been seen as viable alternatives to 'traditional' verified photomontages. Before we started we wrote a specification for our ideal city model – a 'wish-list' which was to form a standard to work towards in the years to come.

If it was to be a worthwhile exercise, GMJ CityModels had to be:

- accurate – more accurate than Ordnance Survey data;
- detailed and topographic – representing the real world, not a symbolic abstraction of it;
- realistic – the cities needed to be recognisable;
- modelled quickly – we needed to cover very large areas, over many cities;
- intelligent – the models needed to easily form part of a Geographical Information System;
- low polygon – to facilitate as interactive an experience as possible.

The most important part of the process was to be our method of gathering site data, both dimensional and visual, and without recourse to maps of any kind. We settled on high-resolution aerial photographs as our base information. These were more than capable of providing the detail we required and covered the whole of the UK. In fact, in London, some of it captured details down to 10cm and even 5cm in size. By commissioning our own surveys we created a network of real-world coordinates to anchor the photographic tiles to each other and to the Ordnance Survey National Grid very accurately. In fact, any point on each photograph could now be measured to within 300mm accuracy over 100m. This was acceptable in plan, but we also needed to gather height data and found that we could use a property of the way the images were captured to our advantage.

The photography is taken from an aircraft as it passes over a specific area; the rate at which the images are captured is set to produce a large overlap between each photograph. This provides enough duplication to allow eventual blending between shots when stitching photographs together over large areas. Image-pairs can also be used to provide a stereo view of the city and heights can be gathered by analysing the offsets (or parallax) between each shot, a process called photogrammetry. We used Erdas Stereo Analyst software to enable this and set about producing a pilot of around one square kilometre of London. Carefully, we started tracing the entire area, manually in 3-D.

The first problem we faced was of our own making. We had set our initial resolution to be one metre and had decided to model everything we could see of this size or greater. This was to be the compromise regarding the size of the finished model file; also, we imagined, this tactic would speed up the modelling process. It seemed to take a surprisingly long time. In fact, we found it was quicker to model everything we could see, whatever size it was. This removed the time-consuming decision process of what to trace and what not to trace. We knew this approach would create larger models, but took a gamble that, by the time we had finished, we would find a platform powerful enough to play the model back interactively, or at least a software routine clever enough to reduce the complexity of the datasets for us.

Another big problem was file management. To meet the 'intelligence' part of our specification we delineated the models by postcode. In this way we would be able to access the 3-D model of any building by typing in its address. In itself this is not a huge problem but it is compounded by the number of steps required, going in and out of several different pieces of software (Stereo Analyst, MicroStation, 3-D Studio Max being just three) each file format having its own peculiar restrictions. Files and labels were over-writing each other and what was recognised by one system wasn't recognised by another. Eventually the original pilot area was created over and over in many different ways until we found a suitable workflow.

Photogrammetry had another positive aspect. Being based on photography it was possible to reuse the imagery on the model data itself, giving us a good degree of photorealism on the finished model, as long as we looked at the model from the air. But the fact that our model was based on aerial photography let us down when it came to elevation detail. We had beautifully detailed roofscapes and very accurate heights, but blank façades. Given that the most important views of a new development were usually at street level, we set about finding a technology that would let us get a comparable level of façade detail.

The quickest and most accurate way of getting detailed street-level surveys in 3-D was using ground-based LIDAR. These laser scanners, positioned every 10 metres or so along the street, gather 'clouds' of three-dimensional points 3mm or so apart with astonishing, near-absolute, accuracy. When strung together these scans provided fantastic levels of detail along whole streets. However, they came with three main problems. Firstly, three-dimensional points are not an efficient way to describe surfaces, and a laser scanner has to establish millions of them to describe one 'flat' wall. Secondly, the data is notoriously 'noisy' or prone to tiny deviations, making it even more difficult to rationalise. Finally, to minimise obstructions like people and cars, the scans were taken at night, meaning we could not gather photographic detail at the same time. All in all, it was almost impossible to use.

Returning to site to get our street-level photography was to provide us with a solution. To obtain the volume of façade imagery we would require to cover whole streets, traditional cameras were no use as a great deal of work was required to stitch the photography together before it could be applied to the buildings. We employed a very high resolution digital 360 degree camera, typically used by forensic teams to collect crime scene data. Gathering 600–700MB photographs every 10 metres along the street gave us a wealth of image data which was considerably more useful than a plethora of lower resolution snapshots. This was so useful, in fact, that we found we could model from the photographs themselves. A 360-degree photograph has no field-of-view issues to match; knowing a few key dimensions, along with our tripod height, meant we could trace model detail from the photographs themselves in a similar way to how we worked with the aerial photography. The models were inaccurate but they looked very realistic once covered in the source photography. Our laser point cloud was then used to constrain the models to some real and accurate dimensions. We completed our pilot and, feeling confident in our process, we sought and were granted a patent for it. We then started presenting the sample area to clients.

The London Borough of Southwark asked us to create an area of south London's Elephant and Castle district to help Make Architects with the design of a masterplan for the area. We produced 5 square kilometres of aerial model in 2005 and started using it to inform the viewpoints for the Castle House planning application, followed by one for Newington Butts – both part of the original masterplan. Our intention had been to model the area from both the air and the ground, but the council found the aerial model so useful that instead we spent the time working out to a larger area – covering the whole of Southwark. Realising that if Southwark found it that useful, then so might other boroughs, we carried on modelling north of the river to include the City, the West End and further west to the Serpentine. The model now covers 35 square kilometres of London and includes every feature of the city that is visible from the air, including trees, lampposts (although not all are visible depending on occlusion with buildings), walls, roads, pavements and, of course, buildings. Trees are modelled as flat canopies positioned at the highest point of the tree, ready to be fitted with 3-D parametric shapes.

We have acquired photographic texture data for every surface, albeit only from aerial photography, and currently have programs filtering the thousands of images and organising them by postcode. Once complete, we will have two 'unwrapped' images per postcode: one for the roofs (containing adequate photography), and one for façades (containing the distorted imagery). In this way we

Fig 1 Partial view of GMJ's digital model of London, looking west. The model currently covers 35 square kilometres

can return to a building and upgrade or update its façade photography quickly.

Our original model was based on photography captured in 2000 so a streamlined updating process is important. We have found a system that can compare the 2000 photography with more recent images and notify us of areas of change. In the 5 square kilometres of the City of London we were surprised to find over 2000 areas of change over just six years. Remodelling these areas is considerably quicker than starting from scratch. It is intriguing to think that our model already has a historic aspect to it; this will grow as we update again. We also use it as a base repository for all the proposed developments we come across (whether we have been involved in them directly or not) so in that aspect the model is capable of being wound forward.

We have also modelled Liverpool and are working on the city of Newport. At the time of writing, we had modelled just a few areas in detail with ground-based lasers. Compared to the speed with which we can cover cities from the air (around one square kilometre per week), it is a time-consuming process. In 2005 GMJ received a grant from the Department of Trade and Industry to research this area alongside academics from London South Bank University with a view to automating the process as much as possible. The arrangement has also enabled our software developers to find ways of using the model in GIS systems and, in cooperation with ArcGIS developer ESRI, some exciting tools have started to emerge which allow the city to be queried as you would a database. By 2010, we expect our expanded London model will cover an area of 100 square kilometres.

Robert Graves is creative director of GMJ.

VISUALLY
VERIFIED MONTAGES.
NADI JAHANGIRI,
M3ARCHITECTS

VISUALLY VERIFIED MONTAGES.

NADI JAHANGIRI,
M3ARCHITECTS

m3architects typically creates visually verified montages (VVMs) for clients as part of the requirement to produce an environmental impact study (EIM), an important element of a planning application or appeal. We define a VVM as 'an accurate and independently verifiable visual representation of a proposed development shown in its intended context'. By implication, our definition implies that a VVM is projected onto a photograph of an existing scene and is not created completely within a computer space.

Our process is bespoke for each project and image and, we believe, offers the most accurate way of indicating the visual impact of a proposal from selected viewpoints. There is no reason why a complete computer model of London (see chapter 3.2), or any city, cannot be used as a resource to assess the macro effect of a development, but we believe that this creates as many problems as it solves. We use the 'bridge to America' analogy; it is technically possible, fantastically expensive and completely unnecessary. While a total model solution would, among other things, free the image from the constraints of gravity (viewpoints can be created from the air or from the tops of buildings from which access might usually be denied), the accuracy and currency of the model would need to be constantly maintained. If large areas or distances were involved, what allowance would be made for the earth's curvature, for instance?

A complete computer model of our towns and cities is a worthwhile resource and would have many useful applications at the town-planning scale. For the vast majority of projects, where just a simple series of images of the scheme from specific viewpoints is usually required – to indicate to planners, planning committee members and the public what the architectural proposal looks like – such a model would be unnecessary.

Methodology

The process that we use in creating VVMs (figures 1, 2, 3 and 4) essentially involves creating a 'CADspace' that accurately reflects the space shown in the photograph, and then placing an accurate model of the proposal into that space. The simplest and most accurate way of doing this is to survey a series (usually around six but up to a dozen per view) of fixed, permanent control points within the photograph. These points are located by GPS satellite technology and the Ordnance Survey Active Network to an accuracy of plus or minus 10 millimetres. By surveying these existing points and locating them in space, it becomes unnecessary to create a full model of the context as the photograph describes the environment accurately enough.

In tandem with the surveying and photography process, an accurate CAD model of the proposal is created and located within the CADspace. There is then an opportunity, prior to the application of materials and colours, to create a 'line in the sky' impact study (figure 3) which shows just the outer extent of the building. This is a quick and simple way of assessing the impact of the proposal, not

Fig 1 Photograph of a site, set for redevelopment, for which a VVM is required

Fig 2 Control points are added to the streetscape, in preparation for the VVM

just for planners but for the design team as a whole, before going to the time and expense of a photorealistic render.

Once materials and colours are applied and the precise date and time of the base photograph (to create an accurate shadow impact) are fed in, a full render can be projected onto the photograph. It is at this point that those parts of the rendered model that are obscured by existing foreground buildings, trees, buses, and so on, can be masked out in Photoshop. The image is then complete. The process is completed with the creation of a datasheet for each image that contains a complete set of information regarding surveyed control points, camera positions and lens settings. This information is provided to allow a suitably qualified third party to re-create the views.

m3architects often makes the point that a reasonably good architect would be able to draw the visual impact of their building onto a photograph provided he or she could locate the base and key it into the existing surroundings. If the architect then moves around the corner so that the building base is not visible, and there are no other visual prompts, his or her intuition for the impact of the building also disappears.

We often cite the case of the architect who had, without the benefit of the VVM process, tried to make a judgement about the impact of his building from some distance; our work demonstrated he had designed a building 1.5 storeys lower than

it actually would have been. He had based the design on a mistaken premise and had potentially 'under-developed' his client's site.

The future

Access to the creation of quick and cost-effective VVMs means that many more types and smaller scales of development are able to be assessed in this way. Many architects could (but most don't) produce VVMs in-house and could use them as a tester for the design. Particularly where the viewpoints are at some distance from the site, it can be a powerful tool early in the design process.

The creation of VVMs will remain in the hands of specialist companies who will continue to provide this service to the construction industry. This perception of VVMs as an independently produced service is important to the idea of third-party verification. The requirement for VVMs will doubtless continue to expand. The movie equivalent of a VVM, where the building appears in a moving picture, is now possible and arguably gives a much better 'perception' of the proposal. The costs currently exclude all but the largest and highest-profile projects, but this will change as computing power continues to rise and costs to fall.

Nadi Jahangiri is a founder of London-based architecture practice m3.

Fig 3 A 'line in the sky' is drawn, outlining the new development   **Fig 4** The completed VVM, showing the impact of the proposed building on the site

THE MODELLING
AND DEPICTION OF KNIGHTSTONE ISLAND.
JONATHAN REEVES,
JR ARCHITECTURE

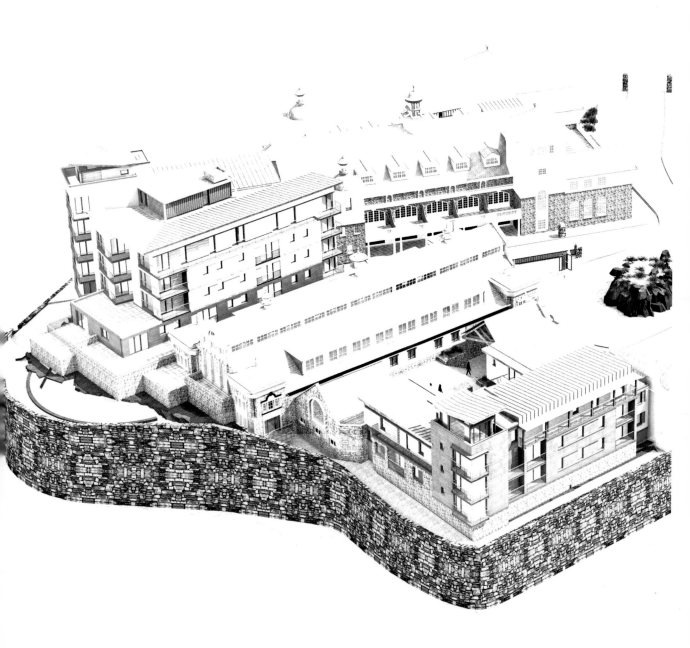

THE MODELLING AND DEPICTION OF KNIGHTSTONE ISLAND.
JONATHAN REEVES, JR ARCHITECTURE

Knightstone Island in Weston-super-Mare, in western England, is a unique man-made island that is linked to the seafront by a causeway. Its popularity as a seaside leisure destination has long since passed, leaving three grade II listed buildings in a dilapidated state. An invited design bid competition was organised by the local authority and English Heritage to select an architect/developer team to develop the island's buildings for mainly residential use.

Acanthus Ferguson Mann Architects and Redrow Homes formed the team that appointed JRA to help with the competition submission and presentation. From the beginning of the project it was important that any new buildings proposed for the site needed to be designed in context with the existing pavilions. 3-D modelling of the island and the existing buildings was undertaken during the early stages of the project as a way of understanding and informing the conceptual design stage. Each building, and two new proposed buildings, were then developed in separate VectorWorks files that could be referenced into the main site model. This meant that it was possible to work on each building as a single entity but also to see the massing and spatial relationships between the buildings as they were updated into the site model. Modelling the different types of building required the use of different tools and techniques, as the existing buildings were more traditional with high

levels of ornament and detail. By contrast, the proposed buildings were modern and rational, and easier to model with traditional CAD tools. In general, residential developments contain a lot of repetition of elements such as doors, windows and balconies; VectorWorks' libraries of unique symbols to represent such repetition increased the efficiency of creating and amending the model (which was subjected to considerable revision during the design process).

A significant benefit of 3-D modelling is, of course, the ability to generate two-dimensional drawings directly from the model. Knightstone Island has a complex geometry, and each building is rotated at a different angle. This meant it was very difficult to draw meaningful elevations of the proposed buildings and adapted existing structures. However, the accuracy and detail of the 3-D model meant that any elevation could be set up and rendered either as an image file, or as a hidden line view that could then be further edited.

The island is a distinct landmark from many areas of the promenade, and English Heritage requested a number of key views of the proposals from various positions around the town. By importing a .dwg file of local survey data, it was possible to accurately set up virtual cameras in the same position as the required key views. These viewpoints were also photographed to allow the production of

Figs 1 to 4 Early studies for JRA's Knightstone Island visualisation project. The entire project was modelled in VectorWorks and rendered in Artlantis and (for the later stages) Cinema 4D

1

2

a number of high-quality photomontages. These were used to show the impact of the scheme on the proposed skyline and existing buildings.

The final competition assessment required competitive team presentations. JRA prepared a digital presentation which featured transitions between the key-view photographs which faded into the proposals. This was an effective way to communicate the sensitivity of the design in relation to the existing buildings. Also, before and after elevations were produced directly from the 3-D model. Two animations were also presented showing the island from an imaginary helicopter ride, while another showed the view while driving along the causeway and arriving into the courtyard. This dynamic form of presentation enabled the jury to understand the nature of the proposals, and the bid was successful in winning the competition. Following the competition win, 3-D modelling was used throughout the design process in the form of quick massing studies that could be developed into more detailed models as the scheme progressed. These revised models were used to set up new key views and the elevations of the final planning submission.

Following a successful planning application, the developer commissioned a comprehensive series of marketing visuals to help promote interest and promote early sales even before work had started on site. The original 3-D model was worked up in more detail and exported to Cinema 4D for rendering, using advanced global illumination and rendering techniques. These high-resolution images were montaged into photographs via Photoshop. This stage was essential in making the image sit realistically within its backdrop, while final tweaking of colour and saturation was essential.

To complete the package of CGI material, detailed models of a number of the apartments were also created, rendered and animated. All of this visual material was brought together for the printed brochure, a CD-ROM, a dedicated website and, eventually, television advertisements. Within just a few weeks, more than half of the apartments had been sold – months before the project even went on site. The effective use of creative 3-D modelling and visualisation during the design process is now essential in architectural practice during all stages of the project, not just as a marketing tool. Furthermore, developing an expertise in digital techniques provides an opportunity for small practices like JRA to collaborate (and even compete) with larger practices on projects of a scale they would not normally get involved in. By harnessing today's hardware and software, small- and medium-size practices are able to ignore traditional boundaries and punch way above their weight in the global economy.

3

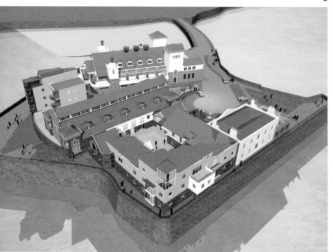

4

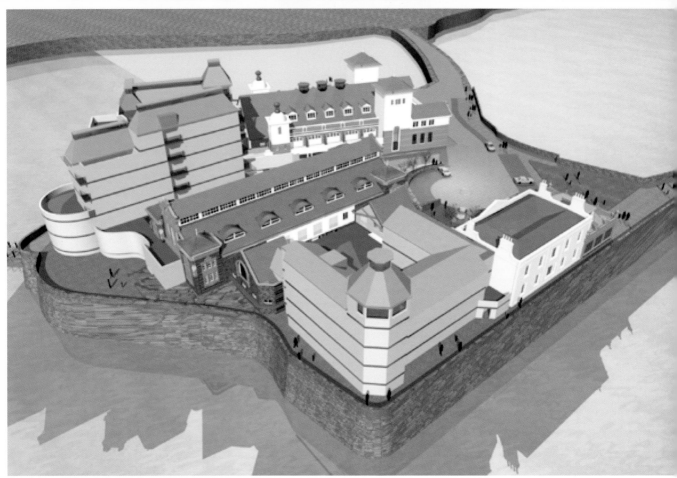

Fig 5 A massing development study for Knightstone Island, showing more detail and resolution than the earlier models

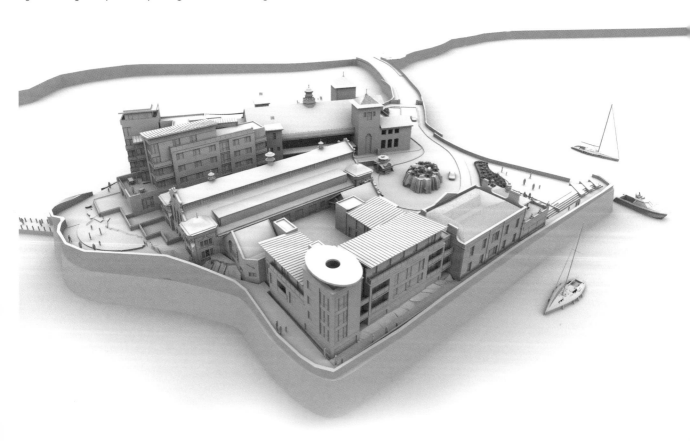

Fig 6 'White Card' render of the scheme, emphasising form and mass

Fig 8 A montage of model and photograph, illustrating the scale and impact of this development

It is easy to take contemporary information technology for granted. However, this is a relatively recent phenomenon. I have always been fascinated with the potential of digital technology to empower the creative individual. First-generation video games such as *Space Invaders* and *Pac-Man* were formative experiences for me; these early games provided a powerful, exciting (and addictive) experience of how digital technology could be used to represent and manipulate virtual environments. The next revelation came with the arrival of the ZX Spectrum, a 48k colour computer that cost £125. Even with that miniscule amount of memory, the machine was capable of opening a new world. This computer was programmable, which meant that it was possible to create drawings and interactive environments using a simple language ('Basic'), albeit with painstaking efforts.

1984 was a watershed moment with the introduction of the Macintosh, the first mass-market personal computer with a graphical interface and a range of software applications that allowed drawing via a mouse and keyboard. These early drawing programs, such as MacDraw Pro, were sophisticated compared to earlier tools. Suddenly the technology no longer imposed limits on the creative imagination. This exponential evolution in capabilities of hardware and software has propelled us along a trajectory to where we are today.

Jonathan Reeves is an architect based in Bristol. He runs his own design practice and delivers bespoke visualisation and training packages to architects.

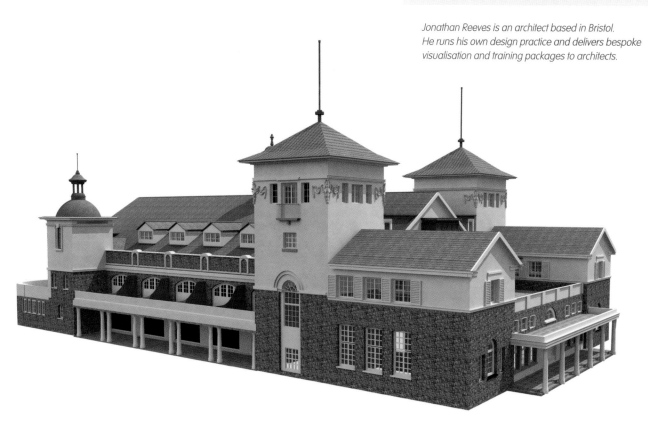

Fig 7 A study of a single building element – a pavilion for Knightstone Island

TECHNOLOGY AND FABRICATION

If the digital model has been well-made, and analysis demonstrates that it is an object of integrity, then it can be fabricated. Whether through rapid prototyping, full-scale manufacture or the cutting of components and templates, almost anything that can be modelled can be made. Indeed, complex forms need not be composed of complex components. Flat surfaces can be twisted, folded and otherwise manipulated into a collection of elements that combine to create three-dimensional forms that belie their elemental nature. Furthermore, digital processes can provide a new degree of certainty within manufacturing – if the pieces fit together in the model, there is no good reason why they should not fit together on site. Better than that, computing opens up the possibilities of mass customisation. Large economies of scale may no longer be necessary to make a component financially viable; architects can create bespoke forms from bespoke components without requiring fantasy budgets.

FROM MODEL
TO MANUFACTURE.
TIM LUCAS,
PRICE & MYERS
GEOMETRICS

It is now possible to create almost any form imaginable in 3-D modelling software, and almost any form can be built. However, some forms are easier to make than others. Creating buildings with interesting and unusual forms has always been possible, if expensive and time-consuming. This chapter examines 3-D geometry that can be simply and economically constructed using standard materials, through modern methods of design and manufacturing. The same computer-driven technology can aid the quick and accurate assembly of manufactured components into the finished building.

The surfaces that make up a building, bridge or sculpture can be formed in a number of ways, depending on the scale, material and constraints of the surface's geometry:

- cutting or carving a block of material to form finished surfaces;
- casting or applying a material against another surface;
- forming a surface by distorting a flat sheet of material.

The first method is generally constrained to stone-based architecture. The second applies to concrete and finishes such as render. The third method is central to the way many things are built, from aeroplanes and cars to buildings. The computer can assist in all these modes of surface making – computer numerically controlled (CNC) routers can carve stone or sculpt blocks of expanded polystyrene into concrete formwork based on almost any surface geometry. The process of folding and curving flat sheets into interesting forms is slightly more constrained, but has the potential to allow simple sheet materials such as steel and plywood to take on extraordinary forms. When you think of a ship's hull – where sheets of steel and lengths of timber take on complex forms – the possibilities are obvious. In a building project, however, these processes are usually prohibitively expensive and simpler methods must be found. One of these methods is to create the building's geometry from ruled surfaces.

Anatomy of a ruled surface

Forms made from sheets that are curved in only one direction across their surface are simple to make – just curve a sheet of paper to form a lamp shade or a tube, for example. These single curved surfaces are known as ruled or 'developable' surfaces, as they can be developed or unrolled into flat sheets. They can curve, twist and skew. In fact, any surface that can be described by moving a straight line through space is developable.

Buildings formed from ruled surfaces can very greatly in their complexity. A barrel-vault roof is perhaps one of the simplest, and requires no computing power to flatten. The developed shape is simply a rectangle with one side equal to the length of the vault and the other side equal to the circumference of the arc or curve forming the vault's cross section (figure 1).

A ruled surface, simple to model in almost any modern 3-D CAD program, normally has two underlying components which define its geometry in either direction. One of these components must be made up of straight lines for the surface to be developable. The examples shown in figures 2, 3, 4 and 5 illustrate different ruled surface geometries and their development. The red lines on the surfaces are isoparametric curves, or 'isoparms'; they are curves parallel to either direction of curvature that makes up a surface. Importantly, in all these examples the isoparms in one direction are straight – therefore the surface is curved in only one direction and can be developed.

These simple geometries can be combined into complex-looking forms that are made up of various developable surfaces. These surfaces can be trimmed into patches or strips and joined together to form a composite, more adaptable surface. The Bullring Spiral Café we helped design with Marks Barfield Architects, for example, comprises a complex sweeping and twisting form that was rationalised into developable strips (figure 6). Many programs such as Rhino and Digital Project contain functions able to unroll ruled surfaces. Other stand-alone programs are available (such as Pepakura Designer) and can be found on the internet.

Fig 1 The barrel vault – a developable surface of a simple rectangle

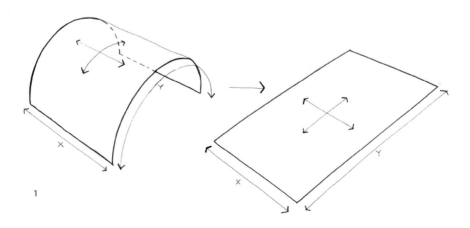

1

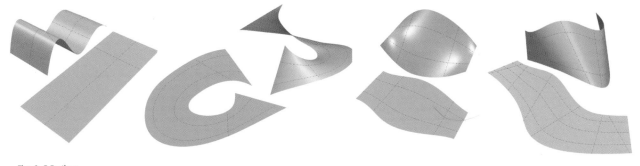

Figs 2–5 Further developable surfaces – a rectangle developed into a bend, a revolved surface, curves and a twist

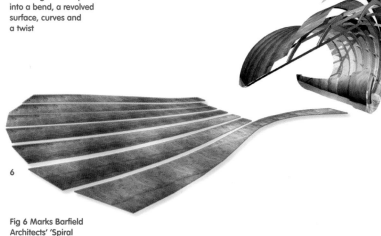

6

Fig 6 Marks Barfield Architects' 'Spiral Café' in Birmingham, shown as a series of developed surfaces

Fig 7 The Bandstand at the De La Warr Pavilion, designed with Níall McLaughlin Architects, was conceived as a developable stressed skin of plywood, fixed to ribs that work structurally with the skin and define its shape

Manufacturing developed surfaces

When unfolded, the shape of a developed surface is often quite irregular. Elements must be precisely cut out, especially if the finished form comprises several developable surfaces that fit together when assembled. An ideal way to make the flat components is with a CNC cutting machine that can read the shape required via a 2-D CAD file and cut it out of a sheet material. Cutting can take the following forms:

- laser-cutting (steel, plastic, aluminium);
- plasma-cutting (steel);
- router (timber panels – including plywood – can also carve rebates, etc.);
- waterjet (almost all materials, including steel, stone, glass, timber, etc.).

A key aspect is being able to assemble the cut-out surfaces in the correct orientation to form the finished building. This can be achieved in a number of ways, but a jig is normally required. This can be something that is made just for assembly purposes and discarded afterwards. However, a more satisfying and sustainable approach, especially for a structural engineer, is to make the jig part of the finished structure. This principle was employed in the construction of the acoustic canopy of the Bandstand at the De La Warr Pavilion, designed with Níall McLaughlin Architects. Here, a developable stressed skin of plywood was fixed to ribs that both work structurally with the skin and define its shape (figure 7). As with the surface itself, the jig (or ribs) needs to be precisely and robustly manufactured in order to allow the flattened, cut-out surface to be applied and permitted to regain its true three-dimensional shape.

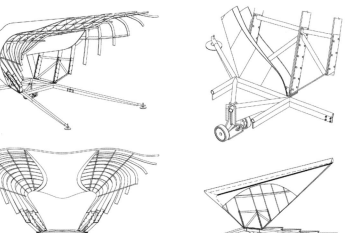

7

FROM MODEL TO MANUFACTURE.

Fig 8 Angel Wings sculpture, Islington, London, designed by Price & Myers with Letts Wheeler Architects and artist Wolfgang Buttress

Angel Wings sculpture, Islington, London
designed with Letts Wheeler Architects and artist
Wolfgang Buttress

This stainless steel sculpture (figure 8) is made
up of two large 'wings' supported on arched legs.
The sculpture stands over a small cylindrical kiosk
building (figure 9) To clear the kiosk, the legs arch
from front to back while curving inwards towards the
centre of the kiosk, where they meet the wing ribs.

The aim was to achieve a sculpture which was
structural in itself without requiring a separate frame
obscured by cladding. We therefore devised a form
for the legs that could be simply made in structural
stainless steel. This form was modelled by extruding
a curved profile from front to back and then cutting
up through this to create the arches that would reach
the springing point of the wings and not clash with
the kiosk building. The form of the arch also tapers
in response to the structural forces induced by

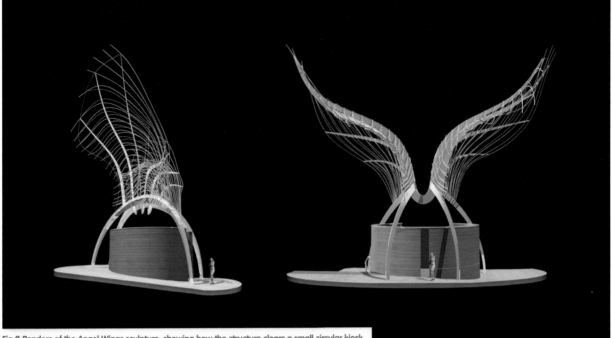

Fig 9 Renders of the Angel Wings sculpture, showing how the structure clears a small circular kiosk

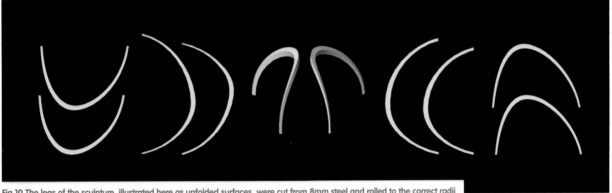

Fig 10 The legs of the sculpture, illustrated here as unfolded surfaces, were cut from 8mm steel and rolled to the correct radii

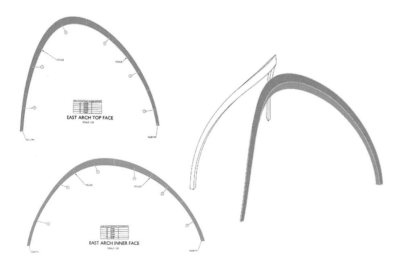

EAST ARCH TOP FACE
SCALE 1:20

EAST ARCH INNER FACE
SCALE 1:20

Fig 11 As a result of the extruding and trimming process, the arch ends up forming a parallelogram

the wings. Each face of the arches is made by extruding a curve along a straight line, and as such is developable. The unrolled shapes were laser cut in 8mm thick stainless steel before being rolled into the radii forming the arch's surfaces (figure 10).

To assemble the four skins, a simple jig was made, allowing the curved plates to be welded together to form the three-dimensional arch structure. The cross-sectional shape of the arch ends up being a parallelogram as a result of this extruding and trimming process (figure 11)

Electric Wharf footbridge, Coventry

This small bridge contains an 18-metre-high feature arch with a span of around 30 metres (figure 12). As well as supporting the bridge deck over the canal, the arch has to support itself from blowing over, which it does by cantilevering out of the ground. To provide the optimum form, the cross section varies from a deep triangular profile at the ground, where it cantilevers, to a more equilateral form at mid-span. The cross-sectional shape varies constantly but is always based on a triangle (figure 13).

The method used to make the arch is a refinement on the Angel Wings' legs. The structure is set up with steel rods at the apexes of the triangle, linked by steel bulkheads, which allowed the accurate setting-out of the corner rods and are the parts of the structure that carry most of the load (figure 14). Infill plates were then cut from 6mm steel to fit onto the faces of the arch between the rods (figure 15).

The surface of the arch was modelled in Digital Project. It was offset 6mm into the arch, and trimmed against the surface of the rod forming the

Fig 12 Electric Wharf footbridge, Coventry, spanning 30 metres

Fig 13 The cross-sectional shape of the bridge varies, but is always based on a triangle

Fig 14 Development perspective of the elements which form the bridge's arch

12

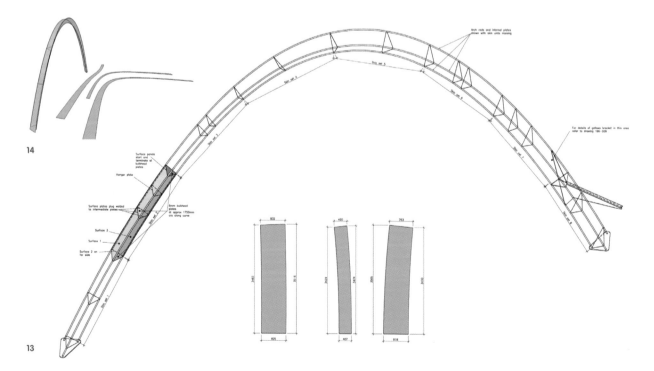

14

13

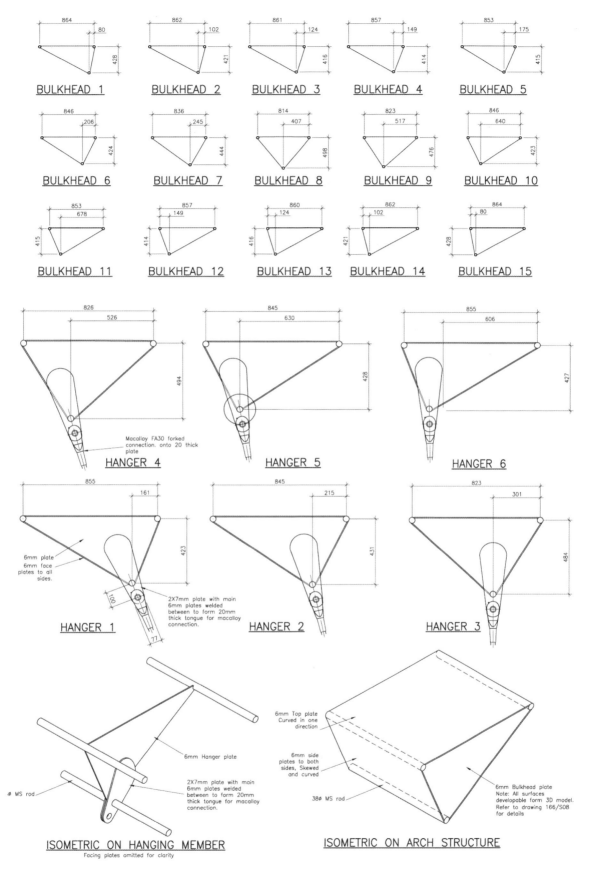

Fig 15 Arch sections of the Electric Wharf bridge

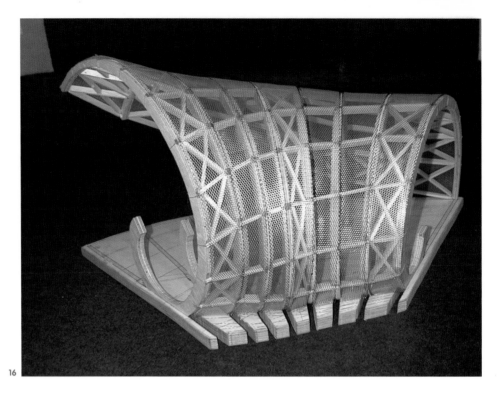

Fig 16 Model of
the Spiral Café,
Birmingham. The
form of the café
was generated by
running a surface
through eight
Fibonacci spirals,
which are fanned
out in plan and
progressively tilted

Fig 17 The geometric
development of
the Spiral Café,
illustrating the
emergence of a
composite surface

16

corner. When assembled, a v-shaped groove was left between the edge of the plate and the rod; this groove was later filled with weld to provide a sound structural connection and smooth finish when ground down.

Bullring Spiral Café, Birmingham – Marks Barfield Architects

The shape of this small building is based on the Fibonacci or 'golden section' spiral. Generated by running a surface through eight Fibonacci spirals fanned out in plan and progressively tilted, the resulting form was built up as ruled surfaces between each spiral (figure 16). This collection of surfaces was trimmed against each other to form a composite surface (figure 17).

A crucial part of constructing a building based on irregular surfaces is setting them up accurately in their 'folded' orientation. As with our earlier Bandstand project, the structure was based on

ribs that both hold the building up and provide a template on which to form the cladding surfaces. These profiles had unusual curving forms when developed, which was due to the skew over part of the surface (figure 18). This form was constructed by effectively setting up the geometry that generated the 3-D model in laser-cut steel ribs. Manufactured entirely using CNC cutters from coordinated fabrication information meant that the steel frame was a direct facsimile of the 3-D model. This not only allowed the plywood and copper-clad surfaces to be laid down on the spirals, but also meant that all other elements could be generated from the 3-D model in the sure knowledge that they would accurately fit onto the real building. This process is something like the full-scale 'rapid prototyping' of a building. By cutting everything down to the bolt holes in the structure using computer controlled machinery, there is the potential to produce intricate and complex buildings in a simple, predictable and economical way (figure 19).

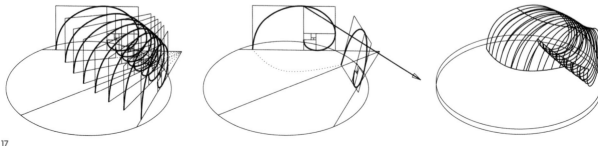

17

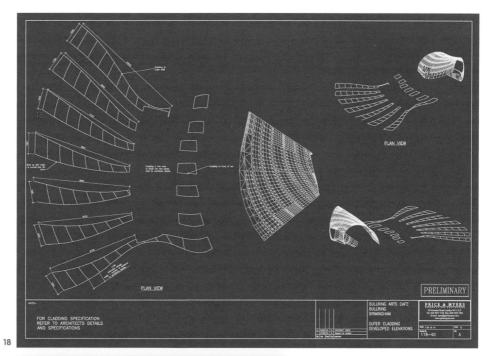

18

19

The opportunity to create interesting, beautiful forms through the fusion of digital modelling and computer-controlled cutting machines is at an early stage in the construction industry. The cost of people's time is almost always the biggest financial constraint in realising a building project. The use of this technology means that the process of making a building is no longer entirely dependent on a craftsman's skill in accurately making and fitting together the component parts. Robotic manufacture of components and assembly jigs that are mass-customised rather than mass-produced makes a whole new typology of form economically viable. Providing that certain geometrical principles are adhered to on the design side, the opportunities for architectural expression and structural ingenuity are immense.

Tim Lucas is a partner with Price & Myers Geometrics.

THE MAKING OF
ARTIFICIAL ECOLOGIES.
MARCO POLETTO,
ECOLOGICSTUDIO

4.2

The passage from the era of the 'machines' to the so-called era of 'ecology' has brought with it a new level of complex thinking and the understanding of its main characteristic: non-linearity. This shift has opened up new interpretations of technology that are able to overcome both the extremes of modernist exaltation with efficiency and a parallel postmodern rejection. Technology in the age of ecology can be interpreted as a new instrument for both thinking about and manufacturing architecture; it is a tool to redescribe the current modus operandi and to evolve new forms of learning and practising architecture itself. Digital design tools, rapid prototyping and manufacturing technologies, nanotechnology and material innovation (as well as interactive and responsive systems) are, within this logic framework, all components cooperating towards the definition of new modes of eco-logic architecture, or architectures for the age of ecology.

During what has been defined an 'epochal transition', a multitude of attitudes within the discipline of architectural design have developed; among the most prominent we can name the 'green hi-tech', where digital design and building technologies have been exploited to embrace the new paradigm of sustainability (intended as the final step in the escalation towards optimal strategies of human inhabitation of the globe). An opposite tendency has been the 'vernacular' approach, where the return to nature has been interpreted as literally as possible, and technology has been either rejected or hidden to symbolise an aversion towards the current trends of human development. A third, rather interesting, tendency can be defined as the 'metaphorical' attitude, where technology has been exploited to support the reproduction of nature and its seductive beauty.

These three quite different attitudes have all developed a strong 'ethical–political' position in relationship to the culture of our time and are using technology as a tool to serve their scope. Our design approach at ecoLogicStudio (eLS) moves instead from what we could define a 'philosophical' position and exploits technology as an instrument of exploration, a means to constantly redefine its

Fig 1 Canopy proposal for Venice's Marco Polo International Airport

design agenda, its production and its practice. From this point of view technology is at the same time secondary and crucial; it doesn't define a design style or a process a priori but it is always present in the definition of every design outcome or design development process.

Redescribing design methods:
the making of artificial ecologies

One of the sediments left by five years of iterations across various projects is a series of 'methodological steps' (see box later in the chapter) that support the re-engineering of architectural types and their derivative domains. In the extension of Marco Polo International Airport in Venice, for example, mapping techniques were deployed from day one; the task was to capture the effects produced by the main programmatic conditions of the project when applied to the typology of a shading canopy (figure 1). The project involved the extension of the check-in area of the airport to occupy the outdoor space framed on the other side by the parking and drop-off buildings. The brief was to enclose this space while maintaining the feeling of the outdoors – that is, by including natural lighting variations and fresh breeze. A field of shading tiles was digitally distributed (and animated with the conditions of sun and people movement) and tracked to guarantee shading potential and views of the sky simultaneously. The emerging animated wave was then processed to negotiate contrasting exigencies in a static configuration (dictated by budget constraints); differentiation was implemented via rotational difference of self-similar shading louvres. The so-called 'cut-off angle' became the parameter to be manipulated to control solar and light access as well as sky views.

At this stage the model was completely redescribed and parameterised to allow a more direct feedback between the evolving architectural configuration and the performative effects generated by the emerging roof (figure 2). Solar radiation and lighting tests were performed to study ranges of variation of cut-off angles acceptable for various activities on the ground floor: the two existing pools, for

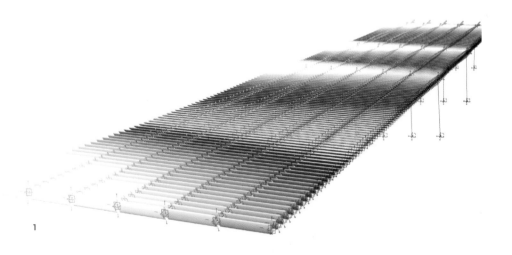

1

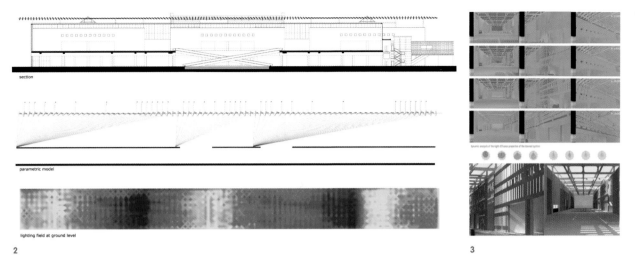

section

parametric model

lighting field at ground level

2

3

Fig 2 Performative design study for the airport canopy, showing solar penetration against a section of the proposed space

Fig 3 Radiance testing of the airport canopy

Fig 4 ecoLogicStudio's Lightwall project, a contemporary version of a traditional, heavy masonry wall with parametrically developed, light diffusing window cavities

Fig 5 STEM, eclogicStudio's 'living screen' system of bottled water and algae, in context

instance, were addressed by a sudden response in the louvres' orientation to allow some direct light to spill through the space and generate reflection games in an area of large people transit (figure 3). Check-in desks were addressed by a progressive reduction of cut-off angle to reach a level of high light diffusion and solar control. Three areas of the ground floor, where the maximum flow of people was modelled by circulation tests, enjoy full views of the sky as the blade orientation converges towards those points.

Among a multitude of potential virtual configurations the final one was bred out of a process of sequential negotiations; parametric relationships, environmental constraints and material properties all contributed to the definition of the breeding environment.

Redescribing architectural typologies: the evolution of architectonical prototypes

The second principal level at which technology plays a crucial role in the work of eLS is the redefinition of conventional architectonical typologies as new prototypes. Prototyping is a term that comes from the field of industrial design. It refers to a replica of a product (or part of it) that – rather than referring to the final product as a representative

copy (a maquette) – is capable of reproducing key properties of the initial product's concept and, in relationship to these properties, can be tested. In the same way, architectonical prototypes do not represent a particular configuration of the final preconceived types but rather are a testing ground for new material organisations that may spill out of existing decomposed typological conditions when subjected to specific performative requirements. The potential for large-scale prototyping has been radically expanded in the last years by the evolution of CAD–CAM platforms for the architectural design environment; nevertheless, the real shift is achieved only when parametric modelling and rapid prototyping technologies are synthesised and made capable of redescribing the way architectonical typologies are investigated and evolved.

eLS's new prototypes include the Lightwall (redescribing the typology of a massive Italian stone wall with small window insertions, figure 4), Stem (a living screen system where solar screening and air oxygenation are incorporated in a novel semi-biological stacking system, figures 5 and 6) and Aqua GardenA (a rain collection and gardening system developed via deformation of a branched tensile structure performing as a percolation device, figures 7 and 8). But it is in the project for a library in

4

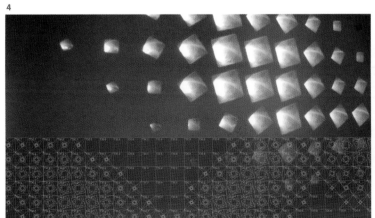

5

THE MAKING OF ARTIFICIAL ECOLOGIES.
MARCO POLETTO, ECOLOGICSTUDIO

Fig 6 Stem,
ecoLogicStudio's
'living screen' system
of bottled water and
algae

Figs 7 and 8
Aqua Garden: an
architectural machine
for the collection
of rainwater and
the conditioning of
outdoor microclimates

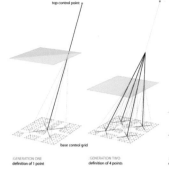
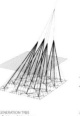

top control point

base control grid

GENERATION ONE
definition of 1 point

GENERATION TWO
definition of 4 points

GENERATION TREE
definition of 16 points

GENERATION FOUR
definition of 64 points

first generation

second generation

third generation

fourth generation

: PLANAR VIEW

water storage and gardening

: MODEL VIEW

7

8

6

lighting levels [lux]

direct incident solar radiation [Wh]

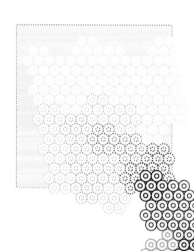

Cirié, near Turin, Italy, that the consequences of such a technological influence can be appreciated at a larger scale.

The library space sits within an existing warehouse building covered by a beautiful shed roof and enclosed on two sides by large windows opening onto public spaces below. The light field and the privacy gradient quickly became defining elements of an otherwise undifferentiated space. At the same time, the concept idea of the library intended as a 'forest of culture' started to materialise and was presented to the public (successfully). But rather than presenting the design as a metaphorical reference, eLS turned the 'forest' concept into a real mechanism of material organisation capable of being transposed via computational techniques in a layout scheme that was free from traditional typological constraints and segregations. At first, reading tables were made to compete for optimal light locations, and clusterisation was triggered in more sociable areas (i.e. near the large windows according to a sociability gradient field). Shelving units were distributed to frame the space around the tables and differentiated by table dimension, subject matter, book dimension, ergonomics (children's shelves occupy just two levels) and incorporated IT equipment. The resulting paths and trajectories across the 'forest' were selected for their degree of straightness and length. The resulting layout (figure 9) promoted both integration and differentiation, along with the emergence of a multitude of micro-spaces (niches), allowing users to find the ones which best suit their needs.

After researching library furniture it immediately became evident that such a layout idea could be implemented only thorough ad hoc furniture, designed with the previous process in mind. A parametric modelling technique was implemented to allow the translation of a 'shelf+table+corridor' prototype into a differentiated system with multiple possible configurations responding to layout requirements (figure 10). A population of 26 different instances was selected as the 'fittest' and went to on to be manufactured. The fabrication was maintained within budget by designing a set of common parts for each shelf and table, mounted on a number of different laser-cut supports (figure 11). The forest of culture concept was therefore materialised not through metaphorical mimicry but through its embodiment into a new architectonical prototype capable of exploiting technological inputs. The natural growth process of a forest became translated into an architectural organism (figures 12 and 13).

Redescribing the practice of architecture: collaborative design and design networks

The development of an innovative design methodology and related prototypical devices has opened up the potential for collaboration that goes far beyond the typical system of 'architectural signatures'. At the core of our work lies a methodological sensibility supported by extreme technological innovation. Collaborative design has therefore evolved as a potential condition for the effective implementation of eLS qualities. Within this format we aim to redefine and optimise our role to

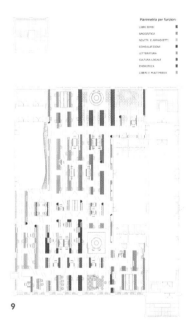

9

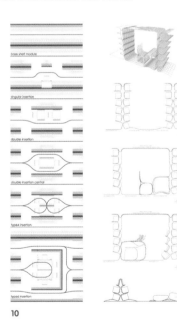

10

12

13

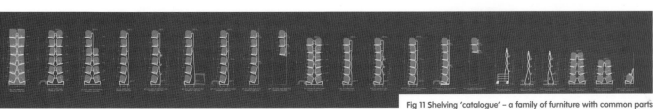

Fig 11 Shelving 'catalogue' – a family of furniture with common parts

THE MAKING OF
ARTIFICIAL ECOLOGIES.
MARCO POLETTO,
ECOLOGICSTUDIO

suit project requirements, increasing the potential for 'value for money' in ever differing circumstances. eLS has so far practised as design architect, concept architect, design consultant, research consultant and educator.

One of our latest projects illustrates how this format can work: the design of an urban pavilion for Istanbul World Capital of Culture 2010 (figure 14). This project was initiated with a workshop involving students from London and Istanbul working under the guidance of eLS and local architect Tuspa, with the support of structural engineers Adams Kara Taylor. The initial design concept for a 'fibrous pavilion' was abstracted in a matrix containing a set of digital/ physical modelling/construction techniques (figure 15). Within this framework the students produced five very different families of pavilions, each capable of generating a multitude of configurations related to specific sites, timeframes and budgets (figure 16). The technological specificity of the physical prototypes encouraged the involvement of a wide range of organisations, including a sponsor (Lafarge), local organisations (Arkitera), universities (ITU), the media (CNN) and art galleries.

The immediate consequence of this strategy was that the design process was enlarged to encompass a wide range of participants, increasing the potential for innovation and final success. Within this modus operandi, the potential for innovation is not directly related to the size of the single design practice; this means that small practices are potentially as innovative, perhaps even more so, than much larger ones.

Design methodology: the four ingredients for the making of artificial ecologies

1 Mapping – from the object to the field: mapping shifts the attention from the perception of the environment as a series of segregated objects to the field of forces that define its dynamic state:

• from site reading to site indexing: maps are at the same time analytical and design tools;

Fig 14 The fibrous room installation, in the Garanti Gallery, Istanbul, a machine for the manufacture of woven structures

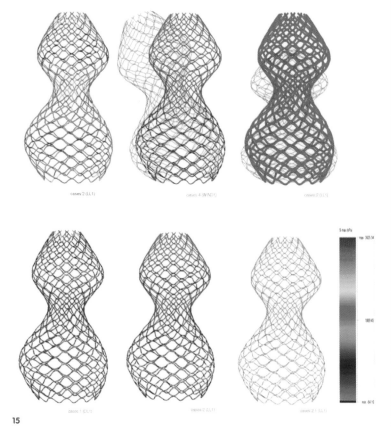

15

Fig 15 Structural testing of the fibrous pavilion, an exercise aided by engineers Adams Kara Taylor

Fig 16 With just a handful of elemental components and rules, ecoLogicStudio and students compiled a large number of configurations for the pavilion

Branching Structure Catalogue

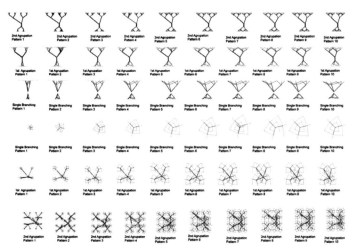

16

- their computational nature allows the emergence of behavioural patterns;
- maps are at the same time scientific objective measurements and architectural subjective acts of representation of reality.

2 **Prototyping** – the era of ecology is not about rejecting technology but is about embedding its quality or characteristics within the designed system:

- the result is a seamless integration between the technological value and the behavioural quality of the system itself (i.e. its phenotypical appearance);
- under such an assumption technology is transposed into a technique and its evaluation no longer operates under linear performative assessment or optimisation, but instead works through its degree of differentiation in response to the environment;
- we define as 'eco-machine' the heterogeneous technological assemblage of design/simulation techniques and their related physical systems/ processes.

3 **Action plan and simulations** – parametric modelling technologies become instruments of design which support this transposition from the object to its differentiated field and from the single solution to its corresponding 'virtual multiplicity':

- under this premise the proliferation of the eco-machines in the site environment is happening as a real simulation; compositional rules are substituted by simulation parameters and their ranges of tolerance and variations;
- the embedded computational power of the eco-machine is exploited to describe dynamic design scenarios.

4 **Testing** – there is no stage of design in which the project has the tendency to converge to a single solution; rather, new trajectories are constantly selected through the latent virtual multiplicities:

- what matters most is the emergent pattern rather than its specific form;
- the testing and evaluation, or feedback, is a process of recognition and further specification of the pattern.

Marco Poletto is an architect and founder partner of ecoLogicStudio.

THE DESIGN AND FABRICATION OF A SPIKY POD. TAREK MERLIN, SMC ALSOP ARCHITECTS

Fig 1 Spiky pod, Queen Mary College's Blizard Building, East London

Fig 2 Interior of Spiky pod, a 40-person seminar space

Queen Mary College, University of London, aspired to create a world-class medical school at the cutting edge of teaching and research. After appointing SMC Alsop and Amec to design the new Institute of Cell and Molecular Science, we conducted a series of workshops to tease out the client's aspirations for what is now called the Blizard Building. The scientists' ideas and emotions were encapsulated into a series of working diagrams that grew into the plans and sections of the building. Completed in March 2005, this research centre accommodates nearly 400 scientists, inhabiting over 9,000 square metres of space. The building comprises a series of laboratories, write-up offices and a 400-seat lecture theatre.

Perhaps the most dramatic elements of the scheme are the four pods that sit over the central void within the glass pavilion. Each of the four pods has its own personality. Different in function, form, materials and construction method, they each presented their own challenges and complexities:

- 'Centre of the Cell' is to be fitted out as an interactive exhibition for local school children;
- 'Mushroom' was conceived as a ground-floor meeting area;
- Cloud' is split into a pair of separate ten-person meeting rooms;
- 'Spiky', a 40-person seminar space (figures 1 and 2), is perhaps the most striking in terms of form.

Design development

Spiky pod was always conceived as a tensile fabric structure that would be pushed and pulled in different and opposing directions to create a form that was as dynamic and visually exciting as possible. During the development of the design we had to consider the constraints on the form-finding process. The pod sits over a void within a glass pavilion, so not only did we have to hit four points on the edge of the void, but the form also had to duck and dive under, over and around the columns that hold up the pavilion (figure 3). The final form comprises 13 spikes: four clamped to legs bolted to the walls of the building; three supported via projecting struts; and six supported by tension cables connected to the main building's structure. Detailed coordination between structural engineer and load analysis of the fabric was paramount. Furthermore, within the fabric enclosure sits an elliptical platform with an acoustic balustrade wall that not only rakes back at an angle from floor level, but also undulates in height around the plan. From the very beginning, form-finding was both challenging and integral to the success of the project.

In the early stages of form-finding, the design team struggled to build a working computer model that took the surrounding physical constraints into account while allowing us to tweak the form with ease. Our initial CAD models were clunky and gave no flexibility or a true representation of how fabric behaves. We found that the only way to successfully replicate this movement was to create a physical model using actual fabric (figure 4). With a pair of nylon tights, some dowelling rod and a foam ball we were able to create a flexible model of Spiky and place it within a physical model of the building. We could push and pull the rods, change their angle and position – and the fabric would follow. Although we knew that we would eventually have to return to the computer, this approach was wonderfully liberating and became the fundamental basis of finding the three-dimensional form.

Particularly challenging was the production of a suitably irregular and dynamic computer model

Fig 3 Section drawing, showing the pod within the context of the wider building

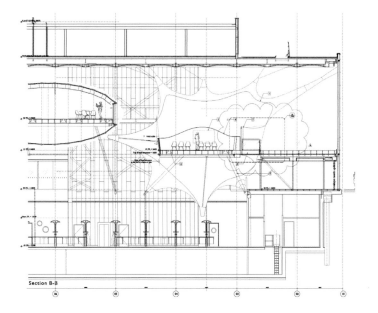

Section B-B

THE DESIGN AND FABRICATION OF A SPIKY POD.
TAREK MERLIN, SMC ALSOP ARCHITECTS

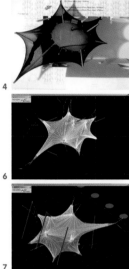

4

6

7

Fig 4 Early model of the pod, made from stretching fabric over dowelling. This form became the basis of the digital model

Fig 5 3-D representation of the physical model, which was then exported into specialist surface-modelling software

Fig 6 The final fabrication geometry for all aspects of the tension structure were derived from a single computer model

Fig 7 Each fabric panel has its own individual geometry, and every piece is a complex shape

that represented the physical one. Without access to a 3-D scanner we simply used a scale rule to establish the locations of the ends of the spikes in relation to a predetermined grid; we then fed the coordinates into a CAD model (figure 5). This was then translated into specialist surface-modelling software.

We worked very closely with specialist subcontractor, Architen Landrell, and its engineering analysis consultants Tensys, whose director David Wakefield developed the 'inTENS' software. Employing the method of 'dynamic relaxation', inTENS is founded on the principle of nodes. Coordinates are traced for each node, all of which are interconnected by data that represents different elements of the tensile structure such as the membrane, cables and beam components. Every time a node is moved the data is updated; during the form-finding process a holistic load analysis is easily achieved for every iteration. Furthermore, the software applies some constraints on the form-finding process that are integral to achieving a successful outcome, such as resisting geometrical inaccuracies and eliminating kinetic energy from the model.

In Spiky's case some of the principles of traditional tensile structures had to be expanded. The PVC fabric itself behaved in a slightly perverse way, unique to tensile structures. Although it appears as if the skin is being pulled into shape, that isn't the whole truth. The traditional tensile engineering logic is not applicable in this case because there is no lower boundary to which the object can anchor itself before tensioning. Unusually, this meant that a tensile stress field existed somewhere within the space defined by the outer form; in order to modify the outer form, this internal membrane stress field had to be adjusted. Of course, one is defined by the other, so the model became extremely sensitive. In changing one point to satisfy an aesthetic concern or respond to a clash detection, another problem would emerge. This was borne out through the extensive collaborative process of reviewing iterations. A typical fabric tension structure might require around ten iterations to make it work; in Spiky's case the number was almost 200.

Fabrication geometry

Once the 3-D model had settled, however, the progression from computer model to factory floor was rapid, although this transition was not without

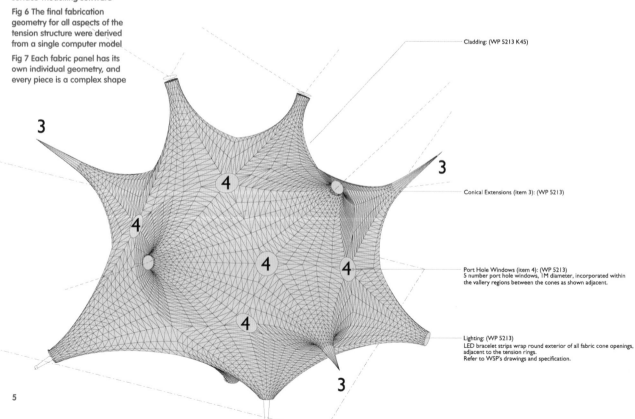

Cladding: (WP 5213 K45)

Conical Extensions (item 3): (WP 5213)

Port Hole Windows (item 4): (WP 5213)
5 number port hole windows, 1M diameter, incorporated within the vallery regions between the cones as shown adjacent.

Lighting: (WP 5213)
LED bracelet strips wrap round exterior of all fabric cone openings, adjacent to the tension rings.
Refer to WSP's drawings and specification.

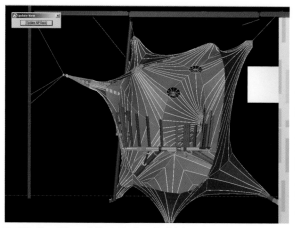

Fig 8 Section of the pod, illustrating how the fabric envelops the internal structure

Fig 9 The fabric cladding was brought to site as a single 407 square metre piece, with an opening in the underside

Fig 10 A pure and crease-free form, believed to be the only 360 degree tensile structure in existence

complications. The final fabrication geometry for all aspects of the tension structure derived from a single computer model – including details of the fabric panels, the boundary and support cables, associated accessories and the projecting support struts. Each fabric panel has its own geometry, and every piece is a complex shape (figures 6, 7 and 8). The three-dimensional geometry of any particular fabric panel was flattened out by successively unfolding triangular geometries within itself. The inTENS program created a pattern-cutting schedule; the fabric was cut and heat-welded into one piece off-site at Architen Landrell's factory. Small-scale models were made along the way to ensure that everything would come together precisely and that all seam lines would read as part of the overall definition of the shape.

Installation sequence

The fabric cladding was brought to site as a single 407 square metre piece, with an opening in the underside. The entire skin was placed on the deck platform, the lower part of the fabric was dropped over the side like a skirt and the opening zipped up from underneath (figure 9). Specialist rope-access installers then began the intricate process of raising the cones up and out towards their final positions. The final tensioning process was extremely challenging because of the many parameters at play. The membrane itself needed to be as taut as possible, but this had to be done in a delicately synchronised process to avoid overloading any one connection point to the main building structure, while ensuring that undue stress was not put upon any part of the fabric skin.

The resulting form pushed the limits of what is possible with tensile structures, resulting in a pure and crease-free form (figure 10). We believe this to be the only 360 degree tensile structure in existence.

Tarek Merlin is an architect at SMC Alsop Architects.

THE TERRAIN MAP
AS FAÇADE.
RODI MACARTHUR, SHEPPARD ROBSON

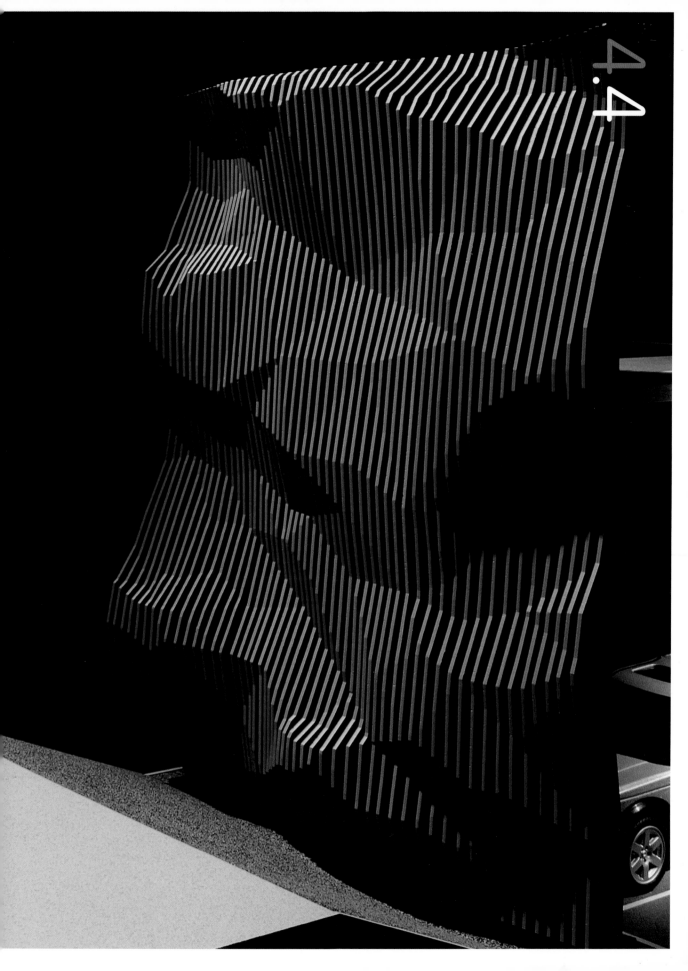

THE TERRAIN MAP
AS FAÇADE.
RODI MACARTHUR,
SHEPPARD ROBSON

Set against the eye-catching backdrop of England's Lake District, it seemed natural, in developing our proposals for the multi-storey car park (MSCP) in Penrith, to establish a dialogue with the scenery and topography on the doorstep of the town. The car park is part of a larger retail, commercial and residential masterplan for the redevelopment of the town centre of Penrith, based around a new market square (figure 1). The £7 million, 1006-space building is being designed for Lowther Manelli Properties Ltd. We felt that the geographic location of Penrith – sitting at the gateway to the Lake District – provided ample reference material to generate an exciting, challenging and unique design. The proposal, however, requires facing up to a number of challenges in order to translate the initial idea into a describable, achievable result. The beauty of the extreme landscape variation within the Lake District was something we wanted to reproduce as accurately as possible in the design of our façade. In order to do this we needed to find an accurate digital representation of the topography of the area, extract a piece from this data to act as our façade, make it conform to the shape of our building and finally give the surface some depth.

The process of locating and selecting a strip of terrain to form the basis of the design for the façade

was relatively straightforward. It became apparent early on in the process that the information available via Google Earth was not of a suitably high resolution to allow an accurate representation of the Cumbrian landscape at the dimensions required. It was important, therefore, to locate an alternative source of accurate, good resolution digital terrain map data. Help was at hand in the form of NASA, which has (perhaps frighteningly, although conveniently) mapped most of the globe at three arc-seconds three-dimensional resolution – i.e. a data point fired from space recording height information at 90-metre horizontal intervals (figure 2).

This allowed us to locate our topography with a sufficient level of detail, containing the individual peaks within the mountain ranges of the Lake District without generating so much data that the resulting model would prove unwieldy (figure 3). The strip that we chose runs from the area directly to the south of Penrith, due west until it hits the Irish Sea, passing over Helvellyn – one of the Lake District's highest and most dramatic peaks. Once identified, it was necessary to extract the strip of topography that was to form our façade and scale it down by the appropriate amount to allow it to fit around the visible faces of the building (figure 4).

2

3

Fig 2 Topographical map of Cumbria, from which Sheppard Robson drew the undulating strip on which the car park's façade was modelled

Fig 3 Strip of terrain selected to wrap around the car park as a façade

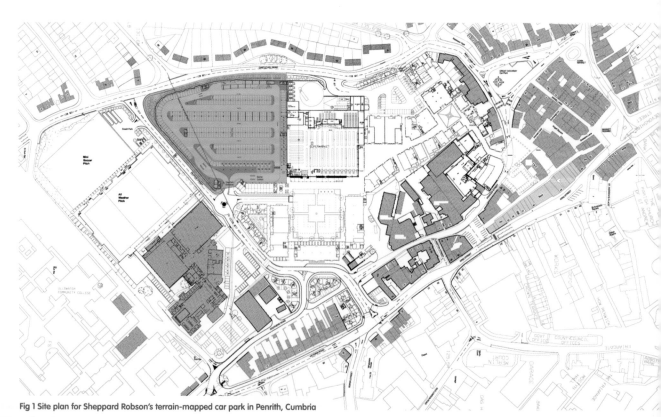

Fig 1 Site plan for Sheppard Robson's terrain-mapped car park in Penrith, Cumbria

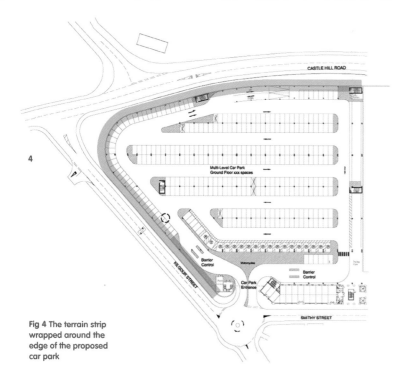

Fig 4 The terrain strip wrapped around the edge of the proposed car park

In order to extract the strip of topography, it was first necessary to convert the raw digital terrain model data into a workable CAD format. The data exists in a format more useful to GIS software users, but a free download from the internet allowed us to save the data as a .dem (digital elevation model) file which could then be imported into Google SketchUp and further exported as a .dwg file. Once converted into the common .dwg file format the terrain map could be opened in MicroStation V8 and developed further. At this stage the model was a large mesh with no thickness; furthermore, we needed to edit the mesh in order to remove areas of the landscape that were extraneous to the façade design (figure 5). It would also be necessary to convert the mesh to a solid model representation of the material to be used in the end result, with depth and thickness (figure 6).

The potential logistics involved in creating each individual panel from the existing surface model were daunting: due to its length, the façade would consist of more than 2,500 individual panels – each one 50mm thick with a gap of 100mm to the next, representing a sometimes dramatic, undulating landscape. Each panel was therefore unique and, conventionally, would have been produced individually with 3-D modelling software. This

5

Fig 5 The strip of England's Lake District formatted as a façade model, from which extraneous detail has been removed

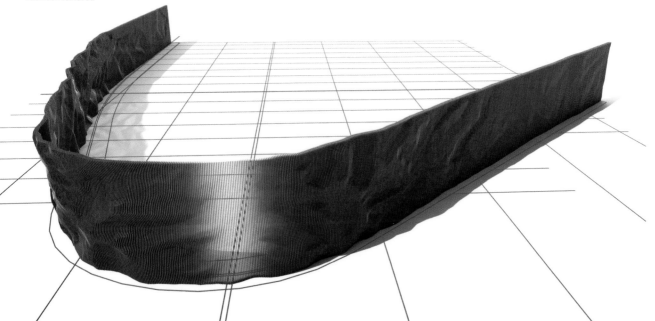

Fig 6 The terrain strip can now be modelled as a curved element, to wrap around the perimeter of the site

THE TERRAIN MAP
AS FAÇADE.
RODI MACARTHUR,
SHEPPARD ROBSON

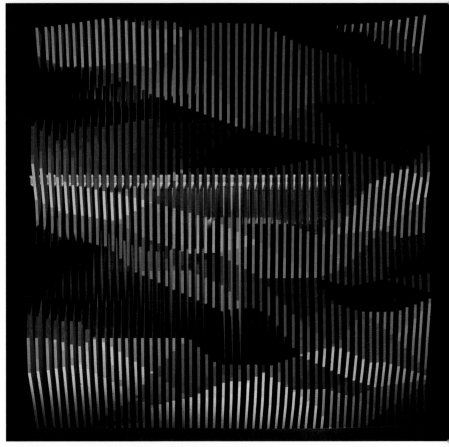

Fig 7 Once the terrain-mapped façade is notionally in place, it is divided into separate timber strips, giving the façade de

Fig 8 Full size sample of the façade, a CNC-cut assembly made possible only through 3D modelling and scripting

clearly didn't represent an appealing – or cost-effective – proposition. With this in mind, with our CAD technical support partners Cadventure we developed a Visual Basic script that could run within MicroStation. This automated the more tedious and technically challenging aspects of accurately modelling individual panels and ensured the array of panels would adhere to the curve of the building footprint (figure 7). Once complete and debugged, the working script reduced the time taken to model the key elements of the façade from a number of days to a matter of minutes. In addition, the script allowed us to explore a number of proposals in order to determine the optimum thickness and depth of panels, as well as the spacing between panels. This tool has already proved its worth, but may yet become invaluable should the need arise to explore any value-engineering options for the design of the façade.

When it came to considering the fabrication method for this façade, the processes we had evolved to generate the complex design solution naturally suggested that a computer-controlled prefabrication process would be appropriate. It is hoped that this will ensure that the quality of the end product remains high while maximising the efficient use of raw material by minimising waste.

Timber seemed an obvious choice of material, not least because the local planning authority had expressed a desire to see this type of material used but also because it is an abundant, relatively cheap and highly workable raw material. We began researching timber products that might be appropriate for this type of installation. It quickly became apparent that solid timber might not be appropriate: the (average) dimensions of an individual panel are 8m(h) x 50mm(w) x 300mm(d). In order to produce a typical profile from sawn solid timber we would need to joint smaller pieces to achieve the height. Also, we would need to cut from lumber which is 500mm deep (minimum); this would produce a large amount of waste when cutting the profiles. Additionally, we were not satisfied that we could source timber of a high enough quality in large enough volumes to produce the 2,500 individual strips required. Through necessity, we explored other timber products, including laminated, engineered boards. One manufacturer, Finnforest, suggested Kerto Q. The standard sheet dimensions of Kerto Q are 1.8m x 20m with sheet thicknesses ranging from 12mm to 90mm. Their manufacturing facility in Aichach, outside Munich, has a complex CNC cutting machine that is able to take data from our model and accurately reproduce the individual profiles at full scale. The large sheet size of Kerto Q is also attractive since it gives us the opportunity to optimise the number of pieces cut from an individual sheet, reducing the amount of wasted timber. Offcuts are used by the factory as fuel to provide heat and power.

Having advocated the concept of the façade design, we needed to demonstrate the proposals with a physical model. The process of building a physical model would, we hoped, allow us to prototype some of the processes that could be involved in manufacturing the actual façade. We began to investigate how our model makers could best make use of our three-dimensional information. They required the outlines of each panel, enabling them to laser-cut each profile from a large sheet. It was necessary for us to take each panel in the 3-D model and rotate and position each one on one large sheet. This was a time-consuming process that could also have benefited from some automation in the form of a script or macro, but on this occasion the task fell to a year-out student.

It became clear that a further iteration of the modelling process was necessary to finalise the level of detail inherent in our data. Currently the model is still relatively complex, with a number of almost imperceptible changes of direction occurring along any given length of panel. These do nothing more than add complexity and cost to our model, without contributing to the overall visual drama. The model will, therefore, have to be rebuilt from the initial mesh stage onwards, using simplified – or rather, optimised – geometry. From the optimised model the manufacturer will require data points giving x, y and z coordinates for the CNC cutting machine. Our proposal for this stage of the process is to once again create a Visual Basic script that exports the x, y and z coordinate information of each key node point (or every change in direction for the cutting arm) along a panel length from the MicroStation model to a spreadsheet application that can then be read by the CNC machine.

It has been something of a challenge to take a solid, immovable, elemental and identifiable part of our landscape and reinterpret and reconfigure it in this way. Without the use of 3-D modelling and scripting techniques (and the help of NASA) it simply would not have been possible to produce the façade in its current guise. We would have had to make some sort of approximation, or simulation, of the topography. This, in turn, could have allowed the idea to be diluted in the event that costs became a concern. Using the techniques described here will allow us to produce a visually complex façade, which accurately represents the landscape of the area surrounding Penrith with a minimum amount of wasted material in a time- and cost-effective manner.

Rodi MacArthur is an associate at Sheppard Robson.

MODELLING THE UNSEEN

The beauty of the digital model is that it can encompass that which a two-dimensional drawing cannot: temperature, air flow, the behaviour of smoke, light and acoustics (and even people). It is this facility – one of ensuring that a new building makes its occupants feel safe and comfortable – that makes modern architectural computing particularly compelling. It acknowledges that buildings are not artefacts to behold, but spaces to be experienced. It is an emerging science – wind tunnels are still managing to retain an edge over computer programs, while (for the time being at least) software cannot take full account of human psychology in a panic situation. But they can certainly replicate the process of a fire drill and predict how a structure will perform when set alight. These are things which once lay in the territory of experience and the rule of thumb, but which are now becoming expressed as mathematics.

MODELLING
DAYLIGHT.
ARFON DAVIES
AND FLORENCE LAM,
ARUP LIGHTING

MODELLING DAYLIGHT.
ARFON DAVIES
AND FLORENCE LAM,
ARUP LIGHTING

Fig 1 The solar azimuth and the solar altitude for a given time at a given longitude and altitude can be determined using the equations given in *ASHRAE Fundamentals Handbook*

Fig 2 By joining a series of intersection points a critical shading curve can be drawn on the shading surface

Fig 3 The lower half of the shade is formed by inverting the top half. By symmetry this will shade the opposite triangle of the rooflight. This was the final form used at the Nasher Sculpture Center

Fig 4 Concept model of the shading devices, incorporating the form developed in Figs 1, 2 and 3

Fig 5 Oblique view of the shading devices used at the Nasher Sculpture Center

Fig 6 Prototype of the shading device as a three-by-eight array

Fig 7 Full-scale mock-up of the shading array, eventually used at the Nasher Sculpture Center, Dallas

1

2

3

4

5

6

7

For many years, lighting has been a fundamental mode of expression of designs. The history of architecture is rich in the diversity of its response to light. The lit effect – the interplay of light and shadow – is a response to functional and emotional needs derived from a holistic design approach. Daylight is, of course, an environmentally responsible and energy-efficient source of illumination. There are numerous benefits to a day-lit space. In museums, daylight provides excellent colour-rendering characteristics, which can create a perfect visual experience. In workspaces, classrooms and offices, daylight offers a much healthier visual environment that has been shown to improve productivity. In addition, mounting concerns with global warming and issues of sustainability have brought about a serious consideration of the relationship between daylight and electric light.

An opening in the building fabric, mostly known as a window or a skylight, is more than a link between the inside and outside of a building. Architecturally, it defines a building. Daylighting has so often been at the heart of architecture – both for the qualities that it can bring to interiors and its outward expression through façades, as well as the roof. However, creating a quality day-lit environment can be a challenging task. Exterior daylight conditions vary widely from season to season, hour by hour, as well as by location. The variability of daylight availability can make it difficult to create a consistently lit interior environment. Excessive daylight can cause visual discomfort due to glare, and for museums/art galleries, uncontrolled daylight can be detrimental to light-sensitive artefacts, causing irreparable damage.

An array of physical and computer-modelling techniques are available to assist with the development and design of daylighting systems. These techniques can be used to assist the design team in the design process and to evaluate the resulting design. They can also be used to assist the communication of design concepts and analytical data. These two applications of 3-D modelling techniques have played an important role in the design of a number of recently completed buildings.

3-D modelling and the design process: the Nasher Sculpture Center, Dallas, USA

Engineers have long used rapid prototyping (RP) with a focus on its capability to enhance design and manufacturing process and performance. However, few have addressed the use of this technique in the early stages of the building design process. Over the last few years, Arup Lighting has used RP as a tool for design thought. An example of this is the creation of a full-size model for the sunshades used on Renzo Piano's Nasher Sculpture Center in Dallas.

The building is designed to be a light-filled building of glass and marble, dedicated to the display and study of modern sculpture. Unlike traditional painting galleries, this project was designed to allow a higher level of natural illumination, thus activating the varied

8

forms and surface textures of the sculpture. Its barrel-vault roof comprises transparent low-iron glass overlaid with an innovative cast aluminium solar-shading mechanism. This system was carefully developed and engineered to permit the highest levels of diffused skylight and reflected sunlight while simultaneously blocking-out all direct sun penetration. The design of this slim-line roof skin structure has also allowed maximum visual transparency to the sky.

During the initial concept phase, the sun path diagram for Dallas was carefully studied to create a series of possible forms for the sunshades (figures 1, 2 and 3). Arup structural, services and lighting teams worked closely to develop visualisation images from Rhinoceros, the 3-D modelling program, that brought almost immediate owner buy-in. Through careful design of the digital model, provision was made early on for easy transfer to other applications. At scheme design, the concept model was exported to the Radiance lighting visualisation program for daylight study (figures 4 and 5). What would seem like divergent paths – structural analysis and lighting visualisation – were instead linked in the design development through a physical model generated by rapid prototyping.

Further daylight tests were carried out on a cast aluminium roof-shading panel, which comprises an array of eight-by-three shading elements, made available after the construction of a three-bay full-scale mock up (figures 6 and 7). Physical measurements were taken at an artificial sky laboratory in London to confirm its optical properties and hence to derive a more accurate prediction of interior daylight levels throughout the year. Visual checks on its sun-shading performance were also carried out at 0 degree and ±5 degree elevations to ascertain there would be no direct sunlight penetration throughout the vaulted roof.

Optimisation: the Light House, London

The design of modern building envelopes requires the simultaneous balancing of many different performance criteria. These may include heat loss, heat gain, daylight levels, sun protection and views out, as well as cost. Advanced methods of computer optimisation give new insights into the range of potential solutions. Optimised solutions can be derived via mathematical techniques. These solutions change depending on the relative importance of each parameter to the client. For example, if heat loss is most important to the

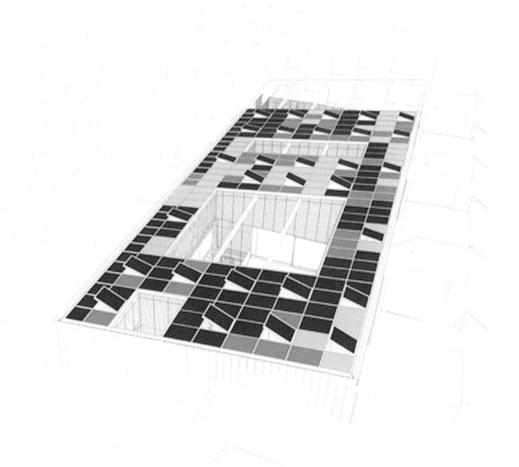

client, then the optimised solution is likely to have smaller windows. Conversely, if views out are most important, windows are likely to be larger. A preassembled set of solutions allows many combinations of parameters to be explored interactively during a design session. By using these techniques, designers can help clients understand the impact of their evolving designs on optimised engineering solutions.

An example of this approach was used for Gianni Botsford Architects' Light House, a new-build home in Notting Hill, west London. The site for the house is enclosed on all sides by surrounding buildings, so daylight only enters from above (figure 8). The bedrooms are located on the ground floor, receiving daylight through courtyards cut into the plan of the building. The living spaces are located on the first floor, with generous daylighting through a fully glazed roof. It is this roof that required a computer-aided optimisation approach in its design.

There were a number of often contradictory criteria for the design of the roof glazing above the living spaces – for example:

- to have a well day-lit living room, but no direct sunlight on the paintings hung there;
- it was desirable to have sunlight in the dining area on winter mornings but not at lunchtime in midsummer;
- in one space, it was desirable to have good views out to the sky, but the space is also overlooked by adjacent properties, and so privacy suggested the use of opaque glass.

Balancing these requirements, along with more practical issues such as cost and solar gain, was further complicated by the interaction of adjacent spaces with each other – sunlight passing through the roof over one space could fall in an adjacent space, as there were wide openings between them. In order to come to a solution, weightings were given to each criterion (e.g. high daylight levels were desirable while avoiding sunlight on the paintings was essential). To achieve these goals, the roof layout comprises four different types of glazing panel ranging from clear glass to a heavily fritted glazing with a low light transmission, good sunlight diffusion and limited views through it (figure 9). The roof itself is made up of 222 glazing panels – to test every combination of these four glazing panels would have required assessment of 4^{222} conditions (a 134-digit number!). Using specially developed scripts and computer-aided optimisation techniques it was possible to home in on a solution that delivered the best performance based on the criteria, weightings and constraints (without analysing all 4^{222} conditions). The solution itself was not the most obvious layout of panels architecturally, but it works well, creating a comfortable living space.

3-D modelling and communicating the design: High Museum of Art, Atlanta, USA

The High Museum of Art, founded in 1905 as the Atlanta Art Association, is the leading art museum in the south-eastern United States of America. In 1983, the museum's Richard Meier-designed building opened to worldwide acclaim, adding 12,500 square metres and tripling the museum's space. At the heart of this new building is an atrium with a west-facing vertical opening and glazed roof. This atrium houses ramped walkways that provide access to three levels of adjoining galleries from the ground-floor entrance lobby. Balconies within the atrium provided long vistas through the building, giving visitors views into the atrium and beyond from adjacent galleries.

In the years following the opening of the building, conservators and curators found that daylight levels within galleries adjacent to the atrium were higher than the maximum limits defined by loan agreements as well as some of their in-house standards. To mitigate this the museum installed fabric shade panels on windows and erected temporary walls across openings to limit daylight penetration into the gallery spaces. Although addressing the need to reduce daylight levels, the museum found these measures had a negative impact on the quality of the internal spaces and removed some of Meier's original design features. The long vistas and connection to the atrium were significantly reduced.

In 2002 the museum began a renovation with the objective of returning to Richard Meier's original layout while addressing the daylight concerns. Arup Lighting was appointed to review the daylight conditions and advise the design team on suitable techniques for controlling daylight penetration. A series of passive shading systems were proposed to control the transmission of windows and façades. These included roller shades and neutral density window films. Following completion of this element of the design it was necessary for Arup to provide detailed predictions of daylight levels to the museum.

Exterior and interior daylight conditions vary widely from season to season, hour by hour. Detailed analysis using the three-dimensional geometry of the building and hourly measured weather data enabled the calculation and prediction of interior daylight conditions throughout the year. This equates to 4,380 individual calculations and data for each point considered. When a series of analysis points are used to evaluate the distribution of daylight on a wall, the number of points increases significantly. Add to this a large number of walls and surfaces that are of interest to the museum and the quantity of data is vast. Communicating the results in a clear and concise way proved to be difficult given the amount of data. The museum wanted to know what the daylight levels at a given

Fig 10 Fish-eye view of the 3-D model of the High Museum of Art, Atlanta

wall would be at a certain time of year, the average illuminance on that wall and also the annual exposure. This would have resulted in hundreds of pages of graphs and charts if traditional techniques were used.

We therefore used the 3-D model (figure 10) constructed for the analysis to develop a new way of communicating the analysis data to the design team. The objective was to give the client the ability to obtain daylight illuminance information for display walls at any given hour of the year within an interactive 3-D environment. The resulting application would enable the client to navigate through this environment and select any wall of interest for interrogation.

A combination of AutoCAD and 3ds Max was used to generate the geometry for the 3-D environment. Radiance was used to calculate the daylight illuminances for a predefined set of walls based on measured weather data. Macromedia Director was then used to build the 3-D environment. Custom scripts were developed within Macromedia to produce false-colour representations of wall daylight illuminance on the fly. Collision detection was also included to prevent the character within the 3-D environment from walking through walls. A simple cylinder was used as the character.

Additional features included the ability to export a graphic showing the distribution of daylight on a wall at any given time; the ability to produce animations on specific walls showing the variation of daylight on a wall for a given day; and the ability to calculate the annual illuminance exposure on a given wall. This last feature provides important information to the museum conservation team and enables them to plan the location and distribution of sensitive objects within the museum. The resulting application enabled the client to browse through a vast amount of analysis data in a clear and graphical way (figure 11). The application also gave them the freedom to obtain the information when they needed it.

Arfon Davies is an Associate Director at Arup Lighting. Florence Lam is an Associate Director at Arup Lighting, and the leader of the Arup Lighting Group, based in London.

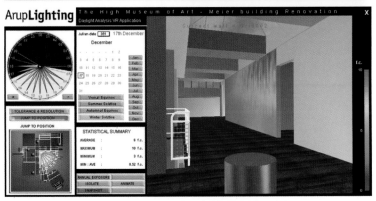

Fig 11 Arup's lighting analysis for the High Museum of Art put a premium on simple and clear retrieval of data through an intuitive graphical user interface

THE DAYLIGHT-OPTIMISED
FAÇADE.
ANDREW MACINTOSH
AND RICHARD PRIEST,
FEILDEN CLEGG
BRADLEY STUDIOS

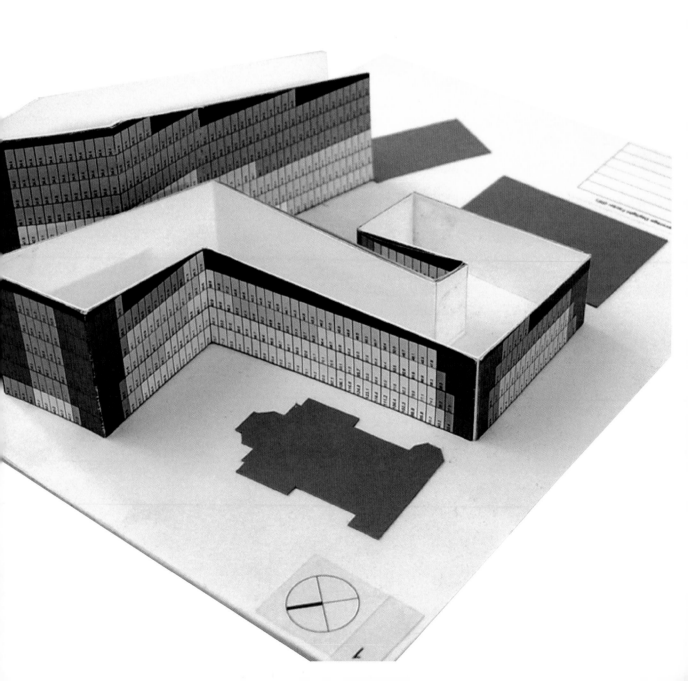

THE DAYLIGHT-
OPTIMISED FAÇADE.
ANDREW MACINTOSH
AND RICHARD PRIEST,
FEILDEN CLEGG
BRADLEY STUDIOS

This chapter is concerned with a new academic complex for Leeds Metropolitan University close to Leeds city centre, which combines a wide range of uses in two major landmark buildings, one rising to 23 storeys (figure 1). A major public space linking key urban areas forms a significant landscape element in the scheme. The buildings include new offices and teaching spaces for four departments, which include the Department for Cultural Studies; the Department for Social Science; The Department for Architecture, Landscape and Design; and the Arts and Graphics Department. The 10,000 square metres of teaching and office space is being provided as shell-and-core only, so was treated as open-plan office space for the purpose of the design development described here. Feilden Clegg Bradley have now also been appointed to carry out the fit-out and space planning for the four departments. Other uses include a new Baptist Church, a café/exhibition space and 240 student bedrooms/studios. The scheme was granted planning permission in March 2007.

The external face of the building is a Corten rain-screen façade. The initial concept was for greater quantities of glazing at the lower levels and the façade would become progressively more solid higher up the building (figure 2). At this early stage, the randomised, full-height glazing panels were of varying widths. However, for ease of construction and cost efficiency this was subsequently rationalised to a grid of 1.5m wide panels. The façade study (figure 2) follows an intuitive logic for providing adequate daylight to the internal spaces; upper storeys typically have greater access to light and so need less glazing, whereas lower levels, with more overshadowing from nearby buildings, need more glazing to achieve an equally bright interior. Although this is essentially correct, it was already apparent that it wouldn't be appropriate to repeat the same pattern all the way around the building. The angular plan and complex massing means that existing buildings and the project itself will cause varied overshadowing around the site; and then there is the question of each façade's

**Fig 2 Concept
façade study
and plan**

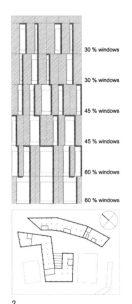

30 % windows

30 % windows

45 % windows

45 % windows

60 % windows

60 % windows

2

Fig 1 Computer-generated image: from Woodhouse Lane looking north

Fig 3 Sketch models (1:500) with the Excel spreadsheets applied as façades

Fig 4 Spreadsheets for two facets of the façade, showing progression of the analysis: (1a) glazing percentages required to achieve three per cent average daylight factor for each module of the façade; (1b) maximum glazing percentages possible without overheating; (2) daylighting versus overheating, and the need for solar glass; (3) final glazing ratios determined as a composite of the preceding analysis

aspect in relation to the sun. All the research, analysis and programming described below is a consequence of the team's desire to test this initial intuition, and a willingness to go where the results took the design.

The light levels within a naturally lit space will fluctuate depending on how bright it is outside, so the light level is normally expressed as a percentage ratio between the internal 'illuminance' and that available outside from an unobstructed sky. This is called the 'daylight factor' but it is an attribute of a particular point in space only; a more commonly used quantity is the 'average daylight factor', taken across the whole room horizontally at desk level. Recommendations vary, but less than two per cent is likely to require artificial lighting and five per cent is likely to be perceived as very well lit.

Based on analysis of a typical section through the building, some preliminary calculations were made for achievable daylight factors and a target of three per cent was agreed as a balance between providing natural light, avoiding overheating (which

is discussed later) and the general solidity of the building's appearance. An initial analysis of the amount of glazing needed on different floors and in different façades to achieve a three per cent average daylight factor confirmed that there was often more variation around the building than there was vertically. The vertical gradation in the percentage of glazing needed was only evident on areas of the façade in close proximity to other buildings. Since the team was keen to progress the façade design on this basis, more detailed data on overshadowing was commissioned from Paul Littlefair of the UK's Building Research Establishment (BRE). This data gave us a 'ø' value (which is a measure of the area of sky from which a window can receive light) for every 1.5 metre module on every floor of the building, from which it was possible to calculate the optimum percentage of glazing for that module. This data in Excel spreadsheets was colour coded and applied as a scaled façade to a 1:500 model to allow us to see more clearly what was going on (figures 3 and 4).

Providing natural lighting to spaces is always

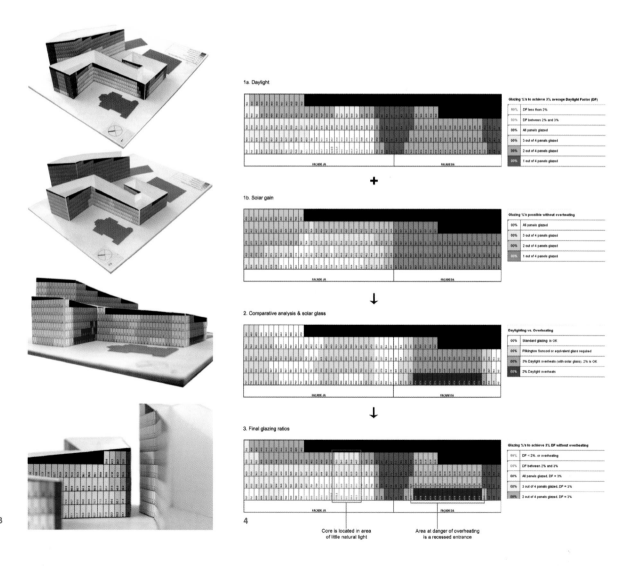

3

4

1a. Daylight

	Glazing %'s to achieve 3% average Daylight Factor (DF)
00%	DF less than 2%
00%	DF between 2% and 3%
00%	All panels glazed
00%	3 out of 4 panels glazed
00%	2 out of 4 panels glazed
00%	1 out of 4 panels glazed

FAÇADE JA   FAÇADE DA

+

1b. Solar gain

	Glazing %'s possible without overheating
00%	All panels glazed
00%	3 out of 4 panels glazed
00%	2 out of 4 panels glazed
00%	1 out of 4 panels glazed

FAÇADE JA   FAÇADE DA

↓

2. Comparative analysis & solar glass

	Daylighting vs. Overheating
00%	Standard glazing is OK
00%	Pilkington Suncool or equivalent glass required
00%	3% Daylight overheats (with solar glass). 2% is OK
00%	2% Daylight overheats

FAÇADE JA   FAÇADE DA

↓

3. Final glazing ratios

	Glazing %'s to achieve 3% DF without overheating
00%	DF < 2%, or overheating
00%	DF between 2% and 3%
00%	All panels glazed, DF = 3%
00%	3 out of 4 panels glazed, DF = 3%
00%	2 out of 4 panels glazed, DF = 3%

FAÇADE JA   FAÇADE DA

Core is located in area of little natural light

Area at danger of overheating is a recessed entrance

THE DAYLIGHT-OPTIMISED FAÇADE.
ANDREW MACINTOSH
AND RICHARD PRIEST,
FEILDEN CLEGG
BRADLEY STUDIOS

Fig 5 Creation and development of the façades: (3) final glazing ratios determined as a composite of the preceding analysis; (4) computer-generated façade; (5) manual adjustments to accommodate cores, entrances and plant area, and to allow for fixing of the panels; (6) the finished façade after a finer grain has been applied

3. Final glazing ratios

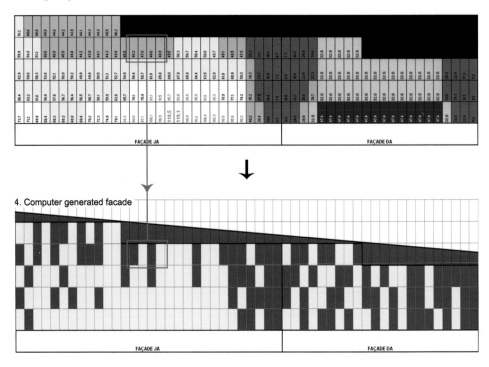

4. Computer generated facade

5. Facade adjustments

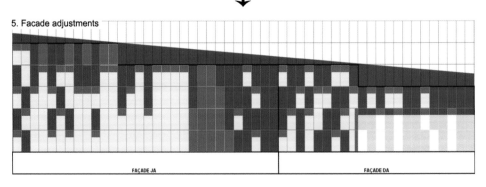

6. Final facade

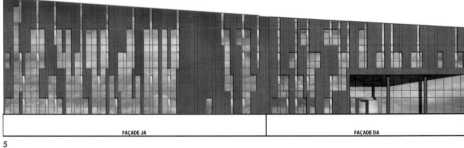

Fig 6 North-west elevation of the project in context

twinned with the danger of overheating them. This problem was addressed by conducting a similar study of the maximum area of glazing that would be possible without overheating. For the Leeds area, Part L of the UK building code recommends limiting heat gains to 41 watts per square metre of floor area (counting only floor area within 6 metres of the façade); 21 watts per square metre were assumed for internal gains, leaving a maximum of 20 watts for solar gain. Detailed data for this was also provided by Paul Littlefair and once again converted into a coloured spreadsheet to visualise the effects. Because these results are dependent on orientation as well as overshadowing from buildings, they exhibit a slightly different pattern from the first model (figure 4:1a Daylight; 4.1b Solar gain). Comparison of the two datasets showed that substantial areas of the building could not allow the desired level of daylighting without overheating. Luckily there was a relatively straightforward solution to most of the problems in the form of solar glass. Solar glass allows only around 40 per cent of solar heat to pass through the glass (compared to around 70 per cent for more typical double glazing). By using this where required, it was possible to keep the required glazing levels around most of the building. Where a conflict remained, considerations of overheating took precedence. A section of façade was colour-coded (figure 4.2): white for regular glazing, green for solar glazing, and pink and red where the level of natural light has to be reduced to avoid overheating. This was considered a problem if the resulting average daylight factor was below

two per cent, but all areas where this occurred could be used for non-work space such as access cores, plant or entrances.

So far, all of the calculations and analysis had been performed using Excel spreadsheets. The task now was to convert all this hard data back into a façade design. This was done by means of a Visual Basic for Applications (VBA) program within Excel, developed using in-house computing expertise. This was chosen in preference to a stand-alone application, as the latter would require more extensive programming and the work might never be re-used. Making this decision also meant that any solution produced must be easily imported into other applications such as MicroStation (the practice's primary CAD package).

The algorithm is a set of recursive conditional statements, making weighted decisions based on the numerical daylighting analysis and its design, at its current iteration. User-defined variables add easy control of how the algorithm responds to the changing design requirements. The algorithm splits the façade up into groups of four 1.5 metre modules. Each group is then averaged to get the amount of glazing required for that section of the building, and assigned a number of glazed panels accordingly (figure 5), which are randomly placed by the program. This process is then repeated for each group of modules all the way around the building. The randomised placing was refined further for aesthetic rather than scientific reasons because the intention was that

THE DAYLIGHT-OPTIMISED FAÇADE.
ANDREW MACINTOSH AND RICHARD PRIEST, FEILDEN CLEGG BRADLEY STUDIOS

the Corten – generally denser at the top of the building – would look as if it were dripping down the sides of the building, thinning out as it went. In order to assist with this, the algorithm produced a weighted decision to arrange the solid and glazed modules based on the surrounding panels, so that the probability of placing solid panels below or diagonally below other solid panels was increased. This created links between the solid panels at the top of the façade and those further down, creating the appearance of the Corten 'dripping' down the façade. This was all executed with a single button within Excel, meaning that lots of options could be

created very rapidly and a preferred one selected.

The façade design was adjusted manually to accommodate non-standard areas such as plant, cores and entrances. The detailed issue of fixing the Corten panels back to the slab meant that each solid panel had to over-sail the slab below, thereby connecting the runs of Corten and reducing unnecessary areas of glazing. Final manual adjustments were made to give a finer grain (figures 5, 6, 7 and 8). Before doing this, the results were cross-checked with the original figures to see whether the computer program had rounded the glazing area up or down. Where possible, half-

Fig 7 Computer-generated image: from Woodhouse Lane looking south

panels were added or subtracted according to this logic, while in the process allowing some aesthetic freedom to adjust the appearance of the façades.

Although it could have been possible to link the algorithm within Excel direct to MicroStation to initiate the drawing, using cells made it quick to achieve this manually, and time pressures meant we opted for the safer route. As a progression of these ideas, the radiosity renderer Maxwell has been used to simulate the amount of daylight illuminating the proposed façades on another project. Renderings were made throughout a 24-hour period during summer and winter

solstices, effectively giving a year-round analysis. A stand-alone program was then built to analyse the brightness of these compiled renderings. The results from this experiment were successful in that they mirrored the results of daylighting analysis by the BRE and therefore provide a way of undertaking the whole analysis without external help.

Andrew Macintosh is an architectural assistant and Richard Priest is an architectural software engineer, both at Feilden Clegg Bradley Architects.

Fig 8 Computer-generated image: view of the north entrance into the site

STRUCTURAL
FIRE MODELLING.
BARBARA LANE,
ARUP

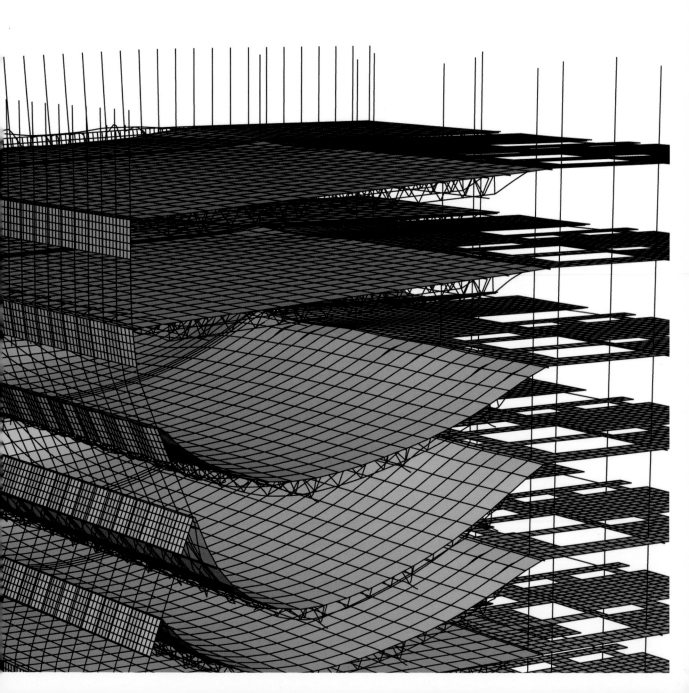

STRUCTURAL FIRE MODELLING.
BARBARA LANE,
ARUP

Buildings are complicated three-dimensional objects. The history of structural design has been a progression in techniques that allow the problem of evaluating the response of a structure under specific load cases (wind, snow, earthquake, people, storage, etc.) to be simplified. Advanced computer analysis is merely the latest technique available to the designers of buildings. When designers now contemplate the effect of fire on structural response, however, the problem becomes even more complex; a fire in a typical office building can easily reach 800°C. At this level of heat the response of materials (such as steel and concrete) is to weaken and, of considerable importance, they also expand. Heating structural members to this degree therefore reduces their ability to resist the existing load due to degrading strength and stiffness; at the same time fire introduces new loads as a result of the expansion. It was these mechanisms that were behind the recent collapse of high-profile buildings such as the World Trade Center towers in New York (figure 1) and Torre Windsor in Madrid.

The complexity of fire loading when contemplated within a three-dimensional framework makes it extremely difficult to calculate the structural response using traditional simplified design

equations. In fact, very few such representations exist for the fire case. Therefore the current approach is to use finite element modelling (FEM) software, which allows the direct evaluation of the full-frame structural response to fire. This is particularly useful when considering tall or unique buildings where structural efficiency is maximised and the consequences of collapse are unacceptable.

Structural fire modelling also provides the designer with a visual representation of the whole building, which proves very useful in the approvals process – while gaining the support and understanding of the statutory authorities (the 'authorities having jurisdiction'), the client and the rest of the design team. Overall this leads to a more efficient building design.

Structural fire design

The aim of structural fire engineering is to ensure that a building will not collapse when subjected to a reasonable 'worst case' fire scenario. The structural response is quantified in this scenario and evaluated against a number of agreed performance criteria; alterations to the design are proposed where behaviours of concern occur,

Fig 1 Modelling collapse of the World Trade Center, New York

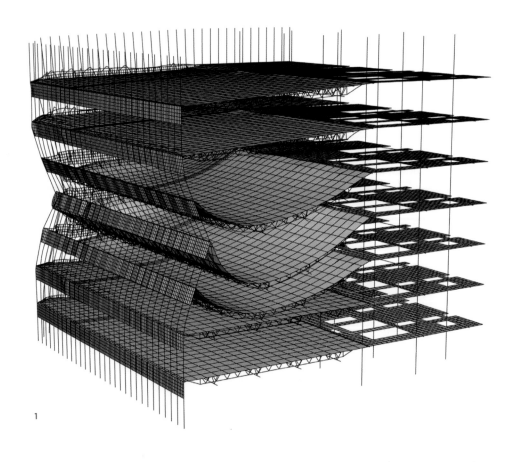

1

or the design is optimised where enhanced behaviours are observed. As the typical approach to protecting structures against fire is to apply fire-rated material to steel structures, or increase thicknesses for concrete structures, any form of optimisation brings with it an associated cost saving. In addition, anywhere that safety can be relied on without the application of additional materials means a more robust solution as it is not reliant on continual maintenance and reapplication.

By using 3-D modelling it is now possible to quantify where a refined fire protection strategy is possible, or to create forms that are inherently more robust in a fire situation. This is a major departure from standard code-compliant design, and brings with it a greater level of robustness.

In the future, as available computing power increases and techniques are refined, it is anticipated that structural fire design will become part of the normal design process – possibly represented by simplified design methods like those drawn up for other complex load cases, such as wind and earthquake loading. Commercial structural modelling projects produce typical results (figures 2 and 3).

Software

There are a number of commercial and research FEM programs available. Due to the complexity of the problem, the program must be capable of calculating non-linear geometries. The modelling program must also be able to handle materials that are non-linear (i.e. allow plastic deformations) and temperature dependent. Arup uses ABAQUS FEM software, a commercially available, general-purpose FEM program with the capability of modelling a wide range of situations. There are versions of the software capable of running on most major hardware platforms and all versions are capable of using multiple processors.

The advantage of using commercial FEM software is that it is already extensively tested. Moreover, these programs are developed to such an extent to allow an engineer to focus on the issues related to the physical problem and detach from the underlying mathematical and computing complexity. ABAQUS models are based on an input file that is acted on by the program. The input fire can be constructed manually using a text editor or graphically using a dedicated graphical user interface. It is possible to come across a problem that cannot be solved using

Fig 2 Column and cellular beam response (part of larger model)
Fig 3 Partial floor structural model

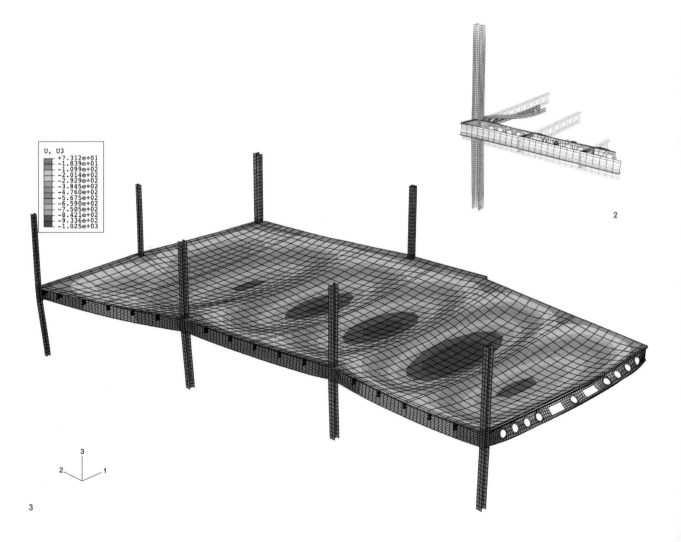

U, U3
+7.312e+01
−1.839e+01
−1.099e+02
−2.014e+02
−2.929e+02
−3.845e+02
−4.760e+02
−5.675e+02
−6.590e+02
−7.505e+02
−8.421e+02
−9.336e+02
−1.025e+03

2

3
2 — 1

STRUCTURAL FIRE MODELLING.
BARBARA LANE,
ARUP

the available tools within a standard FEM program; to get around this, ABAQUS allows the engineer to create user-defined modules that can be used with the main program (figure 3).

Method

A typical structural fire investigation is conducted over four stages:

- **Design fire**: This stage calculates a representative worst-case fire in the building. There are a number of methods available to evaluate the design fire, ranging from following the international 'standard fire' approximations through simple calculation methods to advanced 3D computational fluid dynamics modelling.

- **Heat transfer**: The effect of the fire on the structure is effectively based on the temperatures attained in individual members. This stage takes into account the fire protection applied to the structure and creates a set of thermal loads for each member over the duration of the design fire.

- **Mechanical assessment of structure**: The thermal load curves calculated during the previous stage are applied to the structural model. The response of the model is compared to appropriate performance criteria, generally defined in terms of structural stability and the effect on those elements designed to resist fire spread – floors and walls.

- **Mitigation measures**: these are proposed where needed to resolve poor performance. They include optimisation such as the removal of fire protection or the refinement of section sizes based on enhanced performance.

All stages must be presented and agreed with the authorities having jurisdiction to ensure a successful outcome.

All this is based on the creation of a representative model of the building. It is therefore necessary for the modeller to thoroughly understand how the building structure works under normal loading at ambient temperature. Additionally, an appreciation of the use of the building is needed to indicate the worst-case areas in terms of fire load. Close cooperation is required at this stage between the modelling team and the structural engineer. A significant amount of information is required to create a realistic representation of the structure for analysis, including structural layout, member

Fig 4 Multi-storey structural model mesh

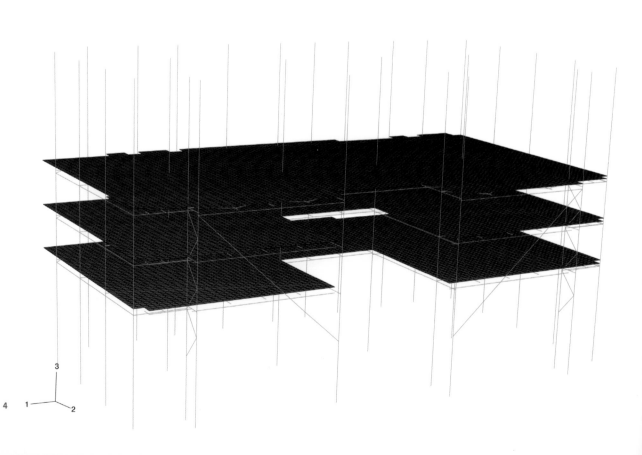

sizes, loads and load patterns, steel and concrete strengths, and so on.

Typically the area to be modelled is chosen as a representative 'worst case' including the least robust features of the building. In some cases it is necessary to model a number of areas in order to fully understand the response of a building.

Case study

A 42-storey office tower is to be built in the City of London. One of the main architectural features of the building is the inclusion of multiple three-storey atria over the full height of the building (figure 4). This allows a number of floors to be connected into a single fire compartment, leading to the possibility of a multi-storey fire. This is not normally considered under UK building regulations and hence required advanced computer analysis. The structure consists of a robust tube structure, designed to resist wind and gravity loading, surrounding composite steel-framed floors.

In a typical design all members in the case study building would require 120-minute protection. The concept behind the proposed design was to increase structural efficiency without compromising building safety. This was achieved by lowering the general level of protection to a 90-minute rating and leaving a significant number of secondary beams unprotected. The case study was evaluated against a design fire assumed to affect office areas simultaneously over three floors. The results of the model indicated that stability was maintained throughout the design fire, including at maximum deflection (figure 5). Similarly, it was shown that horizontal and vertical compartmentation were maintained (wall and floor systems created to prevent the horizontal and vertical spread of fire).

Due to the complexity of the building's response to a multi-storey fire it would be impossible to evaluate a structure to the required level of detail using simple calculation methods. Using a 3-D model meant that a number of similar scenarios could be analysed in a relatively short time, allowing the design to be refined. In addition, the output of the model could be presented in terms of animations and contour plots overlaid on the model geometry. This allowed the results to be presented in a clear and concise format.

Barbara Lane is an associate director at Arup Fire.

Fig 5 Multi-storey model, final vertical deflections

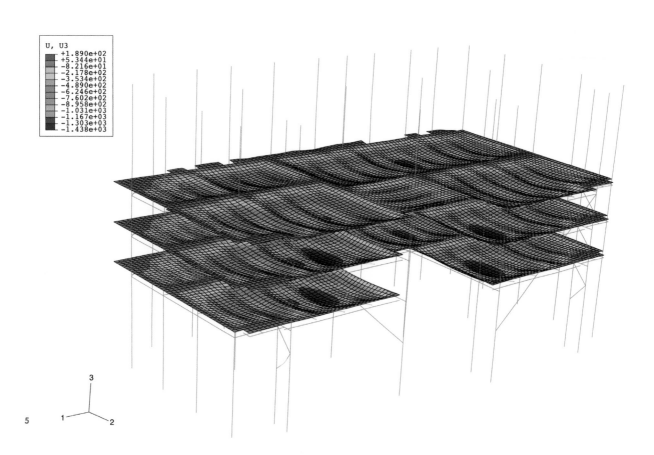

COMPUTER MODELLING
EVACUATION SCENARIOS.
DAVID STOW,
ARUP

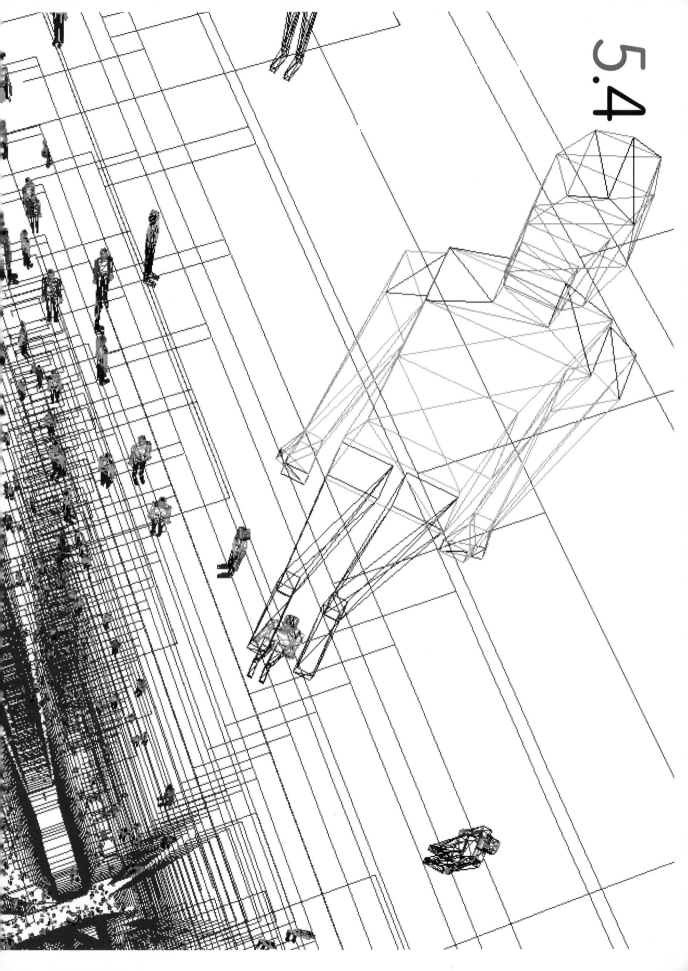

5.4

162 COMPUTER
MODELLING
EVACUATION
SCENARIOS.
DAVID STOW,
ARUP

The layouts of stairs and exits in buildings are typically designed in accordance with published fire safety guidance documents. It is assumed that those escape provisions would perform adequately if there was ever a need to evacuate a building. However, this can be tested only once the building has been completed, leaving it too late for changes to be made to the design.

In some buildings, there is often a desire to test whether the building will perform adequately before it is completed, enabling the layout to be altered during the design phase. An example of this might be a large, complex building where there are a large number of occupants and a variety of different escape routes available. To investigate this, computer-based 3-D evacuation programs can be used to build up a virtual model of a building, and to see how occupants are likely to move through it in an evacuation.

By using evacuation models, a range of design options can be tested to determine the most effective layout and assess where problems may occur, such as excessive queuing, bottlenecks and blockages. Evacuation models can also be used to determine how a building will perform as a whole during an evacuation, for example by enabling the evacuation time from specific areas or from the whole building to be assessed. This information, when presented in a user-friendly graphical form, can be a very powerful tool in explaining concepts or complex design issues to clients, approving authorities, end users and so on.

Evacuation models

There are a number of evacuation models available, including Exodus, Simulex and STEPS. Earlier models tended to rely on a 2-D visualisation of a building, with the user looking down on the model in plan form. As the models became more sophisticated, a more user-friendly 3-D interface was developed to enable the building and evacuation to be viewed from a number of different angles.

Evacuation programs typically take the form of grid-based or agent-based models. Grid-based models divide the design into a number of cells, with occupants being able to move into a cell only if it is not blocked either by another occupant or by the building form itself. Agent-based models calculate the movement of each occupant and their interaction with the space around them, rather than just with the cells surrounding them.

STEPS (Simulation of Transient Evacuation and Pedestrian MovementS) is one of the most recent models to be developed. The program originates from the design of transportation systems, in particular underground rail stations and interchanges, and can be used for the prediction of pedestrian movement under both normal and emergency conditions. STEPS uses 3-D visualisation techniques to produce detailed, real-time simulations that may be easily interpreted. To initialise STEPS, the user must first define the building's geometry based on imported CAD files. Multiple levels in a building are then connected by user-defined stairs, as appropriate to the building design. Exits are added that either take people out of the simulation (a system exit) or transport them from one plane to another (a plane exit). Stairs are defined as planes in the model, thus exits must be used to connect a floor plane with a stair plane. Each plane in the building is then automatically broken up by the software into discrete square cells of a user-defined dimension.

The building's occupants can be given characteristics that affect their movement, such as size, travel speed, patience, group affiliations and awareness of specific exits. STEPS uses the occupants' characteristics, coupled with the defined geometry, to determine how each individual will move. Crowd movement is simply the collective result of each individual's behaviour as they move from one cell to the next. When the simulation is initiated, 'people' move towards exits from the plane they are on, until they ultimately reach a system exit. Cells through which building features pass are referred to as 'blockages' and these will not allow occupants to pass through them. Equally, if one person is in a cell, it is not available for others to move into. People will move at their defined travel speed (which can be set at different values for specific planes for a given individual or group) to the next cell, if it is available, on the way to an exit. If a cell is blocked, an alternate route is taken if possible, otherwise people will begin to queue. The patience level may result in people looking for alternative exits. Generally, each individual will try to get out as fast as possible.

Application

Most tall buildings in the UK use a phased evacuation regime as the basis of their design, meaning that in the event of a fire only those people immediately at risk in the building would be evacuated initially. This typically includes all occupants on the fire floor and the floor above, and any occupants with reduced mobility elsewhere in the building. All other occupants would be alerted to the incident but would be told to remain in the building until such time that the building management team or the fire brigade deemed it necessary to evacuate them. By implementing a phased evacuation regime, it is possible to reduce the number of stairs required in a building because of the limited number of occupants who would be escaping at any one time. If simultaneous evacuation were used, more stairs would likely be needed to cope with the additional escaping occupants in order to comply with the life safety requirements of the UK Building Regulations.

Fig 1 Section of the Leadenhall Building, showing the approximate distribution of people within the tower

In the light of the terrorist incidents that occurred at the beginning of this century, there has been a heightened level of security at most high-profile sites, and occupant evacuation from high-rise buildings was brought to the forefront of people's attention. The fundamental principles underpinning phased evacuation for fire situations were suddenly questioned as to whether they were appropriate for a non-fire or 'extreme' event such as a terrorist attack. Under the UK Building Regulations, buildings have to be designed to withstand fires; furthermore, measures are put in place to prevent the spread of fire and protect escape routes from heat and toxic gases. There is no similar requirement for buildings to withstand an extreme event, where there may be a greater threat posed to a greater number of occupants.

Although not a Building Regulations issue, the owners, operators and occupiers of tall buildings have begun to query whether, in the event of a terrorist attack on their building, they would be able to evacuate people safely in a reasonable period of time. To assess this, it might have been possible to carry out hand calculations using mathematical formulae based on the width of the stairs, the number of floors served and the number of occupants entering the stairs at each level. However, a computer-based 3-D evacuation model such as STEPS can deliver more accurate results by taking into account the effect of merging flows and the interaction of occupants, and allows a greater range of scenarios to be assessed.

The Leadenhall Building

The Leadenhall Building is a high-rise office tower designed by Rogers Stirk Harbour + Partners (formerly the Richard Rogers Partnership) for British Land. The building is to be situated at 122 Leadenhall Street in the City of London and will provide more than 40 floors of office accommodation (figure 1). As a high-profile building in London's financial district, it was considered that a threat existed of an extreme event occurring either at the building or in the area immediately surrounding it. As such, it was queried whether the design of the building would allow all occupants to safely evacuate in a reasonable period of time, or whether the design may need to be altered in some way in order to achieve this.

As the simultaneous evacuation of all levels would not need to be assessed as part of the normal design of this type of building, it was decided to model this scenario using STEPS. The model was set up by importing all floor plates from the CAD model, with the two main 1,200mm-wide stair cores inserted at opposite sides of the building linking each level with the ground floor (figure 2). Once the occupant numbers had been estimated and inserted and their characteristics defined, the model was run to assess where problems might

164 COMPUTER
MODELLING
EVACUATION
SCENARIOS.
DAVID STOW,
ARUP

lie on each floor and determine the time for all occupants to escape.

Because the stairs had been designed for phased evacuation, there were significantly more occupants attempting to use the stairs than would normally be assumed. This quickly resulted in the stairs becoming crowded, although they still allowed a reasonable evacuation time of approximately 30 minutes, without excessive queuing occurring for occupants to leave each floor (figure 3). In the absence of any published guidance on this issue, 30 minutes was deemed reasonable, considering the height of the building and the number of occupants. It also compared favourably to full-scale evacuations that had previously been carried out in similarly sized buildings in London.

Because the modelling was to represent an imminent extreme event, the model was also run with occupants using the lifts to evacuate (figure 4). Lifts are not commonly used for the evacuation of occupants during fire, because of the risk of a loss of power and control. Lifts that are specifically designed to resist the effects of fire are often used to assist fire-fighting operations in a building, and these could also be used for the evacuation of disabled occupants. However, in modelling an extreme event, there could be no reason why the

passenger lifts would not be used by all occupants, as long as adequate lift control procedures could be put in place. This is fast becoming integrated in major evacuation strategies for buildings worldwide.

Therefore, the building evacuation model was set up to assess a full building evacuation via the two 1,200mm-wide stairs and via the three lift banks, each containing eight lifts. Each lift bank either served the low-rise, mid-rise or high-rise levels and was designed to run in 'evacuation mode' in STEPS, meaning that they served the highest levels first and, when full, would not stop at any other levels until they reached the ground floor. Because it could only be estimated what proportion of occupants would use the stairs compared to the lifts, three scenarios were assessed: in percentage terms, 25/75 in favour of the stairs; 50/50; and 75/25 in favour of the lifts. In terms of the total evacuation time, it was found that in each scenario all occupants were still able to escape within 30 minutes. When one quarter of the occupants were modelled as using the lifts to evacuate, the total evacuation time was found to be 25 minutes. This reduced to just over 20 minutes when three quarters of occupants were modelled as using the lifts to evacuate.

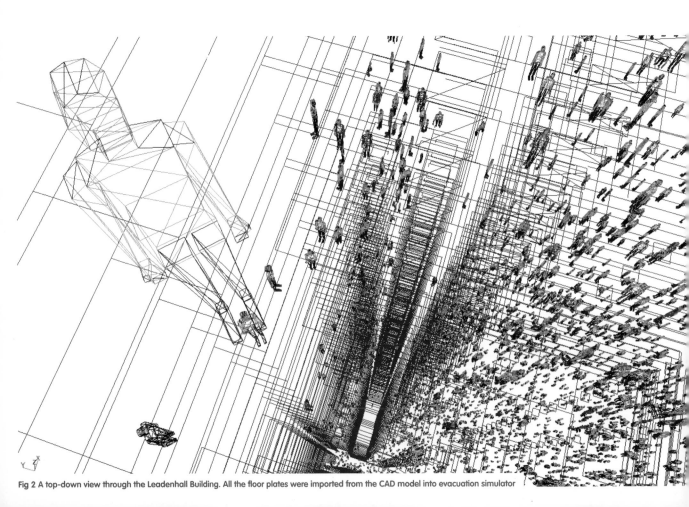

Fig 2 A top-down view through the Leadenhall Building. All the floor plates were imported from the CAD model into evacuation simulator

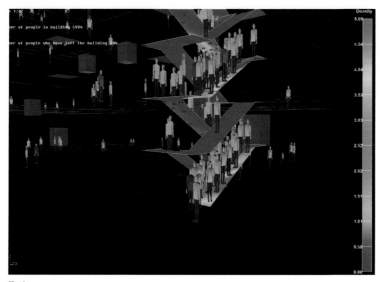

Fig 4

STEPS modelling makes it possible to demonstrate that a total building evacuation could be achieved in a reasonable period of time, with no excessive queuing, bottlenecking or other major problems affecting the means of escape. The evacuation time could be significantly improved if the lifts were also used, but it was demonstrated that this was not essential to achieve a reasonable evacuation time. By carrying out the assessment with a computer-based 3-D evacuation model, the results could be presented to the client and design team in a clear, user-friendly form. Key areas of the evacuation could be focused on and presented as 3-D still images in a report of the study. Separate video clips were also produced showing the evacuation in both real-time and speeded up. This format was very useful for the client to subsequently present to different user groups in the building.

David Stow is a Senior Fire Engineer with Arup.

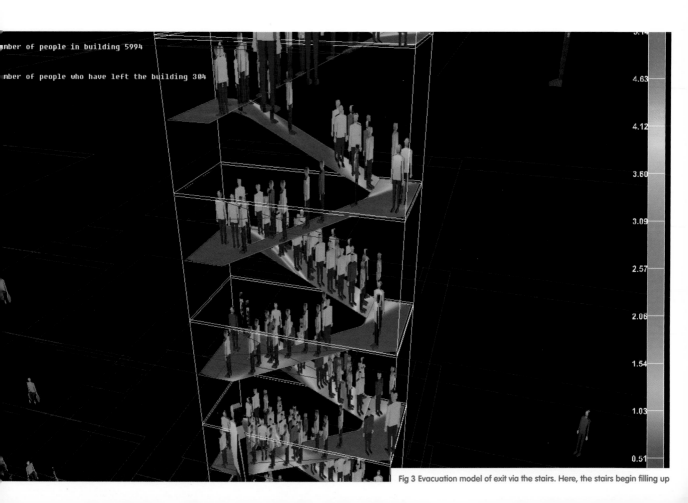

Fig 3 Evacuation model of exit via the stairs. Here, the stairs begin filling up

69

COLLABORATION – SHARING THE DIGITAL MODEL

Collaboration provides a 'dimension' to 3-D computer modelling which, if unexplored, leaves architectural computing an incomplete resource. Collaboration – whether manifested in file-sharing, interoperability, the building information model or anything else – lies at the rather prosaic, workaday end of digital modelling. But it underpins all the analysis, simulation, testing and fabrication described elsewhere in this book. Without any sense of the art of collaboration, the complex and wonderful 3-D model sitting within a hard drive would be ripe with possibility but little else. Proper collaboration requires planning and discipline, but the benefits are considerable: less risk, less error, more certainty and more capability.

INTEROPERABILITY
AND COLLABORATION.
BOB DALZIEL,
3DREID ARCHITECTS

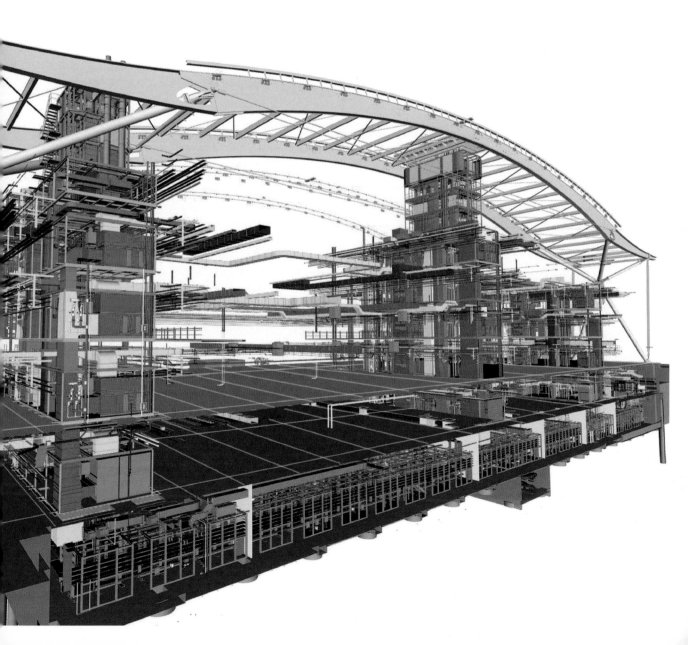

The power of intelligent modelling to simulate building performance (i.e. structural, environmental, constructional and cost performance) is beginning to be realised. From this early work emerges the prospect that a design team representing a variety of disciplines and skills could in future create and operate on a single shared intelligent data structure, rather than on discrete fragments and multiple versions of a project model. I say in future, because the instances of projects in which true integration of parametric inputs from disparate team members have been achieved are rare indeed. It is natural that the art will be advanced by breakthroughs in pockets of the industry, but the potential for innovative, responsive and holistic architecture arising from the application of these advances will not be realised until the contributions of an entire team can be synthesised.

Full collaboration in architecture and building using intelligent modelling, between detached team members, has been an ideal discussed for many years. But the necessary infrastructure to support the concept (the processing power, the appropriate object-oriented and interoperable software, the existence of reliable extranets and the required bandwidth) has only recently become available. We are at a turning point, however, when all of these components exist and are accessible by ordinary practitioners, and for the first time the ideal is really achievable.

To date, the contribution by architects to this enterprise has been somewhat peripheral because their focus on using three-dimensional tools has generally been on the appearance of buildings rather than on their performance. However, recent work by architects and architectural students at, for example, the Architectural Association (AA) and within the Bentley-sponsored SmartGeometry Group suggests there is the seed of a new generation of architects who are fascinated with the power of computing to generate and evaluate form as well as simulate its appearance. Achim Menges, Michael Hensel and Michael Weinstock at the AA say that: 'Rather than being wilful and arbitrary, even the most complex geometry could provide a formal resolution of competing forces and requirements, and could suggest and resolve both structural efficiency and environmental sensitivity.' However, they add, 'advanced material and morphogenetic design techniques call for a higher-level of methodological integration. This poses a major challenge for the next generation of multidisciplinary architectural research and projects. The collaborative task encompasses the striving for an integrated set of design methods, generative and analytical tools and enabling technologies.'

This task has been addressed in different ways and to different degrees in the five case studies described below. No single project can yet be said to represent the optimum or even the fully-realised infrastructure to successfully enable this kind of collaborative working. But each study illustrates an aspect of the problem and provides an indication of future directions and solutions.

One could describe the various software and hardware structures and methods that have been employed to enable this collaboration as 'components'. These components have been used to varying degrees and in different combinations in each of the case studies described in this chapter. The components include:

- **Use of data exchange standards**: simple rules are introduced about the scale, orientation and point of origin of drawing files. Agreement is reached on level and layering conventions, line definitions and notation. These conventions enable team members to exchange working files smoothly without the need to redraw, restructure or heavily amend them, and without significant loss of information.

- **Use of extranets or ftp (file transfer protocol) servers**: data generated by members of a team is stored in a structured way on servers accessible to all designated members of the team. In some cases the ftp server is merely an unmanaged repository providing space for the uploading and downloading of working files. But extranet structuring can include facilities for data tracking which monitor use and provide alerts and red-lining facilities to users.

- **Use of model files**: design information files, representing different elements and subsystems, generated by different contributors, are combined to form a model of the entire project. This is quite different from the common practice of attaching fragments of drawing files from other sources to use as an underlay for subsequent work. Variously referred to as the Building Information Model (BIM) or the Single Model Environment, this approach can be implemented using 2-D and/or 3-D files, but the essential feature is that the files are live (not pdf or plot files), that they interlock to form a whole, and that they represent the most recent iteration of each team player's work.

- **Use of 3-D model files**: many CAD platforms now include object-based products that permit the creation of 3-D models composed of discrete elements, each of which has attributes. Geometry is one of these attributes, but others such as strength, weight, thermal performance and cost can be appended. BIMs composed of such objects can therefore be interrogated in a variety of ways, including the viewing of appearance (both orthographically and in perspective), but also in terms of physical clashing of elements or in terms of a proposal's performance from a structural, thermal or cost perspective. The use of 3-D object files in a BIM offers self-evident benefits, but it requires great rigour in the adherence to collaborative data exchange standards. To address this problem, the international organisation BuildingSmart, formerly the IAI, has established a basis for the definition of interoperable objects called Industry Foundation Classes (IFCs) which can be read from within all common CAD platforms. Also, an integrated 3-D BIM can only really work when all the principal partners in the enterprise are able and prepared to work in this way.

- **Use of parametric objects**: a parameter is a measurement or value on which something else depends. Objects which obey rule systems in relation to each other are referred to as parametric objects. These objects can maintain consistent relationships between themselves as the overall model is manipulated. For example, in a parametric building model, if the pitch of the roof is changed, the walls automatically follow the revised roof-line.

Case Study 1:
Heathrow Terminal 5

Richard Rogers Partnership (now called Rogers Stirk Harbour + Partners) won the competition to design Terminal 5 (T5) in 1989, so the long gestation period for the project has run very much in parallel with the uptake of computer-aided design in architectural practice generally. The early work was all hand-drawn, but Intergraph was gradually introduced for two-dimensional layouts. Some simple exploratory modelling work was done in Modelshop. Digital files were swapped with structural engineer Arup, but initially there was no extranet facility.

RRP was the concept designer for the project, and the team eventually grew to include five principal architectural practices (RRP plus Pascall & Watson, HOK, Chapman Taylor and YRM) and three engineering practices: Arup (structural), DSSR (M&E) and Mott MacDonald (below-ground work). There was also a vast array of managers, subcontractors and suppliers, and an estimated turnover of 25 per cent of staff annually. So the need for consistent and coordinated information exchange became very apparent.

In 1996 the British Airports Authority (BAA) set ambitious targets for the project in respect of design integration and the use of 3-D modelling. The methods and standards employed had grown out of the successful work advanced by Mervyn Richards at Laing Technology for the Heathrow Express Project. In the absence of effective interoperable protocols, it was insisted that all players work in AutoCAD (and eventually ADT), and that the entire core team of several hundred people should be co-located at Longford House near the site. The emphasis on co-location was partly cultural, but also reflected the fact that internet bandwidths then available could not have coped with the quantity and size of files being generated.

In terms of the components of collaboration mentioned above, the project was an early pathfinder because it did use rigorous data exchange standards, it did use managed centralised servers and it did use model files to create a Single Model Environment (or BIM,

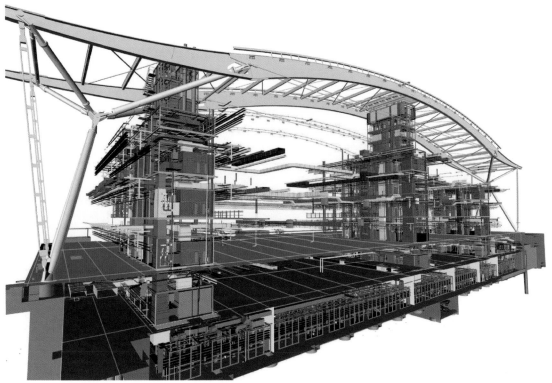

Fig 1 Terminal 5, Heathrow: envelope and services coordination

INTEROPERABILITY
AND COLLABORATION.
BOB DALZIEL,
3DREID ARCHITECTS

see figure 1). Steve Martin, one of RRP's leading architects on the project, remarked that it was often impossible to say who the single author of a drawing was because each drawing represented the active contributions of many players. This is an important characteristic of a true BIM and it is difficult to achieve unless there is some form of global professional liability insurance in place for the project or, as is the case with BAA, there is an explicit no-blame culture that effectively eliminates design-related litigation.

In this project the focus was on efficient digital communication across this extensive professional and construction team, and on the removal of conflicts in geometry rather than on true parametric design. However, there was a limited application of collaborative computer-integrated manufacture involving RRP, Arup and steelwork manufacturer Severfield-Rowen Structures (figure 2). The roof support structure was designed and visualised in 3-D by RRP, checked for structural efficiency by Arup and the design software (Rhino) was then used to drive the fabrication machinery that created the structural elements.

Arup was also involved as coordinator in so-called 4-D planning (figure 3) on a particularly complicated part of the project at the interface of three sub-projects. This was a work-planning process that added time as a fourth dimension to 3-D modelling, creating a real-time graphical simulation of the execution of planned work.

While T5 fell short of a full implementation of all five of the components available for true collaboration using intelligent 3-D modelling, it did give birth to new collaborative standards and processes of a quality that had not previously existed in the industry, and these are soon to become the core of new British Standards for CAD. A DTI-funded organisation called Avanti, spearheaded by the Reading University Construction Forum and by Constructing Excellence, reformatted and rebranded these techniques in 2003; Avanti has since been offering them to project teams in the industry together with expert advice on implementation, with considerable success. BS 1192: 2007, covering both 2-D and 3-D working, will contain 'normative' or recommended standards, and will also explain the suggested methods of working collaboratively using model files.

Fig 2 T5,
clockwise, from
top left: architect's
model; casting
manufacturer's
simulation model;
half-scale physical
prototype; castings
on site

Fig 3 T5 Interchange
4-D model – colours
are contractor/
discipline-specific

3

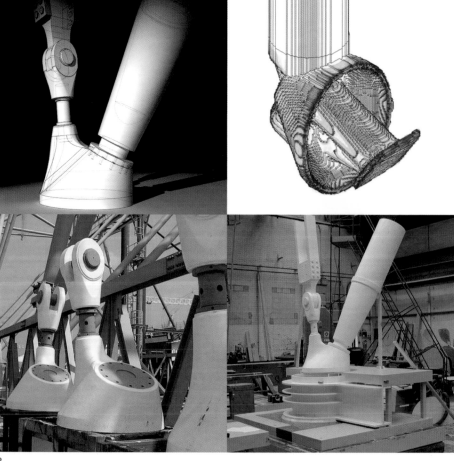

2

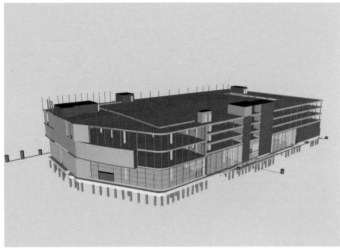

4   5

Fig 4 Enfield town
centre: render of
proposal

Fig 5 Enfield: Tru-
Axis coordination
model

Case Study 2:
Enfield Town Centre Project, London

One of the first projects to employ these standards, supported by Avanti, was a multi-use development in Enfield, north London, designed by Reid Architecture (figure 4). The scheme is characteristic of recent town centre regeneration initiatives across the UK. Funded by ING, it is £25 million of construction, largely retail/restaurant/heath club uses, but it also includes a civic facility incorporating council offices, a library and a public theatre.

In addition to Reid Architecture, the pre-construction consultancy team included structural engineers Gifford & Partners, M&E engineers Hilson Moran and project managers Tweeds. During the early design stages, concepts and drawings were developed conventionally, with Reid using MicroStation and the remainder of the team using AutoCAD. When Costain was appointed as the main contractor the decision was taken to adopt Avanti standards and operate in a shared model environment. Costain's bespoke extranet ICOSnet was employed and the collaborative model was built using active .dwg files (a native AutoDesk format which can nevertheless be effectively created within MicroStation V8).

Critically, the team exchanged and built on live model files, the orientation, origin point and scaling of which were completely aligned, rather than swapping fragments of digital information, PDFs and/or frame (print) files appended to emails. The process of restructuring the previously completed CAD work to achieve this alignment required considerable concentration and effort but the benefits, according to Reid project architect Neil Sterling, far outweighed the initial irritation. Subsequent coordination of the work of subcontractors, all of whom were obliged to participate in using the system, was vastly simplified. Bourne Steel also used the model data,

together with Revit software, as the basis for its own detailed modelling, which was then employed in the manufacture of the structural frame.

The 3-D expression of the shared model was facilitated, managed and updated by a third-party company employed by Costain called TruAxis (figure 5). They assisted the team with the coordination activity, focusing on 3-D clash detection, but also provided construction sequence simulations that were used by Costain to improve the efficiency of construction programming. The model was also used as the basis for photorealistic renderings for marketing.

Costain claims that very considerable cost savings have been made by adopting a BIM approach. There were also very appreciable benefits experienced by the entire team associated with the clarity, simplicity and efficiency of use of the model for the everyday processes of information gathering, design creation and data exchange. The team estimates that at least 20 weeks were saved in the time needed to prepare information for issue to others.

Enfield, like Heathrow T5, has focused on the application of new standards and methods to untangle, enable and streamline the activities of collaboration without fundamentally changing the nature of collaborative design. In particular, although this is an example of early adoption of BIM, there has been limited use of intelligent modelling and no use of parametric design techniques.

Case Study 3:
Beijing Olympic Stadium

In contrast to the case studies described above, the design and construction of the Beijing National (Olympic) Stadium (figure 6) employed the sophistication of parametric modelling; indeed,

Fig 6 The Beijing Olympic stadium – the 'bird's nest'

HERZOG & DE MEURON

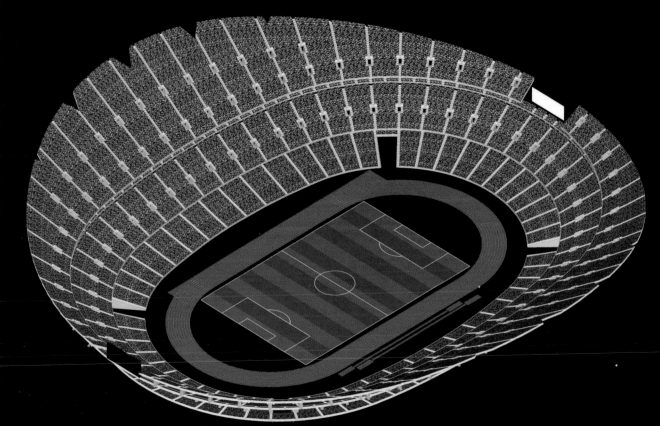
Fig 7 Beijing Olympic stadium: seating bowl parametric model

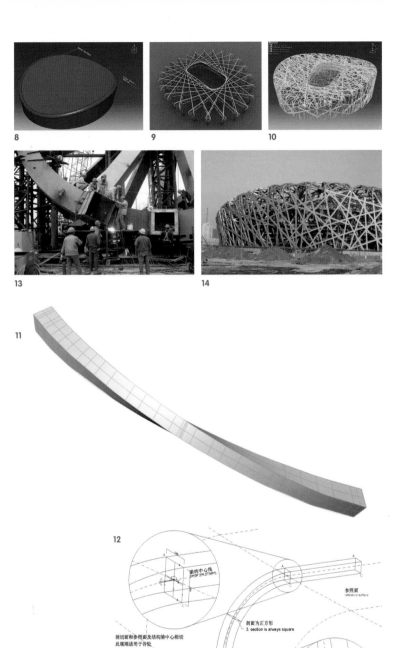

8   **9**   **10**

13   **14**

11

12

Fig 8 Beijing Olympic stadium: outer control-surface model

Fig 9 Beijing Olympic stadium: load-bearing structural model

Fig 10 Beijing Olympic stadium: fully-developed 'bird's nest' model

Fig 11 Beijing Olympic stadium: box-section extracted from Catia model

Fig 12 Beijing Olympic stadium: working drawings exported from Catia model

Figs 13 and 14 Beijing Olympic stadium: site progress, spring 2007

it could not have been realised without it. In fact, the design can be thought of as consisting of one independent parametric model sitting within another.

The inner model controls the seating bowl, created using bespoke software devised by J. Parrish, director of Arup Sport and a long-time proponent of parametric modelling. In the case of the seating bowl, parametric design fixes relationships between seating, supporting terraces and the stadium floor so that the view of any spectator is automatically optimised as a variety of options for bowl geometry are explored (figures 7 and 8). Structural supports for the resulting forms are not necessarily orthogonal. Martin Simpson, the project Associate Director at Arup, commented that even though the final model was exported into AutoCAD for the production of two-dimensional drawings, the geometry of the stadium resulted in very few purely vertical elements, which made the two-dimensional documentation process more complex. Arup also undertook the M&E engineering for the project, so a relatively seamless integration of architecture, structural frame and mechanical engineering was achieved in the complex inner element of the composition.

The outer roof model (figures 9 and 10) contains the now-familiar bird's nest geometry (although the ancient scholar's stone, with its heavily veined surface, is also quoted as a source of inspiration). The two structures, the roof and the bowl, are structurally independent from each other. The bowl is conceived as a series of eight linked segments, whereas the roof is monolithic; this isolation responds to the perceived need to divorce the two structures in case of seismic disturbance.

The architects, Herzog & de Meuron, wished to create a pattern in the surface structure of the roof in which the primary load paths of support could not be distinguished in the composition. The underlying structural concept is highly regular, as is the so-called control surface which defines the outer skin of the roof structure. The primary structure consists of a series of interlocking curved trusses creating a zone a maximum of 12 metres deep. The upper members of the trusses are 1.2 metre square box-section steel beams (figure 11). Interwoven into this structure are secondary box beams of identical cross section (which appear only on the outer surface) and these give the completed structure its organic appearance.

The team used a variety of modelling software products in the early design stages, including Rhino and 3D Studio, and also looked at packages normally used for manufacturing such as Solidworks and ProEngineering, but the final modelling was executed in Catia, which proved to be the only package capable of providing the necessary output for such a complex problem (figure 12). The entire design team, which included

Herzog & de Meuron, Arup and China Architecture and Design Group (CAG), worked on this platform and exchanged files using (unstructured) ftp servers. Catia was able to create the required associations between structural elements so that if the shape or angle of any part of the roof was changed during design development, all of the elements would self-adjust, and all of the box-sections would remain parallel to the outer control surface (itself a complex shape). Catia also enabled Arup to read off the steel thicknesses of the box-beam walls (which varied from beam to beam), and to unravel the beam surfaces into linear strips of complex geometry, demonstrating that they could be cut and welded from plate material. The roof structure model was finally exported to the manufacturer, a ship-builder that used its own in-house software to reproduce this decomposition into strips and, ultimately, to manufacture the sections (figures 13 and 14).

Herzog & de Meuron, Arup and CAG were involved in the first two stages of design, so-called schematic and preliminary design, and CAG then completed the last stage, construction design. This final design stage featured an early application of IFCs. It is likely that the Chinese government will soon adopt this standard as mandatory for future building regulations submissions.

One of the ironies of the project is that the specified deliverables for tender information included a very large number of two-dimensional drawings. These were duly extracted by the consultants from the 3-D model in accordance with the contract. However, the primary source of information relied upon by the contractor, Beijing Urban Construction Group, was not the two-dimensional documentation but the supplementary 3-D coordinate data derived directly from the design model.

Case Study 4: The Water Cube, Beijing

PTW, the Australian architects of the National Swimming Centre for the 2008 Olympics, 'sought to establish a Yin and Yang relationship with the adjacent National Stadium. As a counterpoint to the masculine, totemic image of the National Stadium, the Beijing Aquatic Centre (or Water Cube) appears as serene, emotion-engaging, ethereal and poetic.' The building – a collaboration between PTW, Arup and the China State Construction and Engineering Corporation – is 176 square metres in plan, rising to 31 metres in height (figures 15 and 16).

The surface structure was conceived as an expression of the geometry of soap bubbles. In the words of architect Chris Bosse, part of the PTW design team, this gave 'sophisticated micro details to the monolithic totality'. The scientific basis for the soap-bubble structural system was drawn from the field of theoretical physics. Denis Weaire and Robert Phelan, Irish physicists, were able to calculate that the most efficient way to divide a space into cells of equal volume while minimising the surface area between them was to use a stacked arrangement composed 75 per cent of 14-sided shapes and 25 per cent of 12-sided shapes. This is the fundamental basis for the structure of the building skin, which is composed of 22,000 steel members with 12,000 nodes, sliced to create rectilinear external and internal surfaces (figures 17 and 18), which are then filled with blue-tinted ETFE (ethyltetrafluoroethylene) pillows.

The size and orientation of the cells has been mutated by the architects so that in the finished version there are over 100 distinct shapes. This skeleton provides both primary structure and attachment for the ETFE pillows for the walls and the roof of the building (figures 19 and 20). Within the pillows are foils which can be opened and closed to moderate the amount of solar radiation and natural light entering the interior. The structure, the architecture and the environmental performance of the skin are therefore completely interrelated. In order to manipulate this complex geometric system dynamically, Arup wrote parametric software that

Fig 15 Beijing Aquatic Centre: competition rendering

Fig 16 Beijing Aquatic Centre: 3D Max render of interior

17

TYPICAL CORNER VIEW 1

PLAN ON TYPICAL ROOF FRAME NODES

TYPICAL CORNER VIEW 2

TYPICAL INTERNAL CORNER FRAMING

18

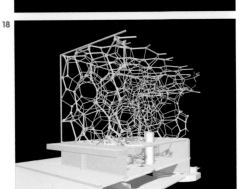

automated the drawing and analysis process. Based on specified design constraints and under 190 different loading scenarios, the algorithm iteratively checked the distribution of forces through the entire structure, based on specific member sizes, allowing the team to test different design configurations and receive feedback within 25 minutes. The result is a spectacular building with a sophisticated structure that is optimised in terms of material weight to strength, achieved with relative ease. The anticipated cost saving associated with the design process alone, compared with traditional processes, exceeds $10 million. From the analysis model the engineers wrote a conversion program that ran inside MicroStation, enabling the team to generate all necessary general arrangement drawings in 2-D.

This is an early example of a construction where the form and structure are completely integrated and fully self-organising. Michael Weinstock of the AA likens this self-organising characteristic to the way that biological processes develop a natural material system. The term biomimetics has been used to describe the way an industrial process can mimic a biological one. Weinstock comments: 'biomimetics is essentially interdisciplinary, a series of collaborations and exchanges between mathematicians, physicists, engineers, botanists, doctors and zoologists. The traditional architectural and engineering way of thinking about materials as something independent of form and structure are obsolete.'

19

20

Case Study 5: The Architectural Association

Under Weinstock's direction, forward-looking research work is being undertaken at the Architectural Association under the banner of emergent technology. This builds on the generative processes described elsewhere in this book, but it has begun to consider how 'the numerous morphogenic design methods, techniques and technologies can be synthesised into a coherent toolset'.

Ying-Tsai Chen, a PhD student at the AA, has been investigating the behaviour of woven structures (figure 21). His interest lies in devising software-driven processes that allow the real-time manipulation of complex architectural forms where the parameters of geometry, resistance to load and physical behaviour are realistically modelled. Starting with the geometry of a woven tube, he

has been able to create script-driven routines that demonstrate how woven tubes will deflect, expand and deform under vertical and horizontal load conditions, while varying the quantity of load, the degree of rotation, the density and thickness of the weave and the location of constraining elements. This involved the use principally of MEL (MAYA Embedded Language) and APDL (ANSYS Parametric Design Language). The results have been tested against physical models to verify that the anticipated behaviours were accurate.

This in itself is an impressive piece of work, which has similarities with the simulation software devised by Arup to model the behaviour of the Beijing Stadium. However, Chen has gone further and has begun to consider the multiple influences of the environment on such structures, and the potential effects on the quality of spaces within.

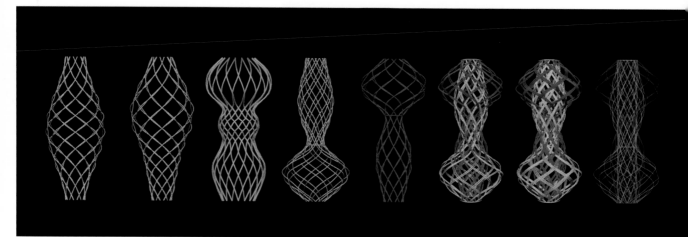

Fig 21 AA research project by PhD student Ying-Tsai Chen: simulations of woven tube deformation under vertical loads

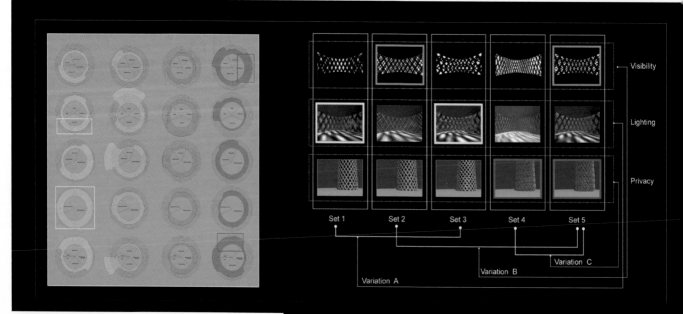

Fig 23 AA research project: comparison of outcomes in façade treatment

In a hypothetical urban building model, which includes two duplex flats and three levels of office space above shops, he has applied the impact of seasonal wind loading and radiation (natural light and heat), and has then created parametric relationships to reflect the needs for visibility, privacy, ventilation (figure 22) and quality of view for each type of use (retail, commercial and residential). These parameters are then merged with the geometric/structural system to produce an integrated intelligent model which will optimise all of the above variables (figures 23 and 24), including structural, environmental and spatial qualities for a given set of loading assumptions and geometry; furthermore, they will allow the user to read off the size, shape and thickness (and indeed cost) of any structural member. Chen has also considered how this information could be used in the manufacture of the structure using computer-controlled machine tools.

This is not yet a 'real-world' proposal, but it is one of a number of contemporary studies demonstrating that the 'formal resolution of competing forces and requirements' referred to at the beginning of this chapter is a realisable proposition. The search to create a self-organising and multiple-performance capacity in architecture places architects in the vanguard of the development of advanced 3-D computing for the built environment rather than at the periphery.

Robert Dalziel is a director at 3DReid Architects.

Fig 22 AA research project: responses to requirements for privacy and air flow

Fig 24 AA research project: model demonstrating resolution of multiple criteria

22

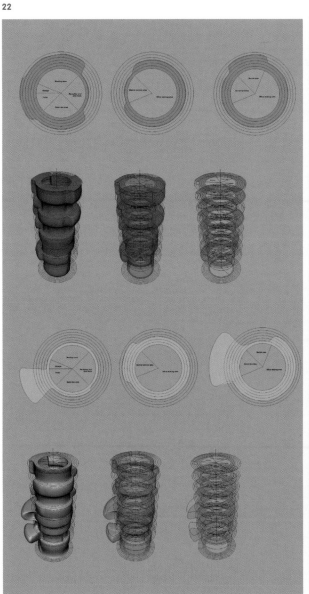

24

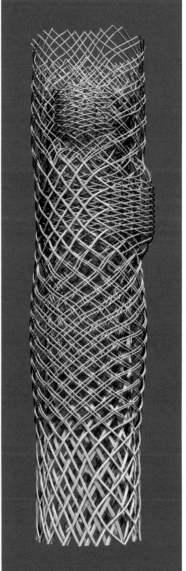

COLLABORATION THROUGH BUILDING INFORMATION MODELLING.

MILES WALKER,
HOK INTERNATIONAL,
AND DAVID THROSSELL,
SKANSKA TECHNOLOGY

COLLABORATION
THROUGH BUILDING
INFORMATION
MODELLING.
MILES WALKER,
HOK INTERNATIONAL,
AND DAVID
THROSSELL, SKANSKA
TECHNOLOGY

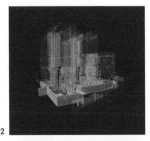

2

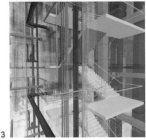

3

Fig 1 The new Royal London Hospital, to be completed in 2012, will include 100 specialist medical departments

Fig 2 The RLH
project was
conceived as a
BIM opportunity
from its inception.
Building design,
M&E and medical
facilities can all be
accommodated in
a single model

Fig 3 Servicing
and circulation
elements within
the centralised
HOK/Skanska BIM
system

When completed in 2012 the Royal London Hospital will be the largest new hospital in the UK. This 905-bed facility will provide London's principal trauma and emergency centre and the city's second largest paediatric unit, as well as 100 other specialist medical departments including the Helicopter Emergency Medical Service. The Royal London's new building is being configured as three towers containing 6,225 rooms across 110,000 square metres of floor space (figure 1).

HOK (appointed as a result of a design competition) is part of a design and delivery team led by Skanska, operating under conditions specified by the UK government's Private Finance Initiative. The project is politically and financially complex, as well as technically demanding. Highly coordinated computing systems based around interoperability and the principles of Building Information Modelling (BIM) have enabled this consortium to create a coherent design which minimises waste and duplication, reduces risk and allows different solutions to be explored quickly and robustly (figure 2). The technical systems, processes and protocols that lie at the heart of the delivery team's operation are designed to tackle two principal challenges: first, to design a building which embodies a dizzying number of coordinated mechanical, electrical, plumbing and medical systems (figure 3); second, to create a set of spaces which are

both humane and conducive to improving people's health and happiness (figure 4).

Before any design was contemplated, both HOK and Skanska established a working methodology based on sharing a BIM dataset via a virtual 'portal' (figure 5). The objective was not only to optimise and seek efficiencies during the design and construction element of the project, but also to provide a useful facilities management asset for the maintenance and operation of the hospital during its first 35 years of life (the term of the PFI contract). Setting up a BIM-based working method entailed an element of risk – preparation for BIM required an up-front investment which was not paid for by the UK's National Health Service. The business case for BIM, built around costs versus perceived value, shows that this working method should considerably reduce the typical 10 per cent overspend attributed to poor spatial coordination, rework and waste for an investment of around 0.5 per cent of the total tender sum. The benefit to Skanska is an increased construction margin; the benefit to HOK is fewer requests for information (RFIs) and hence an increased fee margin; the benefit to the client is a better quality, more robust building. Early investment in BIM is therefore important. Cost benefits are already starting to come through even though construction has barely begun. The business model forecasts that the simplicity of BIM data reuse

Fig 4 The new hospital is designed as a 'set of spaces which are both humane and conducive to improving people's health and happiness'

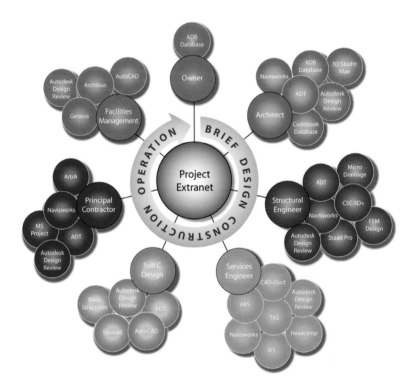

Fig 5 Schematic map of software relationships within the HOK/Skanska project extranet

will save £230,000 on the cost of producing an operations and maintenance manual alone.

The large savings will accrue from avoiding post hoc construction issues – particularly in the mechanical, electrical and plumbing (MEP) realm – which traditionally arise through clashes and inconsistencies discovered on the construction site which were not anticipated or spotted during the design phase. It is our belief that the earlier problems are discovered, the simpler and less costly they are to fix. Furthermore, the sheer scale and complexity involved with delivering over 6,000 rooms will be greatly assisted by making the BIM data work harder for the project team by consolidating the various sources of room information into single room models (figures 6 and 7).

HOK and Skanska agreed in advance to standardise around Autodesk's Architectural Desktop (ADT) modelling tool. All programs used by the key team members, as well as subcontractors, are ADT compatible. Project participants (architects, engineers, contractor, facilities management team and client) have agreed to feed into, and off, a single portal set up and managed by Skanska's central 3-D CAD and Data Management Group.

All computer packages used in the development, analysis, visualisation and management of the

COLLABORATION THROUGH BUILDING INFORMATION MODELLING.
MILES WALKER,
HOK INTERNATIONAL,
AND DAVID
THROSSELL, SKANSKA
TECHNOLOGY

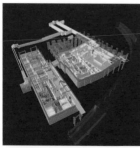

Figs 6 and 7 The sheer scale and complexity involved with delivering over 6,000 rooms will be greatly assisted by making the BIM data work harder for the project team

central 3-D model have been factored into the Data Management Group's 'roadmap'. The central model contains all the data from which, for example, lighting and acoustic studies can be sourced, verified views generated, structures and cladding systems analysed, and services mapped out.

Crucially, the principal ADT models have been linked to Codebook, the software which encapsulates key UK government-sanctioned medical information and requirements. The links between ADT and Codebook do not generate designs automatically; the design of a hospital should embody more sensitivity, creativity and consideration than is made possible by a formula-driven approach. Instead, the Codebook links allow designers to constantly check that room layouts and services fulfil the requirements of medical need. This has saved a considerable amount of design and revision time.

All design work is conducted in 3-D and the two-dimensional drawings required by contractors (largely those in the MEP role) are generated as extractions from the central model. Traditional 2-D CAD packages are not used at all. Even medical planners, who prefer to work in plan, operate within the 2-D mode of the 3-D program – their designs are generated in a manner suited to their way of working while their drawings are 'rich' in data and can be assimilated effortlessly into the central model. 2-D and 3-D working methods are merely different ways of viewing the underlying project data.

The 'clash prevention' and coordination functions of the central model have already highlighted a number of issues that would have become problematic later on. Indeed, the UK's Health & Safety Executive is impressed – the 3-D model

Fig 8 The centralised and highly coordinated approach of the design and construction team ensures that problems are encountered in the digital realm only. Clash detection and simulation systems promise to improve the safety of the finished building

Fig 9 Via the project extranet the building can be viewed on a storey-by-storey basis

Fig 10 Intelligent modelling will provide an important facilities management resource for the end client – as this model of a steam pump demonstrates

generated as an amalgam of the architecture, structure and MEP models has already uncovered potential safety 'blackspots' that would have been difficult and expensive to resolve once the build was complete (figure 8). These safety reviews have been an unexpected success – ordinarily, working in 3-D provides benefits for visualisations, clash-detection and 'fit', but examining our model from the point of view of maintenance personnel (where matters such as railings, access and head-heights are important) will create an environment that is safer and more efficient. Another benefit of working in 3-D has been the ability to plan for the installation of pieces of large medical equipment, which can be 'animated' and 'moved' through a model of the building. At almost every stage of the design process, risk and the potential for error is being minimised.

Considerable efforts have also gone into making the central models easily navigable by individual members of the design team. Through the project extranet, the hospital complex can be viewed as a series of zoned models on a storey-by-storey basis (figure 9). These models, enriched by links to documentation via the powerful ArtrA tool, are regularly combined through Navisworks for coordination checking, clash prevention, 'virtual snagging', operations and maintenance strategy compliance and construction rehearsal.

The NHS's long-term financial interest in the scheme has driven innovative thinking, and we have taken advantage of new technologies to help us manage risk during both the construction and operation of the new building. Certainly, the extraction of materials lists and quantities has led to efficiencies with cost planning, procurement and in support of the project's ambitious waste targets.

The data generated through BIM is designed to be useful beyond the completion of the hospital. As a combination of design/construction and medical information, the model will provide a powerful

resource for facilities management teams; a patient receiving oxygen will be participating in the same information system as the person who installed the oxygen delivery mechanism. Radio frequency identification devices and the embedding of the asset register within a central database (an issue currently being explored by the design team) will boost the value and 'data life' of the BIM to hospital managers of the future (figure 10).

Our 3-D modelling strategy is founded on the principle of 'reuse and share' – it is about data exchange rather than the delivery of drawings. It is an approach which requires discipline, although the standards developed by the UK's Avanti and Construction Project Information Committee programmes have certainly helped guide us in this regard. When fully realised, this collaborative, BIM approach can extract the full benefit from the design data we produce but normally discard once a drawing has been plotted.

For some, the cultural change to BIM has been a natural one, while for others it has represented a challenge; to make this complex project work has relied on 'BIM champions' who could see the benefits beyond short-term technology issues. Now that benchmark solutions are established, future collaboration will come more easily. In fact, BIM is not too difficult to implement and it doesn't cost more; indeed, it leads to reduced risk and less cost. The technology is currently robust and maturing fast – the effort now needs to go into creating a new culture that will encourage people to take the leap of faith.

Miles Walker is firmwide CAD manager and vice president of HOK. David Throssell is Data Management Leader at Skanska Technology.

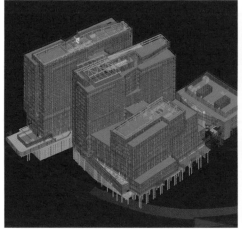

9

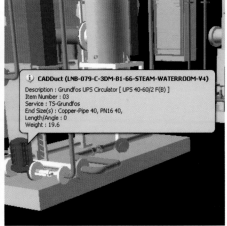

10

INFORMED
SCULPTURE.
RICHARD HYAMS,
ASTUDIO

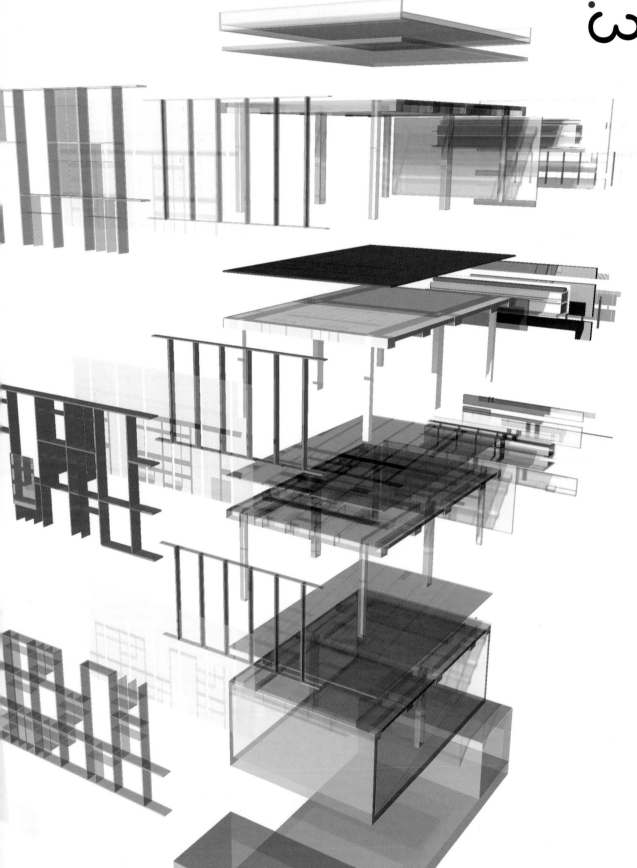

6.3

Fig 1 Skin study for a stadium and physical education teaching facility for Al-Fateh University, Tripoli. All images shown here represent different elements of this project, a collaboration between Astudio and LCE Architects. Model created in MicroStation, exported into 3D Studio Max for final renderings

Fig 2 Section through the stadium model, a combination of MicroStation, 3D Studio Max and Photoshop

Starting a practice with the tools available today is really the most exciting prospect. Due to the potential the computer offers, young practices are capable of delivering a world-class service. With the right skills, a small practice is capable of meeting and beating the output of larger firms (figures 1 and 2). The goal is to ensure we have the maximum amount of time to spend on design, to use technology to help us become more efficient, to streamline processes, to collaborate widely and intelligently, and to produce the best design in the most sustainable way possible.

Ecotect, digital photographs, Google Earth, aerial photography … all in their own way enable a greater depth of understanding of the context in which we build. Running a swift 3-D shadow model generates a simple yet valuable evaluation of first ideas (figure 3). Early analysis of form at the concept stage demonstrates both benefits and inefficiencies while allowing us to test what might be better solutions. Rather like plasticine, digital modelling allows a free expression of form; rapid testing of its attributes is essential.

Once the context is understood, options for the built form and interpretation of the brief begin. The fastest way to get from the moment of inspiration to a representation of it (whether a sketch, a physical model or a CAD model) is the goal. The choice of medium will often depend on what is being designed. A simple sketch is perfect if the diagram can be easily interpreted. However, Astudio is

doing a great deal of sculptural, 'light-shaped' design where the only way to demonstrate the validity of the idea is to build a simple CAD model. Once created and dropped into Ecotect, the model delivers considerable value by calculating (and clearly showing) heat gain, light levels and ultimately the success of the idea (figure 4). This is what can be called 'informed sculpture'.

Generative Component modelling is a promising way forward. It drives a certain rigour through the design process as it makes the designer think clearly about the concept in terms of its principles, interpreted as parameters (both fixed and variable). This allows us to define the form. Of course, developing a design using a 3-D CAD model from the outset will bring enormous benefits for the documentation of the project, as well as tendering, fabrication and construction. If the rigour is set (in terms of drawing discipline) by individuals with a good understanding of how buildings are put together, the result will be not just deliverable but a close match of the original concept (figures 5 and 6). Architects are often accused of selling a beautiful image rather than a reality.

MicroStation is our workhorse CAD program. However, thanks to the compatibility of different CAD software, we often bounce a model between several packages to get the best out of each and enhance the end result. Physical models are invaluable; there is still nothing quite like holding a design in your hands and looking at it from all

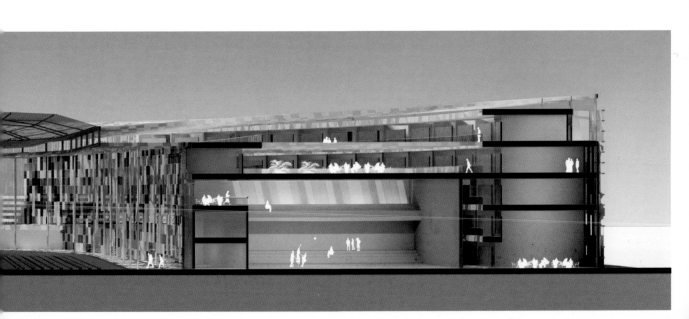

**Fig 3 Early Micro
Station façade
study of the sta-
dium complex**

**Fig 4 Façade sun-
light and shadow
diagram, achieved
by exporting
the MicroStation
model to Ecotect**

angles. I have not yet seen a computer tool that can offer the immediacy of the physical model. We often write macros to undertake simple tasks such as flattening a 3-D CAD model into a two-dimensional drawing, which provides the templates from which a physical model can be made.

Designers in the disciplines that serve the wider built environment profession have their own software to test our designs. However, these applications are increasingly becoming available to architects. Ecotect and IES software, for example, allow us to both interrogate and improve a design. There is, of course, always the danger that these programs make us all experts, but interrogating the output of this software requires a greater understanding of the subjects (lighting, thermal performance, rights to light, etc.) than most architects have. At Astudio

we have an environmental engineer to help us understand this information and use it to improve our projects.

When a Building Information Model (BIM) is truly adopted, 3-D models will streamline the design to tender and construction process. In principle, there is no reason why we shouldn't all be producing our buildings fully integrated in CAD. The façade industry, for example, is ready to receive tenders from architects that simply demonstrate, within a 3-D model, the node points of each façade element. Culturally, architects need to develop their working practices in order to get the best out of the technology they use. Streamlining the process across all disciplines should not only produce a more efficient and buildable project, but also a more economic one.

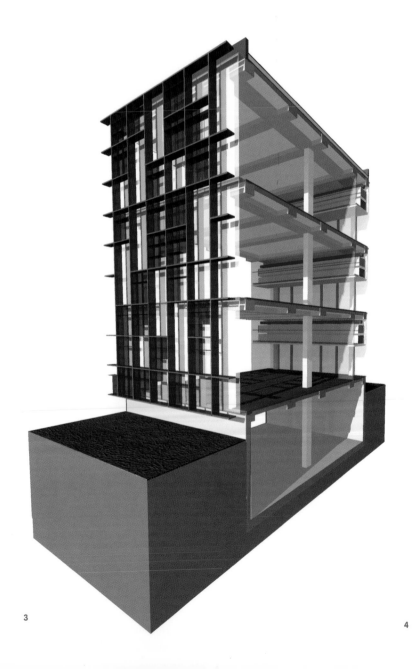

3

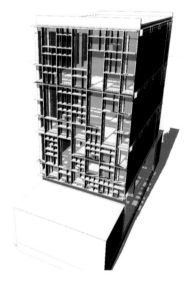

4

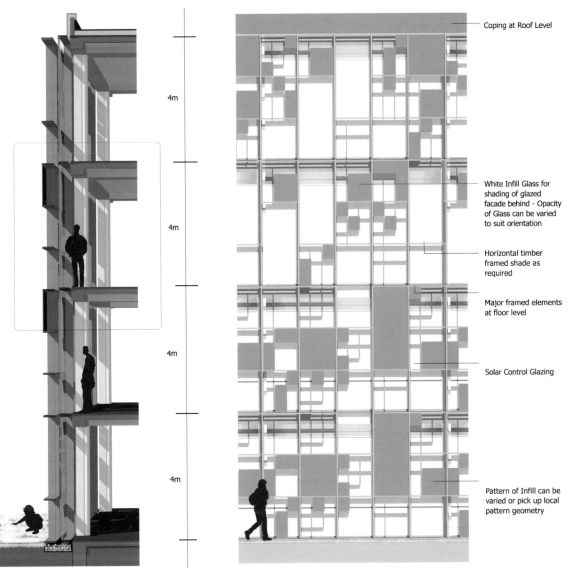

Coping at Roof Level

4m

4m

White Infill Glass for shading of glazed facade behind - Opacity of Glass can be varied to suit orientation

Horizontal timber framed shade as required

Major framed elements at floor level

4m

Solar Control Glazing

4m

Pattern of Infill can be varied or pick up local pattern geometry

6

Facade Section 1:50

Facade Elevation 1:50

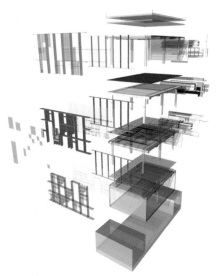

Fig 5 A typical bay of the stadium complex. Model created, exploded and rendered in MicroStation

Fig 6 Technical study of the façade. The model was created and rendered in MicroStation. Images were exported to Photoshop for graphical treatment, then reimported into MicroStation for tagging and plan layout

5

Technology offers fantastic possibilities. Most of us work on computers that can drive many complex processes at once, yet most machines represent a tragic waste of potential. When computers arrived on architects' desk en masse, the race was on to produce the most photorealistic images. This took the focus away from the many more useful offerings the computer brings. Software developers have recently made much more intuitive tools (SketchUp, Generative Components) that put the computer to much more sensible and successful use. Computers are multi-taskers and they perform best when used to map, to sculpt, to test, to share and to build. If used for merely one task, with little reference to anything else, the computer's greatest asset is wasted.

Richard Hyams is a director at Astudio.

PICTURE CREDITS

BENTLEY SYSTEMS, INC.

Bentley Systems, Incorporated is proud to sponsor this innovative book to help architects and engineers as they work to improve and sustain the world's infrastructure. Bentley's comprehensive portfolio of software for building, plant, civil, and geospatial projects spans architecture, engineering, construction, and operations.

Bentley's Building Information Modeling (BIM) and management solutions empower the design, construction, and operation of all types of buildings and facilities, from the conventional to some of the most inspiring projects of our time. They equip project teams to respond effectively to changes – the large ones taking place in the building profession as well as the smaller ones that happen daily on the project site – and to see these changes as an opportunity rather than a challenge (www.bentley.com/bim).

Bentley's exciting new design technology, GenerativeComponents, enables architects and engineers to pursue designs and achieve results that were virtually unthinkable before. Empowered by computational methods, the designers can direct their creativity to deliver inspired sustainable buildings that are freer in form and use innovative materials and assemblies. GenerativeComponents facilitates this by allowing the quick exploration of a broad range of "what-if" alternatives for even the most complex buildings (www.bentley.com/gc.).

Architects and engineers are increasingly utilizing new technologies and methodologies as they strive to deliver the best quality services and ever better buildings. Integrated computational tools and building information modeling, analysis, and simulation software provide feedback on building materials, assemblies, systems performance, and environmental conditions to inform their decisions and inspire their creativity. Bentley is proud to support them with our solutions as they craft space.

All images courtesy of TVS

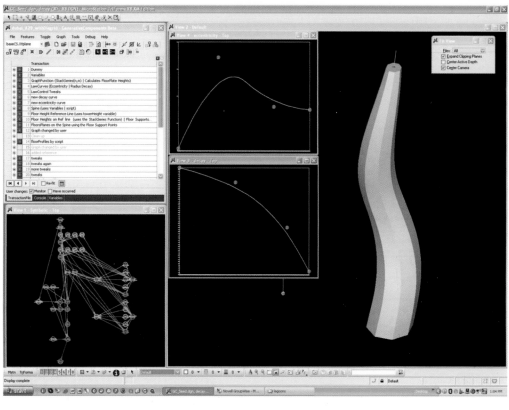